# Windows Me™

**MILLENNIUM EDITION**

# Windows® Me™

**MILLENNIUM EDITION**

**Mac Bride**

**TEACH YOURSELF BOOKS**

For UK orders: please contact Bookpoint Ltd, 130 Milton Park, Abingdon, Oxon OX14 4SB. Telephone: (44) 01235 400414, Fax: (44) 01235 400454. Lines are open 9.00 – 6.00, Monday to Saturday, with a 24 hour message answering service. E-mail address: orders@bookpoint.co.uk

For USA and Canada orders: please contact NTC/Contemporary Publishing, 4255 West Touhy Avenue, Lincolnwood, Illinois 60646-1975, USA. Telephone: (847) 679 5500, Fax: (847) 679 2494.

Long renowned as the authoritative source for self-guided learning – with more than 40 million copies sold worldwide – the *Teach Yourself* series includes over 200 titles in the fields of languages, crafts, hobbies, business and education.

*British Library Cataloguing in Publication Data*
A catalogue record for this title is available from the British Library.

*Library of Congress Catalog Card Number:* On file

First published in UK 2000 by Hodder Headline Plc, 338 Euston Road, London NW1 3BH.

First published in US by NTC/Contemporary Publishing, 4255 West Touhy Avenue, Lincolnwood (Chicago), Illinois 60646-1975 USA.

The 'Teach Yourself' name and logo are registered trade marks of Hodder & Stoughton Ltd. Computer hardware and software brand names mentioned in this book are protected by their respective trademarks and are acknowledged.

Copyright © 2000 Mac Bride

*In UK:* All rights reserved. No part of this publication may be reproduced or transmitted in any form or by any means, electronic or mechanical, including photocopy, recording, or any information storage and retrieval system, without permission in writing from the publisher or under licence from the Copyright Licensing Agency Limited. Further details of such licences (for reprographic reproduction) may be obtained from the Copyright Licensing Agency Limited, of 90 Tottenham Court Road, London W1P 9HE.

*In US:* All rights reserved. No part of this publication may be reproduced, stored in a retrieval system, or transmitted in any form, or by any means, electronic, mechanical, photocopying, or otherwise, without prior permission of NTC/Contemporary Publishing.

Typeset by MacDesign, Southampton.
Printed in Great Britain for Hodder & Stoughton Educational, a division of Hodder Headline Plc, 338 Euston Road, London NW1 3BH by Cox & Wyman Ltd, Reading, Berkshire.

| Impression number | 10 9 8 7 6 5 4 3 2 |
|---|---|
| Year | 2006 2005 2004 2003 2002 2001 |

# CONTENTS

|     | Preface | xi |
|---|---|---|
| **1** | **Introducing Windows Me** | **1** |
| 1.1 | What is Windows Me? | 1 |
| 1.2 | The Desktop | 3 |
| 1.3 | The mouse | 6 |
| 1.4 | The keyboard | 7 |
| 1.5 | Menus | 8 |
| 1.6 | Smart menus | 9 |
| 1.7 | Shortcut menus | 11 |
| 1.8 | Properties, dialog boxes and options | 11 |
|     | Summary | 14 |
| **2** | **The Desktop** | **15** |
| 2.1 | Desktop modes | 15 |
| 2.2 | Customizing the Desktop | 18 |
|     | Summary | 25 |
| **3** | **Working with Windows** | **26** |
| 3.1 | Basic windows concepts | 26 |
| 3.2 | Using the scroll bars | 30 |
| 3.3 | Screen layouts | 30 |
| 3.4 | Tabbing between windows | 33 |
| 3.5 | Adjusting the window size | 33 |
| 3.6 | Moving windows | 36 |
| 3.7 | Closing windows | 36 |
| 3.8 | Shut Down | 36 |
|     | Summary | 38 |

| 4 | **Help!** | **39** |
|---|---|---|
| 4.1 | Help and Support | 39 |
| 4.2 | Application Help | 46 |
| 4.3 | Tips and prompts | 51 |
| 4.4 | Wizards | 53 |
| | Summary | 54 |
| **5** | **Programs and documents** | **55** |
| 5.1 | Definitions | 55 |
| 5.2 | Start → Programs | 56 |
| 5.3 | Other ways to start | 58 |
| 5.4 | Starting from documents | 60 |
| 5.5 | Closing programs | 61 |
| 5.6 | Coping with crashes | 61 |
| 5.7 | Filenames and extensions | 63 |
| | Summary | 65 |
| **6** | **Basic techniques** | **66** |
| 6.1 | Selection techniques | 66 |
| 6.2 | Cut, Copy and Paste | 69 |
| 6.3 | Drag and drop | 71 |
| 6.4 | Scraps | 72 |
| | Summary | 74 |
| **7** | **Files and folders** | **75** |
| 7.1 | Disks and folders | 75 |
| 7.2 | My Computer | 76 |
| 7.3 | Windows Explorer | 77 |
| 7.4 | View options | 81 |
| 7.5 | Displaying and sorting files | 82 |
| 7.6 | Folder Options | 84 |
| 7.7 | File Types | 87 |
| 7.8 | Organizing folders | 89 |
| 7.9 | Creating shortcuts | 92 |

| | | |
|---|---|---|
| 7.10 | File management | 93 |
| 7.11 | The Recycle Bin | 98 |
| 7.12 | Search | 99 |
| | Summary | 102 |
| **8** | **The Control Panel** | **103** |
| 8.1 | Using the Panel | 103 |
| 8.2 | Accessibility | 104 |
| 8.3 | Add/Remove Programs | 106 |
| 8.4 | Date/Time | 109 |
| 8.5 | Desktop Themes | 110 |
| 8.6 | Fonts | 111 |
| 8.7 | Keyboard | 113 |
| 8.8 | Mouse | 114 |
| 8.9 | Sounds | 117 |
| | Summary | 118 |
| **9** | **Taskbar and Start Menu settings** | **119** |
| 9.1 | Taskbar options | 119 |
| 9.2 | Toolbars | 120 |
| 9.3 | Moving and resizing | 123 |
| 9.4 | The Start menu | 124 |
| | Summary | 128 |
| **10** | **Internet Explorer** | **129** |
| 10.1 | What is the Internet? | 129 |
| 10.2 | Getting online | 133 |
| 10.3 | Internet Explorer | 135 |
| 10.4 | Internet Options | 138 |
| 10.5 | Browsing the Web | 144 |
| 10.6 | Files from the Net | 150 |
| 10.7 | Internet Radio | 154 |
| | Summary | 156 |

| 11 | **Outlook Express** | **157** |
|---|---|---|
| 11.1 | Starting Outlook Express | 157 |
| 11.2 | Reading mail | 159 |
| 11.3 | Sending mail | 160 |
| 11.4 | Outlook Express options | 162 |
| 11.5 | The Address Book | 166 |
| 11.6 | Finding people | 169 |
| 11.7 | Newsgroups | 170 |
| 11.8 | Reading the news | 171 |
| | Summary | 174 |
| 12 | **Maintaining your disks** | **175** |
| 12.1 | The System Tools | 175 |
| 12.2 | Disk Properties | 177 |
| 12.3 | Disk Cleanup | 178 |
| 12.4 | ScanDisk | 179 |
| 12.5 | Disk Defragmenter | 181 |
| 12.6 | Maintenance Wizard | 183 |
| 12.7 | System Restore | 186 |
| 12.8 | Backups | 187 |
| 12.9 | Floppy disks | 188 |
| | Summary | 190 |
| 13 | **Printers** | **191** |
| 13.1 | Adding a new printer | 191 |
| 13.2 | Printer Properties | 193 |
| 13.3 | Printing from applications | 195 |
| 13.4 | Controlling the print queue | 195 |
| 13.5 | Printing from file | 197 |
| | Summary | 198 |
| 14 | **The Accessories** | **199** |
| 14.1 | WordPad | 199 |
| 14.2 | Notepad | 206 |
| 14.3 | Character Map | 207 |

| | | |
|---|---|---|
| 14.4 | Paint | 208 |
| 14.5 | Imaging | 212 |
| 14.6 | Calculator | 213 |
| 14.7 | Phone Dialer | 214 |
| 14.8 | Media Player | 216 |
| 14.9 | Movie Maker | 219 |
| 14.10 | Home networking | 220 |
| | Summary | 223 |
| | **Index** | **225** |

# PREFACE

Windows Me (Millennium Edition) is the latest version of Microsoft's world-beating operating system, and one that takes another step further along the path of making computers easier to use.

*Teach Yourself Windows Me* is written primarily for those people who are new to computers, or are at least new to the Windows way – if you have previously used Windows 95 or 98, the change to Me is very simple. This book introduces the basic concepts of working with **W**indows (the system) and **w**indows (the framed parts of the screen in which programs run). It will show you how to set up your computer to suit the way you like to work – you can control more or less everything from the screen display down to the speed of the mouse's response! You will find out how to manage your files efficiently, organizing your storage so that you can find things quickly and removing unwanted clutter, and how to care for your disks so they continue to perform well for a long time.

The Windows package includes many accessories and applications, both large and small. We will be looking briefly at some of these, and more closely at Internet Explorer and Outlook Express. With these two tools you can browse and download files from the Internet, and handle e-mail and newsgroup articles. Windows Me has been designed for easy Internet access, in fact, integration with the Internet is central to its design. If you choose, and if you have the hardware and the connections to support it, you can almost treat the Internet as an extension of your desktop.

This book does not aim to cover every single aspect of Windows Me, for two very good reasons. There is far too much to fit into 224 pages, and few people will ever use all its features. *Teach Yourself Windows Me* concentrates on the needs of the new user at home and in the office. It aims to cover the things that you need to know to be able to use your computer efficiently, and things that you might like to know because they can make using your computer more enjoyable. Working with Windows is intuitive

– once you know how to 'intuit'! When you have mastered the basics and become familiar with some applications, you should be able to apply your understanding of the 'Windows way' to any other Windows applications that interest you.

Happy Windowing.

*Mac Bride*

*2000*

# 1 INTRODUCING WINDOWS Me

> ### AIMS OF THIS CHAPTER
>
> Windows Me is very easy to use – once you have mastered a few key skills and concepts. This chapter gives an overview of Windows Me and of how it works. It looks at what you see on screen, and how you can respond to it and control it with the mouse and keyboard. It also introduces some essential terminology and the ideas behind them.
>
> If you have previously used any similar computer system – such as Windows 95, NT or 3.1, or Apple Macintosh – you can skim through the next few pages, or skip them altogether, and go straight to Chapter 2.

## 1.1 What is Windows Me?

Windows Me is an *operating system* – and more. An operating system handles the low-level interaction between the processor and the screen, memory, mouse, disk drives, printer and other peripherals. Windows Me has *drivers* (control programs) for all PC-compatible processors and just about every kind of PC peripheral currently on the market – and for some that are still being developed! The operating system is a bridge between the hardware of the computer and the *applications* – such as word-processor, spreadsheet or Internet browser. As a result, whatever hardware you are using, as long as it can run the Windows Me operating system, it can run any Windows Me application. (It will also be able to run applications written for earlier versions of Windows.)

Although the operating system is the most important part of Windows, most of it is invisible to you. You don't even need to think about how it works or what it does as Windows Me has its own routines for checking and maintaining the operating system.

## Plug and Play

These built-in maintenance routines also come into play when you add new hardware, such as a joystick, scanner or extra hard drive, to your PC. Windows Me will normally recognize their presence automatically, and install the software needed to control them. This 'plug and play' approach, introduced with Windows 95, extended with 98 and taken even further with Me, is a vast improvement on earlier operating systems – with those, you could spend hours trying to get the computer to work with new hardware!

## The Desktop

The most visible part of Windows is, of course, the screen or *Desktop*, as it is called. Windows is a graphical system. It uses *icons* (small images) to represent programs and files, and visual displays to show what is happening inside your computer. Many of the routine jobs are done by clicking on, dragging (see page 7) or otherwise manipulating these images, using the mouse or keyboard.

Windows is *multi-tasking* – it can run any number of programs at once. In practice, only a few will normally be active at the same time but that is more a reflection of the human inability to do several jobs simultaneously! A typical example of multi-tasking would be one program downloading material from the Internet and another printing a long report, while you wrote a letter in a third.

Each program runs in a separate area of the screen – a window – and these can be resized, moved, minimized or overlapped however you like. Managing windows is covered in Chapter 3.

## Utilities and accessories

Apart from the operating system, Windows Me contains a large set of programs. Some of these are utilities for managing the system – organizing file storage on the disk, adding new peripherals or fine-tuning the way that they work. Others are applications for your use and amusement.

There's WordPad, a good word-processor, Paint and Imaging for creating pictures and editing graphics, a Calculator, Phone Dialer, some games, a set of multimedia tools and applications for the Internet, including Internet Explorer. All of the essential utilities and the more useful applications are covered in this book.

### Integration with the Internet

Windows Me offers a high level of integration with the Internet – it can become almost an extension of your Desktop. Integration works best within organizations that are connected to the Internet through an ISDN line, giving fast, easy access – and preferably with the line open all the time.

If you connect through a dial-up line – as most home and small business users do – you cannot move smoothly from the Desktop to the Internet. In this situation, you will probably 'go online' (connect to the Internet) once or twice a day to get your e-mail or browse the Web, and this will be quite separate from your other computing activities.

## 1.2 The Desktop

The screen should be treated as if it really were a desktop. This is where you keep your tools – utilities and applications – and you can arrange things so that those tools you use most often are close at hand. This is where you create your documents – and you may have several under way at the same time, in the same or in separate applications. You can arrange these so that you can read two or more at once if you want to compare them or copy material from one to another. If you have finished with an application for the time being, you can tuck it out of the way – but it is still ready to be restarted with a click.

### What's on the Desktop?

What do you see when you look at the screen? The answer will vary, of course, depending upon what you are doing and how you have set up the system, but some or all of these items should be visible.

### Background

This may be a flat colour, a pattern, a picture or a Web page with text and images. It can be changed at any time without affecting anything else.

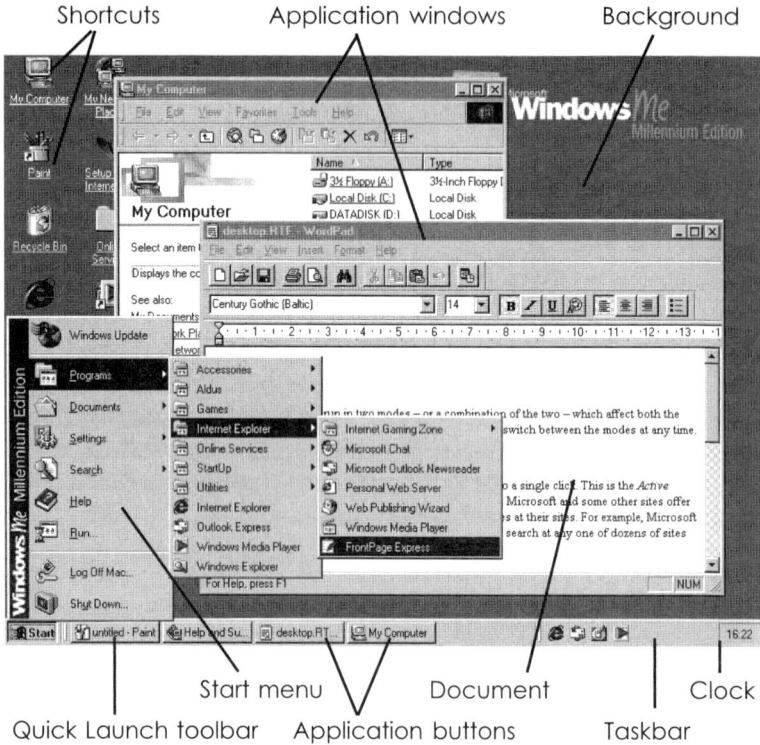

**Figure 1.1** The **Desktop**, in Web mode (see Chapter 2), showing some of the main features.

### Shortcuts

These are icons with links to programs, to *folders* (for storing files on the hard disk) or to places on the Internet. Clicking on the icon will run the program, open the folder or take you off into the Internet. There are some shortcuts there already, but you can easily add your own (see page 92).

### Taskbar

This is normally present as a strip along the bottom of the screen, though it can be moved elsewhere (Chapter 9). It is the main control centre for the Desktop, carrying the tools and buttons to start and to switch between applications.

## Start menu

Clicking on the **Start** button, on the left of the Taskbar, opens the Start menu. Any application on your system can be run from here. The menu also leads to recently-used documents, favourite places on the Internet, the Help pages and other utilities.

## Quick Launch toolbar

Shortcuts can be obscured by application windows, but the Taskbar is normally always visible. The Quick Launch toolbar is just one of the toolbars that can be added to the Taskbar to give you ready access to applications, no matter what the state of the Desktop.

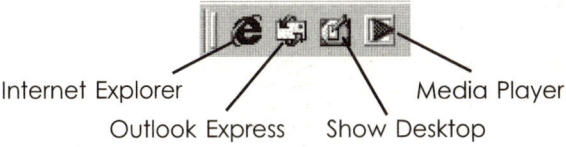

Internet Explorer and Outlook Express are your main Internet applications (see Chapters 10 and 11). Media Player (Chapter 14) plays a wide range of audio and video files. Show Desktop, shrinks all open applications out of the way so that you have a clear view of the Desktop.

## Clock

This is optional, but useful. You should find that the clock keeps excellent time – it even adjusts itself at the start and end of Summer Time!

---

**THE TASKBAR**

The Start menu, Quick Launch toolbar and Clock are all dealt with in more detail along with the other Taskbar features, in Chapter 9.

---

## Application windows

When you run an application, such as My Computer (Chapter 7), WordPad, or Paint (both in Chapter 14), it is displayed in a window. This can be set to fill the screen or to take a smaller area so that part of the Desktop is visible beneath (see Chapter 3 for more on windows).

## Application buttons

When you run an application, a button is added to the Taskbar. Clicking on it will bring that application to the top of your Desktop.

## Document

The letter that you are writing in WordPad, the picture in Paint, the budget you have set out in a spreadsheet – all of these are *documents*. A document is normally only seen in the application that created it, or a compatible one. In the screenshot on page 4, the document 'desktop.rtf' is open in Microsoft Word.

---

### CUSTOMIZING THE DESKTOP

The appearance of the Desktop and the way that you interact with it can be changed to suit yourself. See Chapter 2 to find out how to do this.

---

# 1.3 The mouse

The mouse is almost essential for work with Windows – you can manage without it, but not as easily. It is used for selecting and manipulating objects, highlighting text, making choices, and clicking icons and buttons – as well as for drawing in graphics applications. There are five key 'moves'.

## Point

The easy one! Move the mouse so that the tip of the arrow cursor (or the finger of the hand cursor) is over the object you want to point to. If you point to an icon, and hold the cursor there for a moment, a label will appear, telling you what the icon stands for. If you reach the edge of the mouse mat before the pointer has reached its target, pick the mouse up and put it down again in the middle of the mat.

## Click

A single click of the left mouse button.

## Right-click

A single click of the right mouse button.

# INTRODUCING WINDOWS ME

### Double-click

Two clicks, in quick succession, of the left mouse button. The response of the mouse can be adjusted to suit your double-click speed (see page 114).

### Drag

Point to an object or place on the Desktop, hold down the left mouse button and draw the cursor across the screen.

## 1.4 The keyboard

The keyboard is mainly for entering text, but can also be used for editing text and controlling the system. These keys, in particular, are worth identifying and remembering:

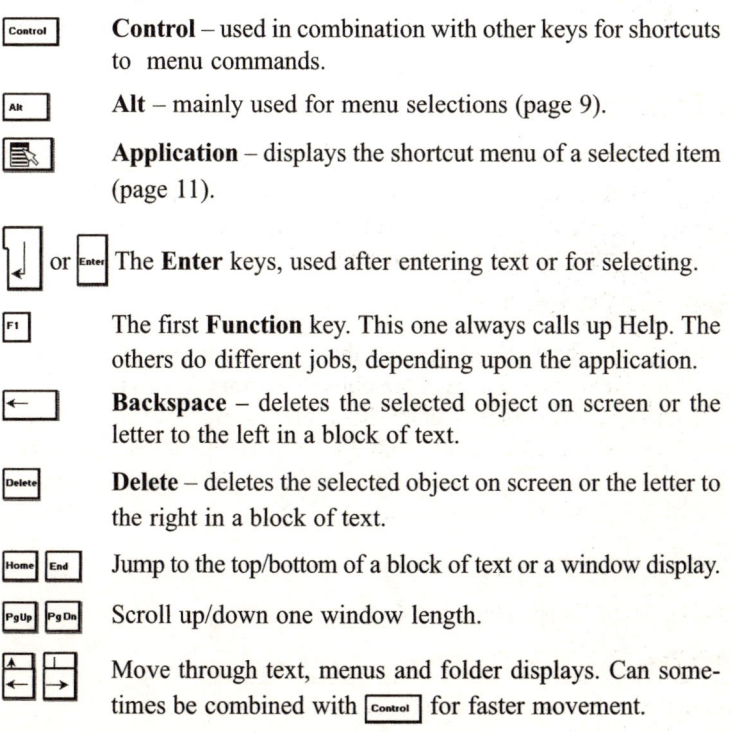

**Windows** – press to open the Start menu. Also used in some keyboard shortcuts.

**Control** – used in combination with other keys for shortcuts to menu commands.

**Alt** – mainly used for menu selections (page 9).

**Application** – displays the shortcut menu of a selected item (page 11).

The **Enter** keys, used after entering text or for selecting.

The first **Function** key. This one always calls up Help. The others do different jobs, depending upon the application.

**Backspace** – deletes the selected object on screen or the letter to the left in a block of text.

**Delete** – deletes the selected object on screen or the letter to the right in a block of text.

Jump to the top/bottom of a block of text or a window display.

Scroll up/down one window length.

Move through text, menus and folder displays. Can sometimes be combined with Control for faster movement.

## 1.5 Menus

In any Windows Me (or earlier) applications, the commands and options are grouped on a set of pull-down menus.

They follow simple rules:
- If an item has an ▶ on the right, a submenu will open when you point to the item.
- If an item has ... after the name, a panel or dialog box (page 11) will open when you point to the item.
- If an item has ● to its left, it is the selected option from a set.
- If an item has ✓ to its left, it is an option and is turned on – click to turn it off or on again.
- If a name is in grey ('greyed out'), the command is not available at that time – you probably have to select something first.

### Menus and the mouse
- To open a menu, click on its name in the Menu bar.
- To run a command or set an option, click on it with the mouse.
- To leave the menu system without selecting a command, click anywhere else on the screen.

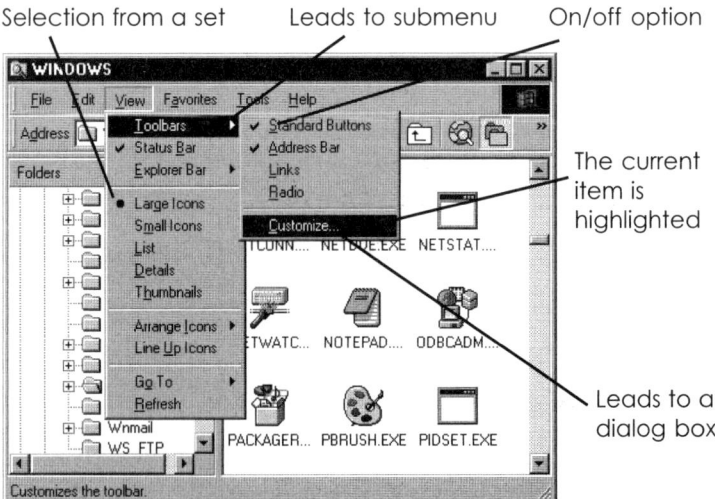

**Figure 1.2** A typical menu (this is in Windows Explorer).

## Menu selection using the keyboard

When the work that you are doing is mainly typing, you may find it more convenient to make your menu selections via the keyboard. Here's how:

❶ Hold down **Alt** and press the underlined letter in the name on the Menu bar.

*either*

❷ Press the underlined letter of the name to run the command, set the on/off option or open the submenu.

*or*

❸ Move through the menus with the arrow keys – up/down the menu and right to open submenus – then press **Enter**.

♦ The left/right arrows will move you from one menu to another.

♦ Press **Escape** to close the menu without selecting a command.

## Keyboard shortcuts

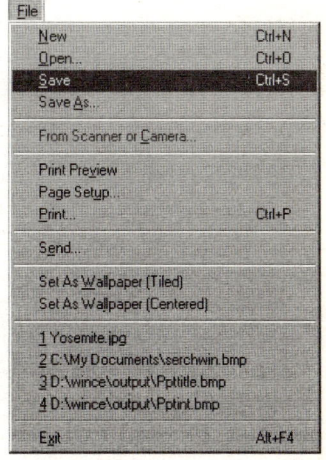

Many applications allow you to run some of the most commonly-used commands directly from the keyboard, without touching the menu system. For example, in Paint, **Control + S** (i.e. hold down the **Control** key and press **S**) will call up the **Save** command; **Control + O** has the same effect as selecting **Open** from the **File** menu.

The shortcuts vary, and some applications will offer far more than others, but some are common to all – or most – applications. If a command has a keyboard shortcut, it will be shown on the menu, to the right of the name.

# 1.6 Smart menus

In Windows Me and in some of the latest software – Office 2000, for instance – the menus are 'smart'! They have been designed to respond to the way you work, displaying at first only the core items and those that you use regularly. The rest are tucked out of sight, but can be revealed either by waiting a few moments or by clicking on the double-arrow bar at the bottom of the menu. If you use a program, it will be added to the menu, and become part of the displayed set in future. If you don't use a program for several days, it will be dropped from the menu. As smart menus are normally much shorter, it makes selection simpler and faster.

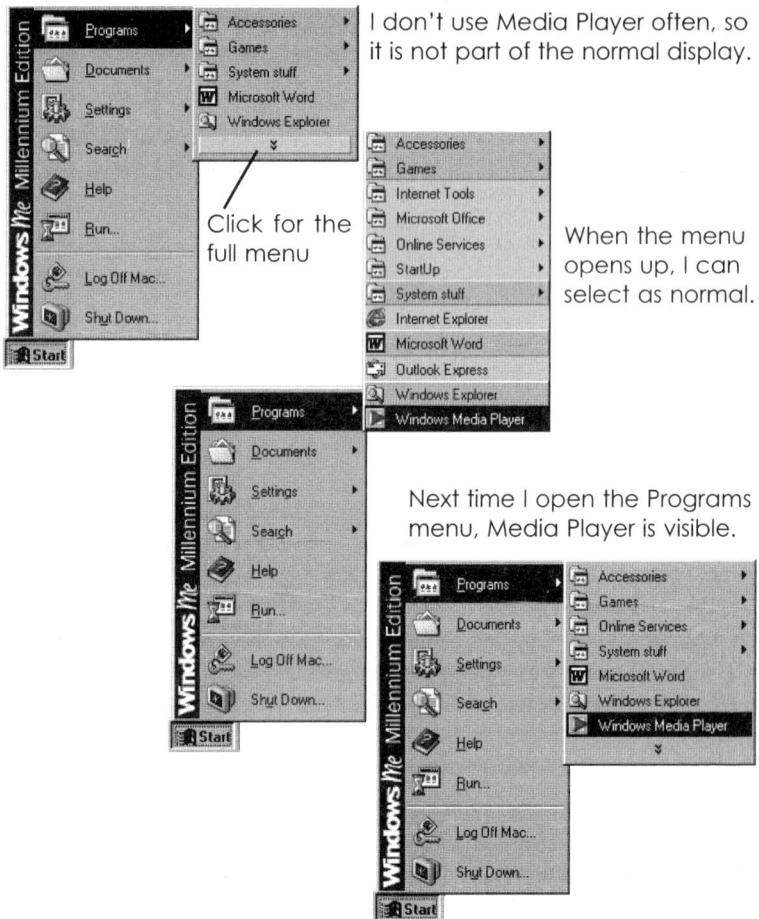

**Figure 1.3** Smart menus in action – it takes a few days for them to kick into action.

INTRODUCING WINDOWS ME 11

## 1.7 Shortcut menus

If you right-click on more or less anything on the screen, or press the **Application** key when an object is selected, a menu will appear beside or on the object. This is its *shortcut* or *context menu* – it will contain a set of commands and options that are relevant to the object in that context. Right-click on a shortcut to a folder, on a shortcut to an application, on the Taskbar or on the background and see what comes up. Don't worry at this stage about what the commands and options do, just notice how they vary – and that some are present on many menus.

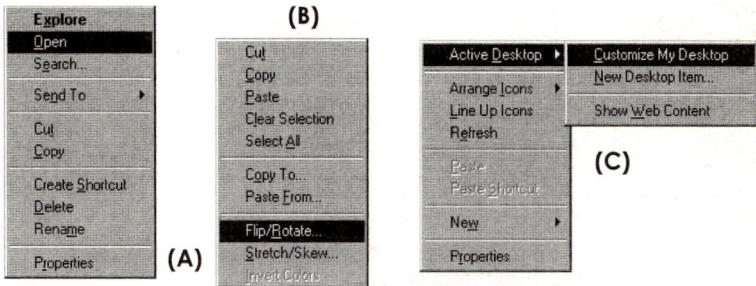

**Figure 1.4** Three examples of shortcut menus, from **(A)** Online services, **(B)** a selected area in Paint and **(C)** the Desktop.

## 1.8 Properties, dialog boxes and options

Almost every object in the Windows Me system has *Properties*, which define what it looks like and how it works. These can be seen, and often changed, through the Properties panel. This is normally reached through the context menu – you will see that two of the menus in Figure 1.4 have Properties as the last item.

Properties panels often have several *tabs*, each dealing with a different aspect of the object. The contents vary enormously. Some will simply contain information – such as the size, date and other details of a file – others have options that you can set in different ways.

♦ To switch between tabs, click on the name at the top.

When a Windows program wants to get information from you, it will do it through a *dialog box*. These vary in size and style, depending upon the information to be collected.

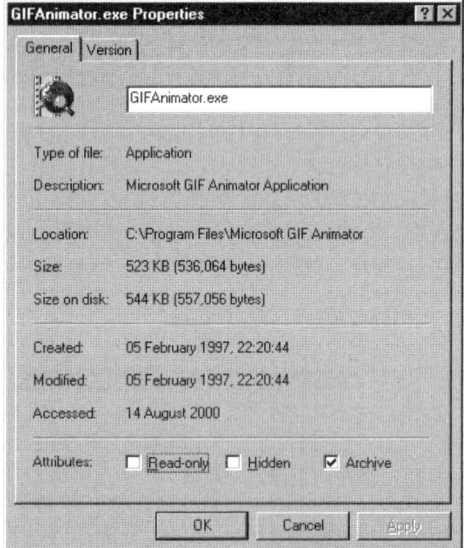

Some tabs are purely for information. This one also has some options in the bottom section.

**Tip**: *As a general rule, leave the Attributes alone! The default settings are probably best.*

Click on the name to open a tab.

Options can be set in many ways (see pages 13 and 14).

When you have finished with a panel, click **OK** to fix your changes, or **Cancel** to leave things as they were before. **Apply** will make the changes but leave the panel open.

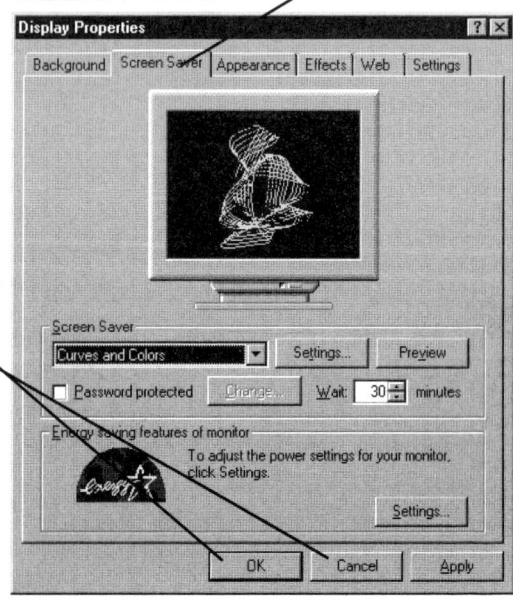

**Figure 1.5** Two **Properties** panels. The top one is from a program, the bottom one from the Desktop (see Chapter 2).

# INTRODUCING WINDOWS ME 13

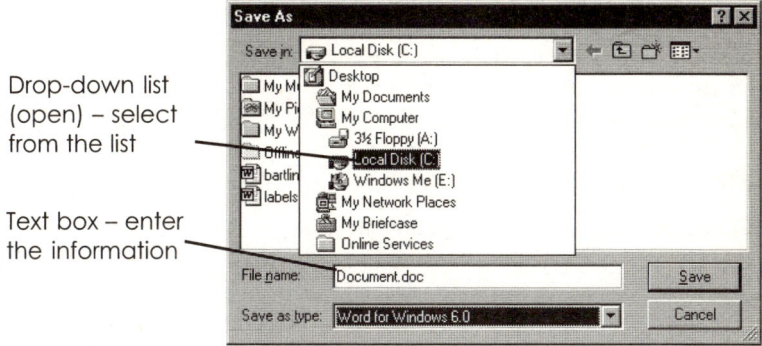

Drop-down list (open) – select from the list

Text box – enter the information

**Figure 1.6** A **Save As** dialog box showing an open drop-down list and a text box. The **Save as type** options are also on a drop-down list.

Windows uses a range of methods for setting options and collecting information in its Properties panels and dialog boxes.

## Text boxes

Typically used for collecting filenames or personal details. Sometimes a value will be suggested by the system. Edit it, or retype it if necessary.

## Drop-down lists

These look like text boxes but have an arrow to their right. Click on the arrow to make the list drop down, then select a value.

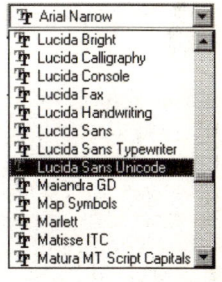

## Lists

With a simple list, just scroll through it and select a value. They sometimes have a linked text box. The selected value is displayed there, but you can also type in a value.

## Check boxes

These are switches for options – click to turn them on or off.

Check boxes are sometimes found singly, but often in sets. You can have any number of check boxes on at the same time, unlike radio buttons.

## Radio buttons

These are used to select one – and only one – from a set of alternatives. Click on the button or its name to select.

## Sliders and number values

**Sliders** are used where an approximate value will do – for example, volume controls, speed and colour definition (actual values may not mean much to most of us

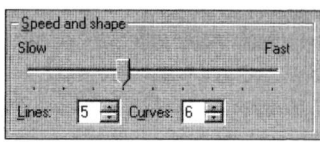

these situations!). Clicking to the side of the slider will move it towards the click point, or you can drag the slider in the direction.

**Numbers** are often set through scroll boxes. Click the up or down arrows to adjust the value. If you want to make a big change, type in a new value.

## SUMMARY

- ✓ Windows Me is an operating system with a package of utility and application programs.
- ✓ The screen is referred to as the Desktop, and should be treated much as a real desktop.
- ✓ The mouse responds to single and double clicks of the left button, and to single clicks of the right button. It can also be used to drag objects across the Desktop.
- ✓ Certain keys serve specific functions.
- ✓ In any application, the commands can be reached through the menu system.
- ✓ The Start menu is smart, adjusting itself to suit you.
- ✓ Some commands have keyboard shortcuts.
- ✓ Right-clicking on an object normally opens a shortcut menu, containing relevant commands.
- ✓ Windows Me has a number of simple ways to set options and make selections.

# 2 THE DESKTOP

## AIMS OF THIS CHAPTER

In this chapter we will look at the Desktop itself, and ways to arrange items on it – experimenting will show you what works best for you in different situations. We will also look at how you can change the appearance of the Desktop, as you should set the screen up to suit yourself before you go any further into your explorations of Windows Me.

## 2.1 Desktop modes

The Desktop can be run in two modes – or a combination of the two – which affect both the appearance and the way that you handle items. You can switch between the modes at any time.

### Web Page mode

In this mode, the shortcuts are underlined and respond to a single click. This is the *Active Desktop*, from which you can reach out into the Internet. Microsoft and some other sites offer *Active Desktop components* which create links to services at their sites. For example, Microsoft offers a Search component, which allows you to set up a search at any one of dozens of sites before you go online.

### Classic mode

In this simpler mode, it takes a double-click to start a shortcut, and the Active Desktop components are not displayed. If you do not have an Internet connection, or you find that you do not make use of the Active Desktop features, this is the mode to use.

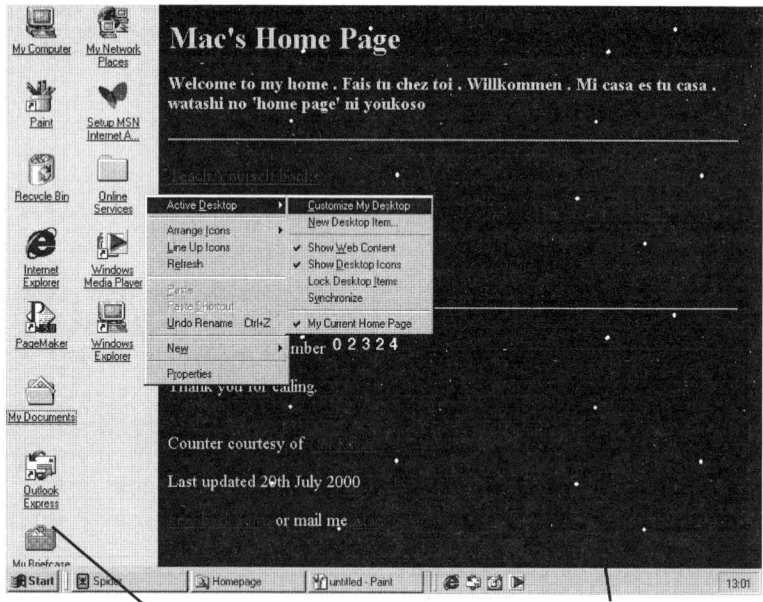

Notice the underlines                    Active Desktop component

**Figure 2.1** The **Desktop**, in Web page mode.

For reasons best known to themselves, Microsoft has put the Web/Classic mode switches inside My Computer. We will dip into it now, to set up the Desktop, and return to it properly in Chapter 7.

❶ Locate the My Computer icon. If it is underlined, click it once, otherwise, click on it twice in quick succession.

❷ Click on **Tools** to open the menu, then click on **Folder Options…**

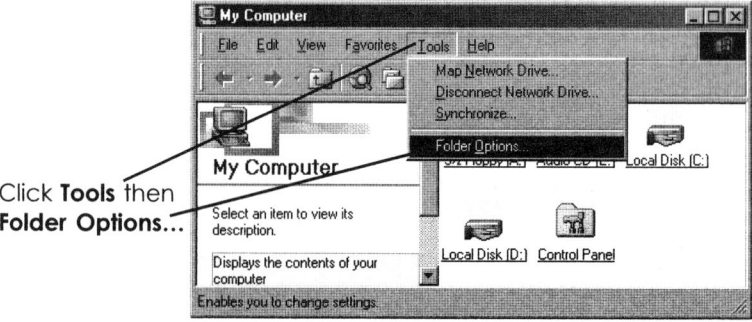

Click **Tools** then **Folder Options…**

# THE DESKTOP

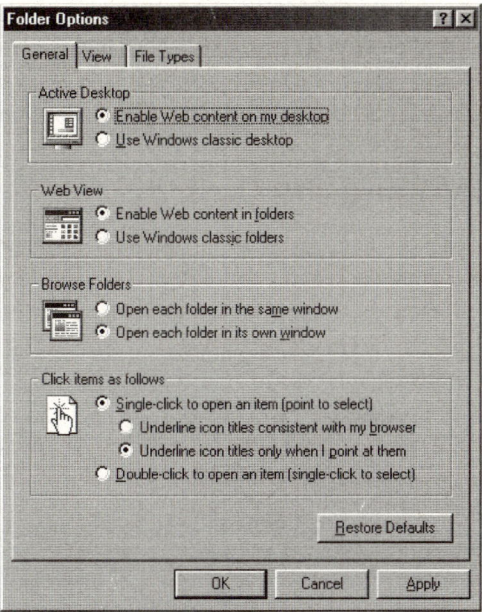

**Figure 2.2** The **Folder Options** panel, opened from My Computer – the same options can also be reached from Windows Explorer (see Chapter 7 for more on these).

## Folder Options

At this point we are only interested in two of the options on the **General** tab. We will return to the other options and the other tabs when we look at files and folders in Chapter 7.

In the **Active Desktop** section, select **Enable Web content on my desktop** if you want to be able to use an HTML page as a background (see page 18), or to run Active Desktop components.

In the **Click items...** section, set how you want the computer to respond to single and double-clicks. The best settings are probably:

- **Open with a single click** if you are a new user – it's simpler. You may want to set it so that you only get underlining when you point at an item – having everything underlined is messy.
- **Double-click to open** if you have previously used earlier versions of Windows – it's the familiar way of working.

Experiment with the variations here, to see which suit you best. But once you have decided, stick with it! If you keep changing the effects of single and double-clicking, you will confuse yourself.

* When you have set the options, click **OK** to close the panel.

## 2.2 Customizing the Desktop

The customized Desktop can be based on either the Web page or classic mode. You can change the settings – and go back and adjust them – at any point without affecting any other application that may be open at the time.

❶ Right-click anywhere on the background of the Desktop to get its context menu.

❷ The top command, **Active Desktop**, leads to a submenu. Point to it to open the submenu and select **Customize my Desktop**.

❸ This opens the **Display Properties** panel, with the **Web** tab at the front.

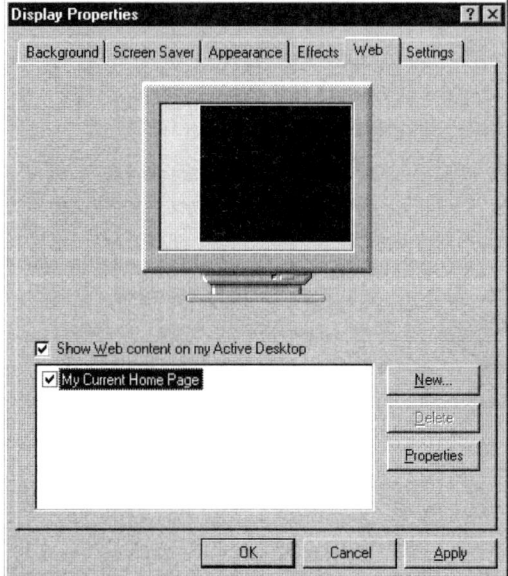

**Figure 2.3** The Web tab. The **New** and **Delete** button refer to Active Desktop elements. If you click the **Apply** button, the new settings will be applied without closing the panel.

## Web

The main option here is **Show Web content on my Active Desktop**. If that is turned on, you can then select which Active Desktop elements you want to include. At first, there will only be one element listed – *My Current Home Page*. Over time you may add many elements, with the effect that the screen becomes impossibly crowded if they are all visible at once. Using this panel to turn them off is the equivalent of clearing stuff off your desk and piling it on the floor (though a bit more organized). The elements are still available and can be turned back on at any time.

The idea of Active Desktop components has not caught on in the way that Microsoft had hoped, but there are some available from Microsoft – and a few other sites. If you want to investigate these, Click the **New** button.

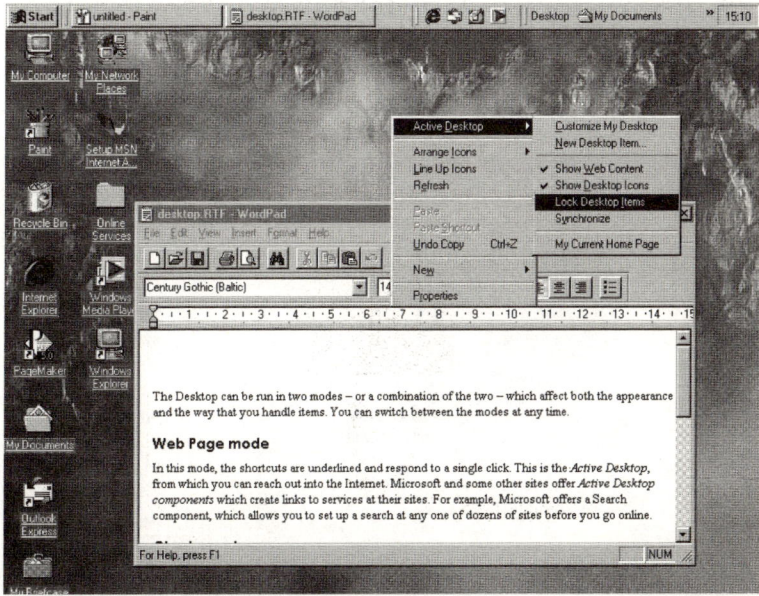

**Figure 2.4 Customizing the Desktop**. This has been given a new background and the Taskbar has been moved to the top of the screen with the Desktop toolbar added to it. This duplicates the icons on the Desktop – which means you can still reach them when an application fills the screen. (Chapter 9 has more on the Taskbar.) Note that the icon names are underlined, showing that they respond to a single click.

This will link you to the Active Desktop area of Microsoft's site, where you have a selection of components for downloading.

## The Background

Click the **Background** tab on the **Display Properties** panel to get to this.

The background is purely decorative! The background can be a plain colour, a single picture, a small image 'tiled' to fill the whole screen or an HTML document. Windows Me has a selection of small and large images (and two HTML documents), but any JPG, GIF or BMP image or Web page can be used.

- ❶ Scroll through the list of images and pages. If you find one that sounds interesting, select it and it will be shown in the preview.
- ◆ With a small image, set the **Display** mode to **Tile**. The image will be repeated across and down to fill the screen.
- ◆ With a larger image, set the **Display** mode to **Center** to see it in its natural size, or **Stretch** to make it fill the screen.

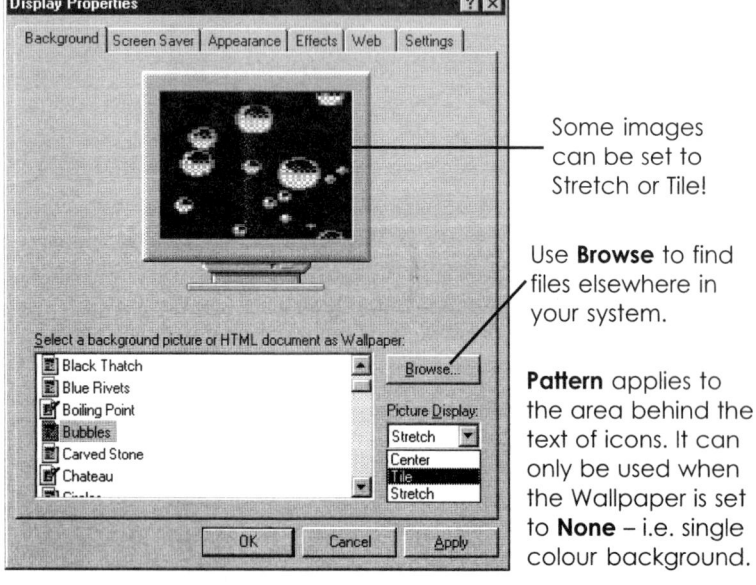

Some images can be set to Stretch or Tile!

Use **Browse** to find files elsewhere in your system.

**Pattern** applies to the area behind the text of icons. It can only be used when the Wallpaper is set to **None** – i.e. single colour background.

**Figure 2.5** The **Background** tab, with the Display options visible – and hiding the Pattern button.

> **HTML**
>
> HyperText Markup Language is the system used to create pages for the World Wide Web. HTML documents can display formatted text and images, and can carry links to other places on the Web or within your own computer or local network. HTML is easy to learn, but if you want a really simple way to create HTML pages, have a look at FrontPage Express. If you do want to learn HTML, try *Teach Yourself HTML*.

❷ Click **Apply** to test the choice. If you don't like it, try another.

*Don't click **OK** yet. If you do, it will close the Display Properties panel.*

If, at some later point, you find an image – perhaps while surfing the Web – or an actual Web page, that you would like to use as your Desktop's 'wallpaper', save it, then reopen this panel and use the **Browse** button to set it as your background.

## The Screen Saver

This is mainly decorative. A screen saver is a moving image that takes over the screen if the computer is left unattended for a while. On older monitors this prevented a static image from burning a permanent ghost image into the screen. Newer monitors do not suffer from this, but screen savers are more interesting than a static image on an idle screen.

> **PROTECT FROM PRYING EYES**
>
> The Screen Saver can be password protected, so that it will lock the screen – and the rest of the system – until the password is entered. This can be useful if you do not want passers-by to read your screen while you are away from your desk.

## Appearance

Use this panel to set the colour and fonts for the Desktop and standard Windows-elements in all applications – the menus, dialog boxes, etc. You can select from a wide range of ready-made colour schemes, and adjust the settings for individual elements.

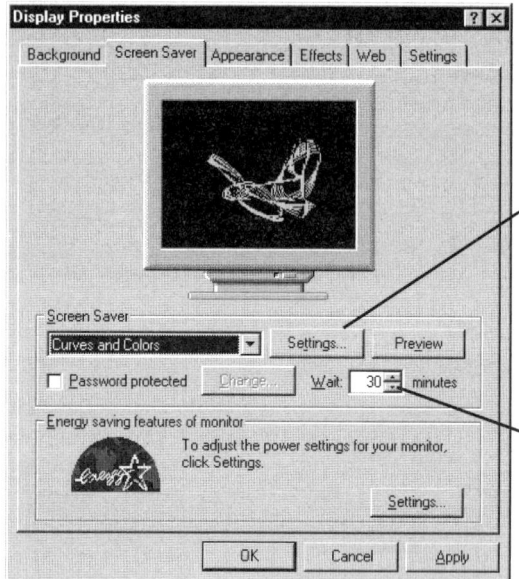

The Settings options let you set the speed, colour, text or other features, depending on the choice of Screen Saver.

How long does the computer have to be idle before the Screen Saver should kick in?

**Figure 2.6** The **Screen Saver** tab.

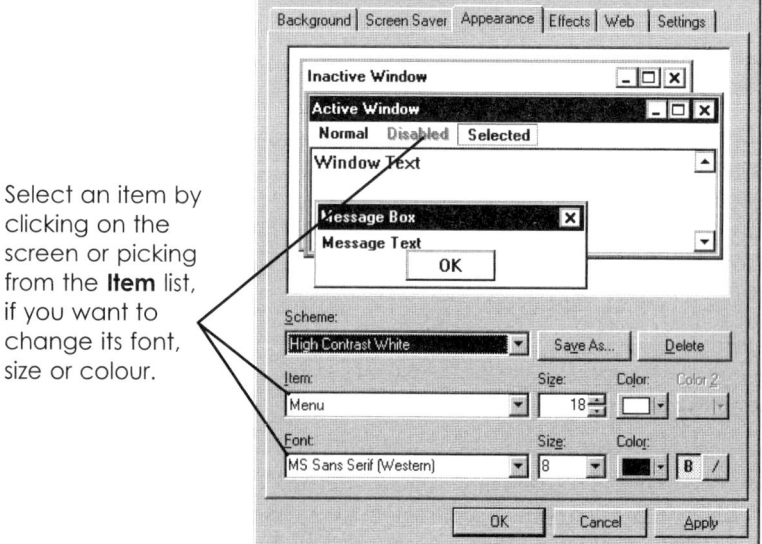

Select an item by clicking on the screen or picking from the **Item** list, if you want to change its font, size or colour.

**Figure 2.7** The **Appearance** tab.

# THE DESKTOP

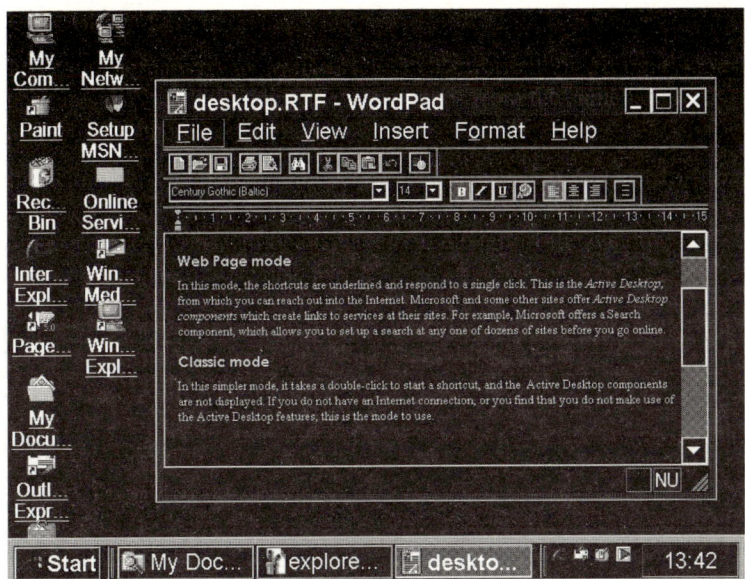

**Figure 2.8** One of the **High Contrast schemes**. For maximum visibility, try the High Contrast White, with extra large fonts.

Some of the colour schemes are miracles of bad taste, others refined and easy on the eye. There are also a number of high contrast schemes, some with large fonts, for greater visibility. Experiment and find one you like.

If it takes you a while to get everything 'just so', click the **Save As...** button on the Appearance tab and save the settings as a scheme. If someone later changes the settings, you can get your desktop back by selecting your saved scheme.

## Effects

Here you can change the images used for the Desktop icons, if you like – though the choice is limited unless you have bought the Plus pack of Windows Me add-ons.

In the Visual Effects section, turn on **Use large icons** if you need the extra visibility. The other options are purely decorative, and can slow things down slightly as they all create more work for the system.

**Figure 2.9** The **Effects** tab.

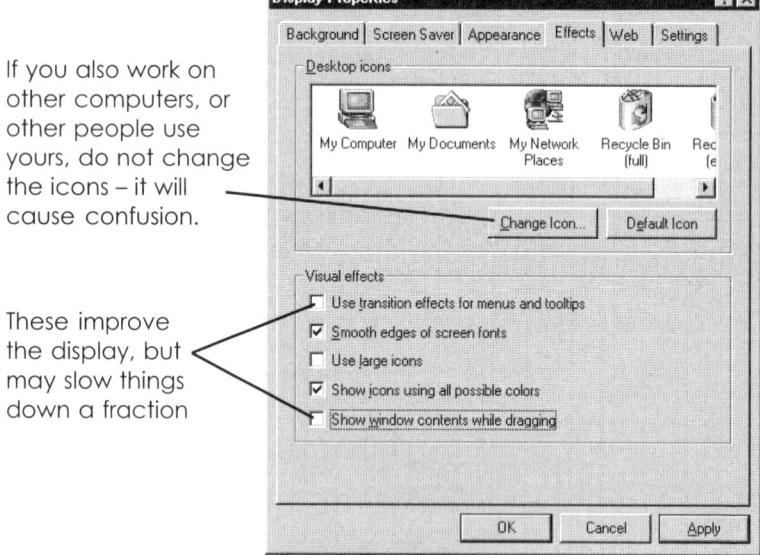

If you also work on other computers, or other people use yours, do not change the icons – it will cause confusion.

These improve the display, but may slow things down a fraction

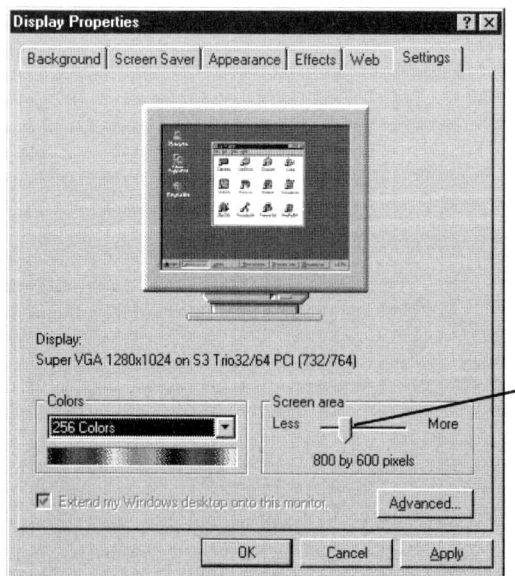

The Screen area is set low here as this works better for the (small) pictures I need for this book. 1024 by 768 or 1280 by 1024 work better on a 17" monitor.

**Figure 2.10** The **Settings** tab.

## Settings

The Settings relate to the size of the screen and number of colours used in the display. They should normally be left alone as Windows Me will select the optimum settings for your system – and the Advanced settings should certainly be left at their defaults unless you know and understand the details of your system. Bad selections here can really mess up your screen!

### SUMMARY

- ✓ The Desktop can be run in Web or Classic mode.
- ✓ If you want to link to the Internet through Active Desktop components, as part of your normal working approach, use Web page mode.
- ✓ Many aspects of the screen can be controlled through the Display properties panel.
- ✓ The Background, Screen Saver and Effects options are largely decorative and have little impact on the working of your system.
- ✓ The Appearance options can be set to high contrast and large fonts if you need to make the display easier to see.

# 3 WORKING WITH WINDOWS

## AIMS OF THIS CHAPTER

If you only use one application at a time, you don't have to think too much about managing your windows – there will only be the one. But this kind of usage does not take advantage of Windows Me, a multi-tasking system. If you want to have several applications open, you must know how to switch between them, and to arrange their windows so that you can work efficiently. This chapter will show you how.

### HOW MANY WINDOWS AT ONCE?

There is no fixed limit to the number of windows that you can have open at the same time. The maximum depends on the amount of RAM memory on the computer and how memory-hungry the applications are. You won't run many big programs at once in a 32Mb machine, but 128Mb should be able to handle far more than you could ever realistically want.

I once had 30 applications running simultaneously, though 26 of these were started accidentally! (Don't lean on the **Enter** key when an application icon is selected on the Desktop...)

## 3.1 Basic windows concepts

A window is a framed area of the screen that exists and is controlled independently of any other windows. All applications are displayed in windows. If an application can handle multiple documents, each document is displayed in its own window within the application.

# WORKING WITH WINDOWS

All windows have these features:
- **Title bar** along the top – showing the name of the application or document;
- **Minimize**, **Maximize/Restore** and **Close** buttons on the far right of the title bar – for changing the mode (page 28) and for shutting down;
- An icon at the far left of the Title Bar – leading to the window's **Control menu** (page 28);
- **Scroll bars** along the right and bottom – for moving the contents within the frame. These are only present if the contents are too wide or too long to fit within the frame.
- A thin outer **border** – for changing the size (see page 33).

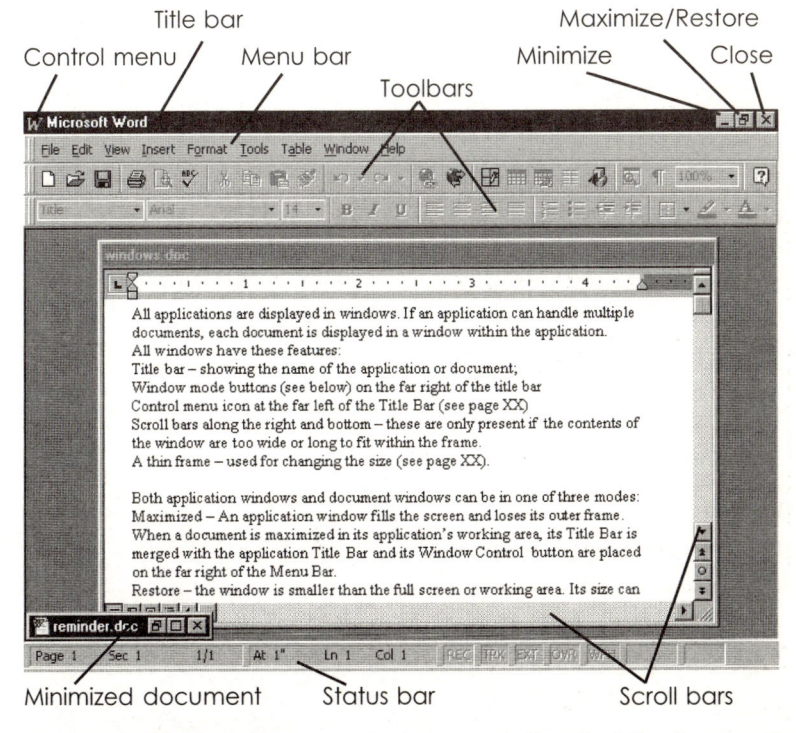

**Figure 3.1** The main features of windows. Notice that the icon and buttons are present in the Minimized document window – the one currently selected – and not in the other.

Application windows also have:

- **Menu bar** – giving access to the full range of commands and options;
- One or more **Toolbars** – containing icons that call up the more commonly-used commands and options. Toolbars are normally along the top of the working area, but may be down either side, or as 'floating' panels anywhere on screen.
- The **Status bar** – displaying a variety of information about the current activity in the application.

Both application and document windows can be in one of three modes, and the simplest way to switch them is with the buttons at the top right:

- **Maximize** – An application window fills the screen and loses its outer frame. When a document is maximized in its application's working area, its Title bar is merged with the application Title bar and its window control buttons are placed on the far right of the Menu bar.
- **Restore** – The window is smaller than the full screen or working area. Its size can be adjusted, and it can be moved to any position – within or beyond the limits of the screen.
- **Minimize** – An application is then visible only as a button on the Taskbar. A minimized document is reduced so that only the Title bar and window control buttons are visible.

**Maximize** and **Restore** are different faces of the same button.

## The Control menu

This is opened by clicking the icon at the far left of the Title bar. But this is really here for keyboard users.

Press **Alt** and the **Space bar** to open the menu in applications, or **Alt** and the **Minus** key in documents.

You can now Minimize, Maximize/Restore or Close by pressing the keys of the underlined letters. (**Alt** + **F4** is a shortcut for Close.)

This is also where keyboard users start to Move (page 36) or change the Size (page 33) of the window.

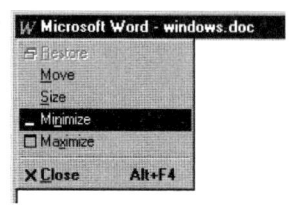

# WORKING WITH WINDOWS

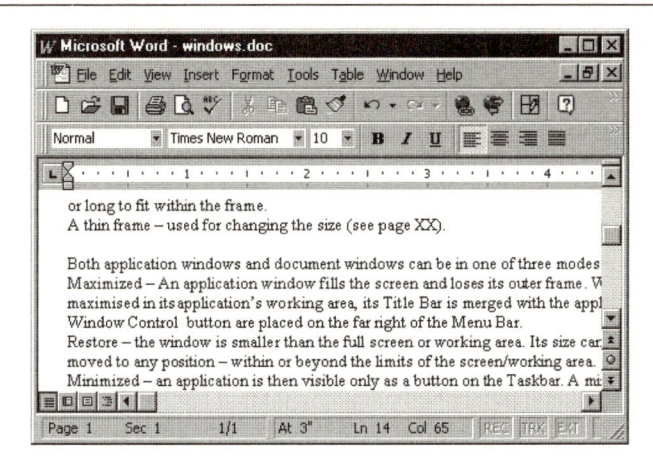

**Figure 3.2** When the document window is Maximized, its Title bar disappears. The document name is incorporated into the application Title bar; the document Control menu icon and buttons are placed in the Menu bar.

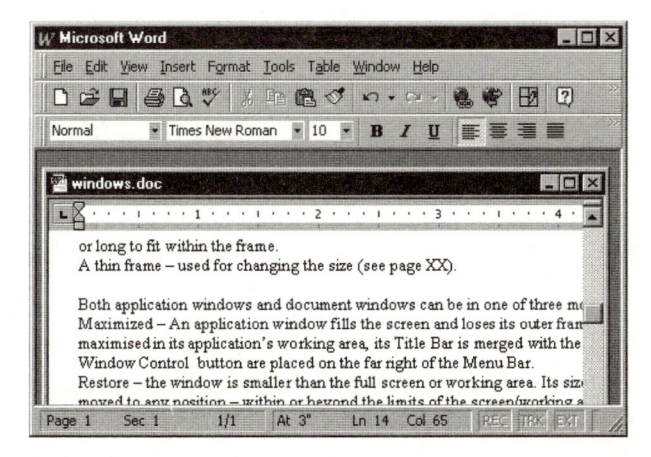

**Figure 3.3** A window can be moved beyond the limits of the visible screen or of an application's working area. Fortunately it never completely disappears, so there is always something to grab hold of to drag it back into view (see page 36).

## 3.2 Using the scroll bars

When you are working on a large picture or a long document, only the part that you are working on will be displayed within the window. Scroll bars will be present along the bottom and/or right of the frame and can be used to move the hidden parts of the document into the working area. They can be controlled in three ways:

- Click on the arrows at the ends to nudge the contents in the direction of the arrow – typically the movement will be a line or so at a time, but the amount of movement varies with the application and document size.
- Click on the bar to the side of or above or below the slider for a larger movement – typically just less than the height or width of the working area.
- Drag the slider. This is the quickest way to scroll through a large document.

Small movement

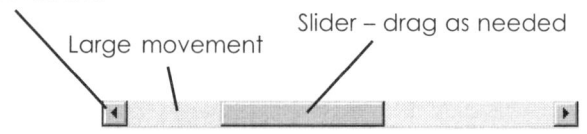

Large movement

Slider – drag as needed

---

**AUTOMATIC SCROLLING**

If the typing, drawing or other movements that you make while working on your document take the current position out of the visible area, the document will be scrolled automatically to bring the current position back into view.

---

## 3.3 Screen layouts

Windows Me allows you enormous flexibility in your screen layouts, though the simplest layout that will do the job is usually the best. You can only ever work on one application at a time – though you can copy or move files or data between two windows and there may be continuing activities, such as printing or downloading, going on in other windows. If you do not actually need to see what is happening in the other windows, the simplest layout is to run all applications in Maximized mode. The one that you are working on will fill the screen, obscuring the others, but you can easily bring one of those to the front by clicking on its button in the Taskbar.

---

### THE WINDOWS KEY AND THE TASKBAR BUTTONS

If you don't want to or cannot use the mouse to click the Taskbar buttons, hold down the **Windows** key and press **Tab**. This will select one of the Taskbar buttons – keep pressing **Tab** to move between the buttons. When the one you want is selected, press **Enter** to activate its window.

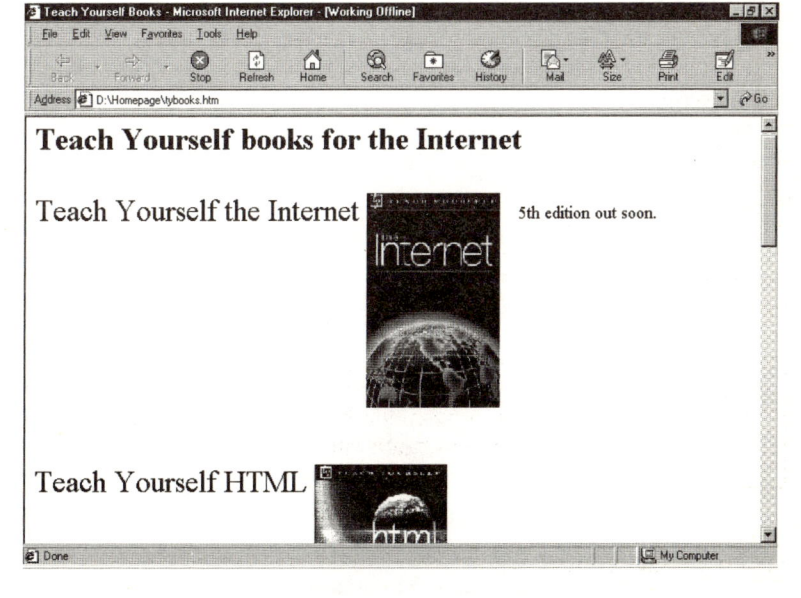

---

**Figure 3.4** If you are only working on one application, you may as well run it in a Maximized window and have the largest working/viewing area. Other windows can be reached, when needed, through their Taskbar buttons.

## Multiple window layouts

Sometimes you will want to be able to see two or more windows at the same time – perhaps to copy material from one application to another or to copy or move files. The simplest approach here is to use the **Cascade** and **Tile** commands. They will take all windows currently open in Maximized or Restore mode and arrange them overlapping (**Cascade**), side-by-side (**Tile Horizontally**) or one above the other (**Tile Vertically**).

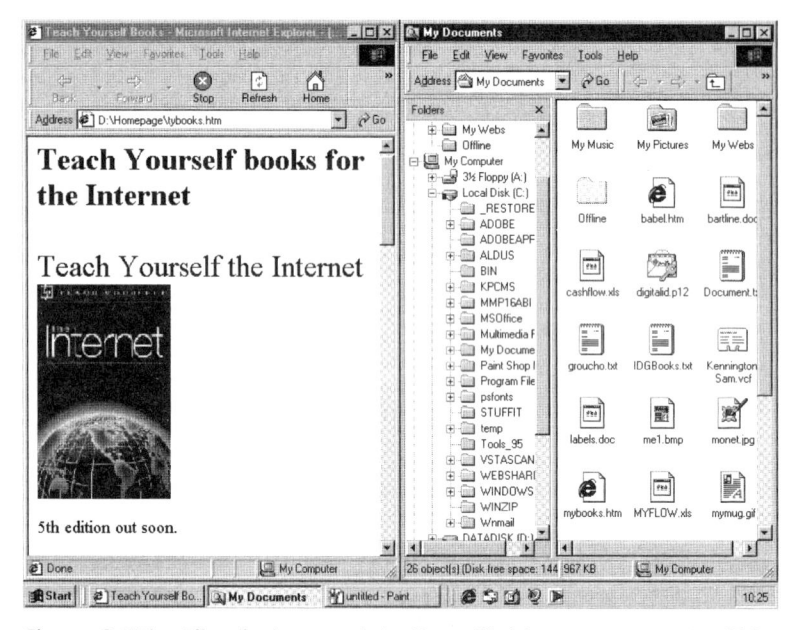

**Figure 3.5** The **Tile** displays work better with bigger screens. An 800 x 600 screen can cope with two windows – more at a pinch.

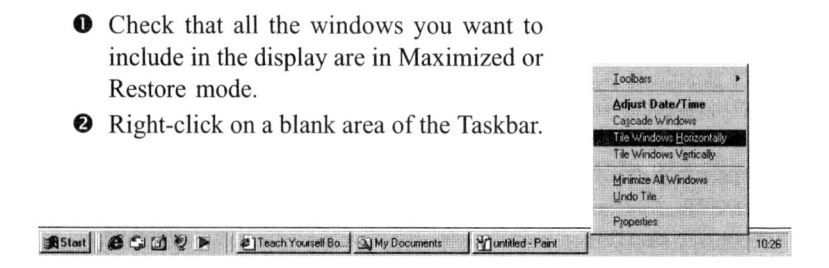

❶ Check that all the windows you want to include in the display are in Maximized or Restore mode.

❷ Right-click on a blank area of the Taskbar.

WORKING WITH WINDOWS 33

❸ Select the **Cascade** or **Tile Horizontally/Vertically** command.
❹ When you want to return to the previous layout, right-click the Taskbar again. The menu will now have an **Undo Cascade** or **Undo Tile** command.

## 3.4 Tabbing between windows

Switching between windows by using their Taskbar buttons is not always convenient. However, there are a couple of neat alternatives. This is the one I prefer:

❶ Hold down the **Alt** key and press **Tab**. This panel appears.

❷ Press **Tab** again until the application that you want is highlighted – if you go off the end, it cycles back to the start.
❸ Release the **Alt** key.

The second alternative is to hold **Alt** and press **Escape**. That also switches between windows and can be repeated until the right one is at the front of the Desktop.

## 3.5 Adjusting the window size

When a window is in Restore mode, its size can be adjusted freely. This can be done easily with the mouse or – less easily – with the keyboard.

### Using the mouse

❶ Select the document or application window.
❷ Point to an edge or corner of the frame – when you are in a suitable place the cursor changes to a double-headed arrow.
❸ Hold down the left mouse button and drag the edge or corner to change the window size. If you have turned on the **Show windows contents while dragging** option (on the **Effects** tab of the **Display Properties**, see page 23), the window will change

size as you drag. If the option is off, you will see a shaded outline showing the new window size.
❹ Release the mouse button.
❺ Repeat on other edges or corners if necessary.

## Using the keyboard

❶ Open the Control menu by holding down **Alt** and pressing the **Space bar** (application) or pressing **Alt + minus** (document).
❷ Press **S** to select Size.
❸ Press the arrow key corresponding to the edge that you want to move. A double-headed arrow will appear on that edge.
❹ Use the arrow keys to move the edge into its new position.
❺ Press **Enter** to fix the new size.
❻ Repeat for the other edges or corners if necessary.

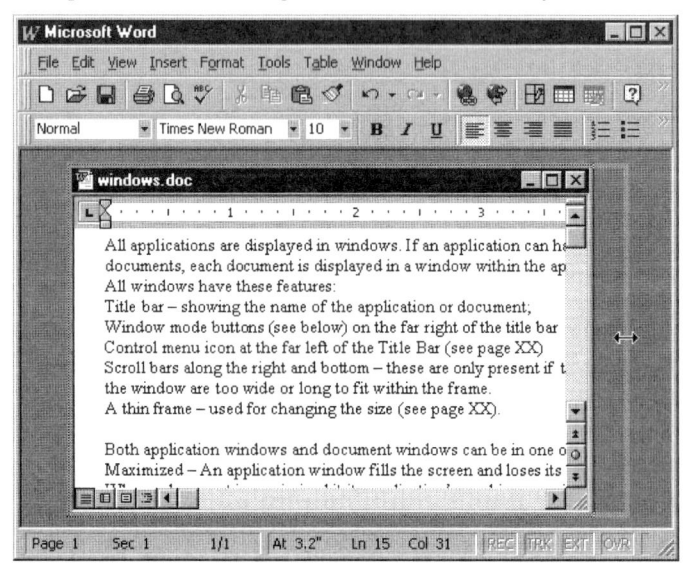

**Figure 3.6** Adjusting the size of a document window. An outline shows the new size as the *Show windows contents while dragging* option has been turned off.

# WORKING WITH WINDOWS

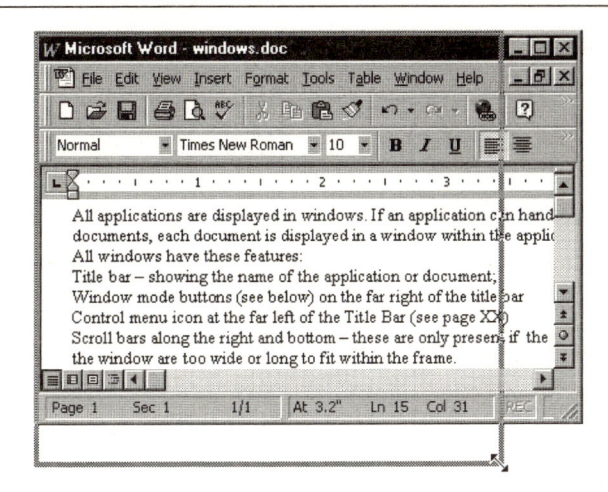

**Figure 3.7** Adjusting the size by dragging on a corner – a more efficient way to change the size, though it can be trickier to locate the cursor at the start.

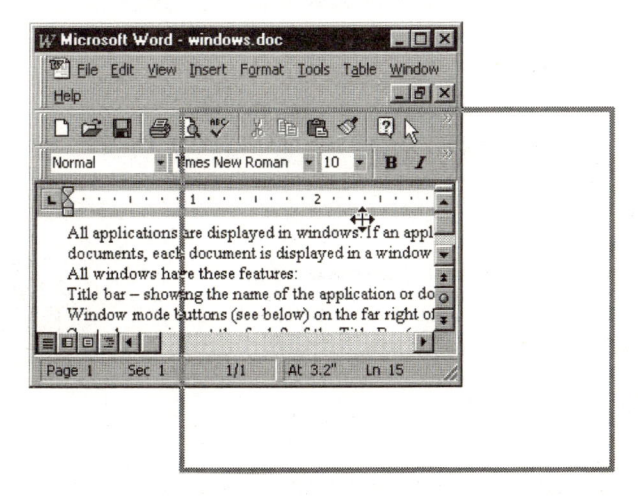

**Figure 3.8** Moving a window. The 4-way arrow only appears when you start from the **Move** command in the Control menu. If *Show windows contents while dragging* is turned off, only the outline moves while you drag – the window then leaps into place when you release the mouse button.

## 3.6 Moving windows

A window in Restore mode can be moved to anywhere on – or part-ways off – the screen (or the working area in an application). The Title bar is the 'handle' for movement.

### Moving with the mouse

- Point to anywhere on the Title bar and drag the window into its new place.

### Moving with the keyboard

❶ Open the Control menu and select **Move**.
❷ Use the arrow keys to move the window as required.
❸ Press **Enter** to fix the new position.

## 3.7 Closing windows

When you have finished with a window, close it. This will free up memory so that other applications run more smoothly, as well as reducing the clutter on your Desktop.

There are three methods which will work with any window:

- Click the **Close** button ⊠ in the top right corner.
- Hold down **Alt** and press the **minus** key to open the Control menu and select **Close**.
- Hold down the **Alt** key and press **F4**.

You can also close a window by exiting from an application (see *Closing programs*, page 61).

## 3.8 Shut Down

When you have finished a working session, you must shut down the system properly – ***do not simply turn off your PC***. Windows Me runs through a shutdown routine that removes any temporary files that were created by the system or by applications, checks the system and closes down safely. If you simply switch off, you may well find that it takes longer than usual to restart, as Windows Me will need to check – and possibly restore –

# WORKING WITH WINDOWS

essential system files. It may even insist on starting in 'Safe mode' and perform a thorough check there before allowing you to start up properly.

To shut down Windows Me:

● Click **Start** and select **Shut Down**. If any windows are open, they will be closed, and you may be prompted to save documents (page 61).

*or*

Hold down the **Alt** key and press **F4** – if a window is open, it will close that, and you will have to press **Alt + F4** again to shut down.

● Select **Shut down**.

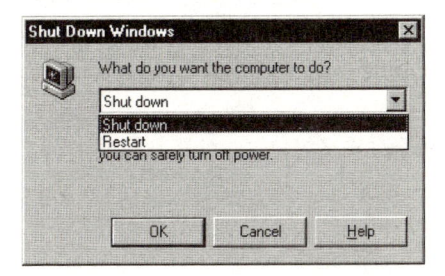

● Wait until you are told that it is safe before turning off your computer – it won't be long.

## Alternative endings

- Some PCs have a **Suspend** or **Hibernate** mode which shuts down the screen and hard drive, but leaves the memory intact. While suspended, the power consumption is virtually nil, but the computer can be restarted almost instantly. This is an attractive alternative to a full shut down.
- If you have had an application crash or freeze up on you, a **Restart** will normally restore order, though on very rare occasions you may need a full shut down and power-off to recover. (See page 61 for more on this.)
- If you are on a network, you can use the Start menu option to log off, leaving the computer ready for the next user.

## SUMMARY

- ✓ Windows can be open in Maximized, Restore or Minimized modes.
- ✓ To switch between the display modes, use the control buttons on the top right of the frame, or the commands on the Control menu.
- ✓ If the contents of a window go beyond the boundaries of the frame, the Scroll bars can be used to pull distant areas into view.
- ✓ There are many different ways to arrange windows on your screen – the simplest is to work with all windows Maximized, pulling them to the front as needed.
- ✓ The Cascade and Tile arrangements will display all Maximized and Restore mode windows.
- ✓ You can switch between open windows by holding down Alt and pressing Tab.
- ✓ The size of a window can be changed by dragging on an edge or corner, or using the Control menu Size command and the arrow keys.
- ✓ Windows can be moved by dragging on their Title bar, or with the Control menu Move command.
- ✓ You must shut down Windows properly at the end of a session.

# 4 | HELP!

## AIMS OF THIS CHAPTER

If you ever get stuck while using Windows, there's plenty of help at hand. Windows Me has its own extensive Help and Support system with 'tours', 'tutorials' and interactive trouble-shooters, and every Windows application has a Help system.

In this chapter you will learn how to navigate through these Help systems to find the assistance that you need. You will also see how to make good use of the other forms of Help that Windows Me offers.

## 4.1 Help and Support

The main Windows Me Help system is reached through the **Help** item on the **Start** menu.

- Click **Start**, select **Help** and you are in.

It will take a little while to load in – get used to it. Help comes slowly, even on a fast machine!

The Help and Support has four sections. *Home* and *Index* are the two most important of these.

### F1 HELP

You can also start Windows Help and Support from the Desktop, or get Help within any application, by pressing [F1].

## Home – the contents list

The Home section acts as a contents list, with many cross-references, all joined together by hyperlinks. These are easy to identify by their underlines. At the top level are a set of major content headings. Click on one of these links to open its page. The links at this level may be to lists of sub-topics, or directly to Help pages (marked by ?) or to Help on the Web (marked by ?) or to 'Tours & tutorials' (marked by ?).

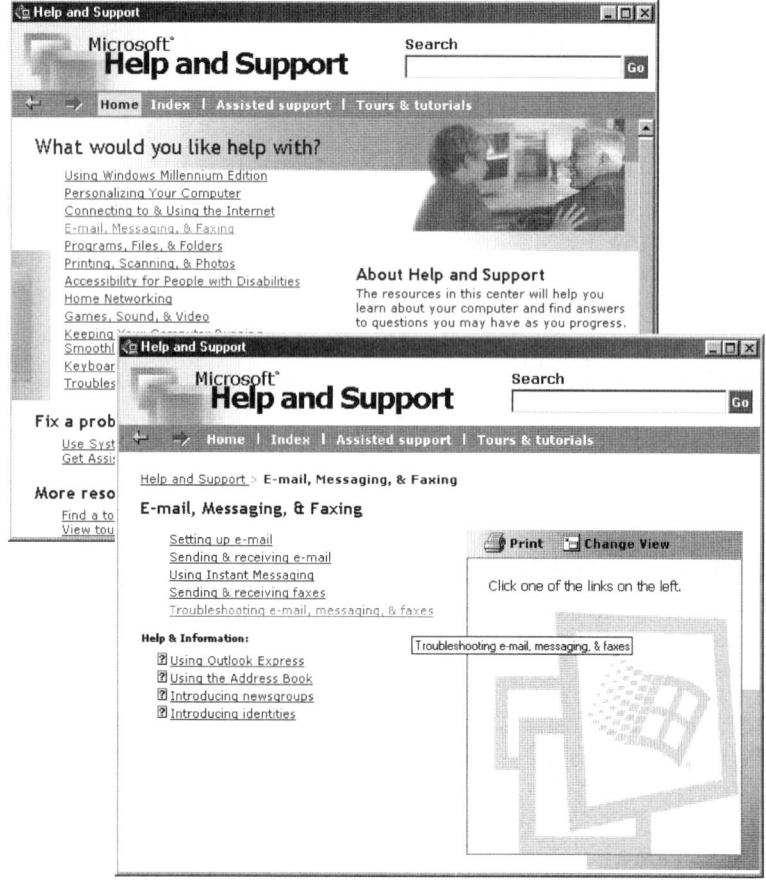

**Figure 4.1** Following the links in the Home section of Help and Support. On the second-level page there are links to five more sub-topics and to four pages of Help.

HELP! 41

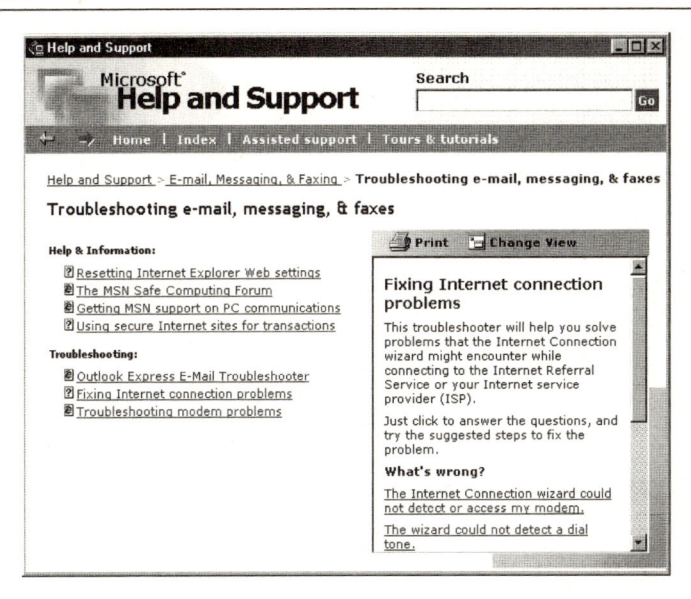

**Figure 4.2** The Troubleshooters can be very useful. They will take you through a series of checks and activities to try to diagnose and cure problems – and they generally work!

If you read to the bottom of a Help page, you will normally then find links to other similar topics. Some pages will simply have the label 'Related topics'. Clicking on this will look up the topic in the Index for you.

## Index

To switch to the Index, click on its label in the Menu bar. This works like the index of a book. To look up a word:

- Drag on the slider or click the down arrow to scroll through the list.

*or*

❶ Start to type the word in the top box. As you type, the system will leap through to the words that begin with the typed letters.

❷ Pick a topic from the list and click Display.

❸ If there are several Help pages for the same index entry, you will be offered a choice – pick one and click Display.

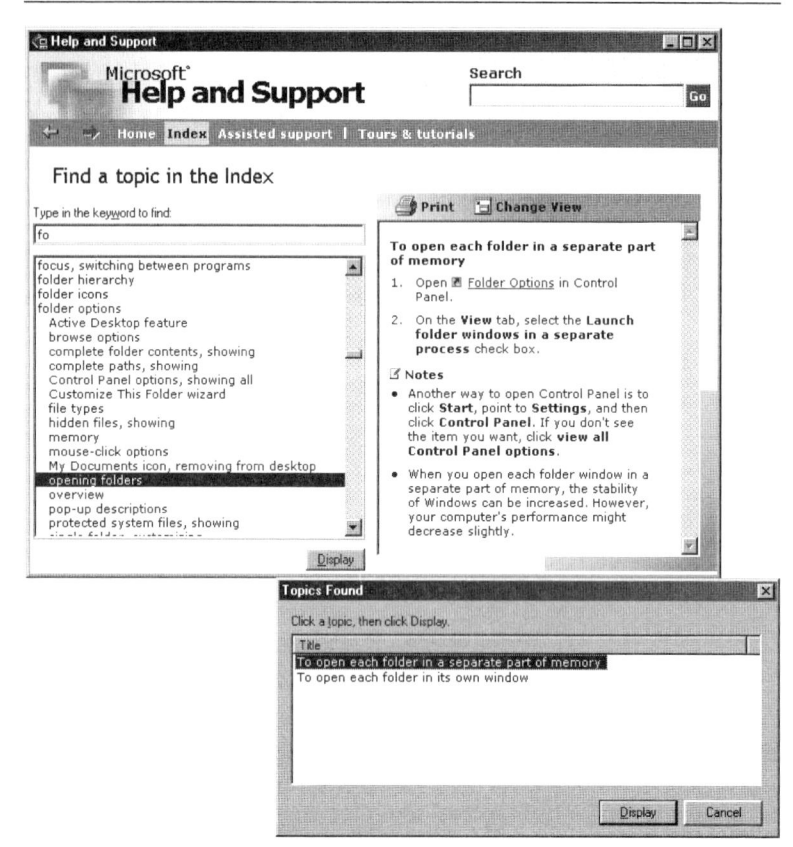

**Figure 4.3** Using the Index. Start to type a word to focus the list, then select an index entry – some lead to several topics.

The Help pages that you find here are the same as those linked from the Home section.

---

### KEYWORDS

When you are asked for a 'keyword' here – and while running searches on the Internet – all that's expected is a word that describes what it is you are looking for. If a word does not give you what you want, try a different word to describe it.

---

## Search

This is an alternative way to find Help on a specific topic. It pretty much duplicates the Index – finding the same pages from the same keywords – but is slightly more accessible.

The **Search** box is present on every page of the Help system. To run a search, type your keyword into the box and click **Go**. A list of pages containing your keyword will be displayed on the left of the window – click one to read its Help topic display.

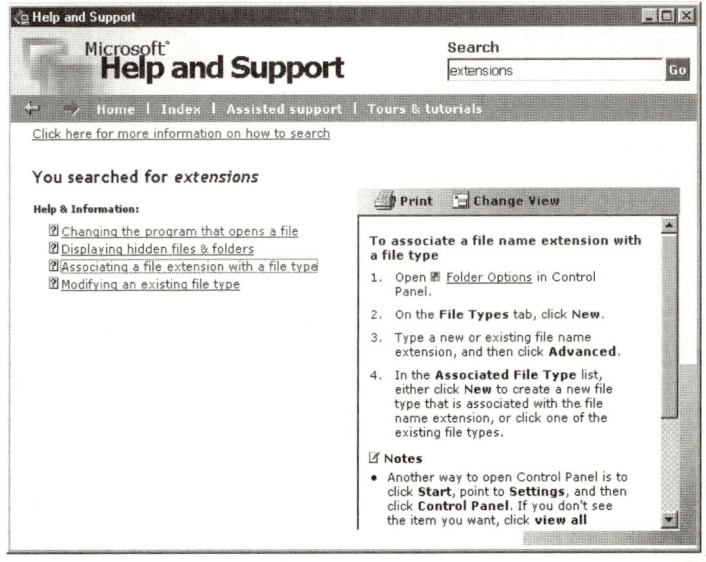

**Figure 4.4** A Search can be started from any page of the Help system. Just type what you are looking for and click Go.

## Change View

On the header bar of the Help topic display you will see **Print** – click on that for a printed copy of the Help – and **Change View**. If you click on this, the surrounding Help and Support window will close down, leaving just the topic display. This can be very useful if you want to keep the information visible while you tackle that tricky job.

♦ Click to reopen the full window when you need it.

**Figure 4.5** The **Change View** option shuts down everything except the topic display.

Remember that this is a window and can be resized to show more of the entry and moved to a convenient part of the screen so that you can still read it while working on whatever you needed the Help on.

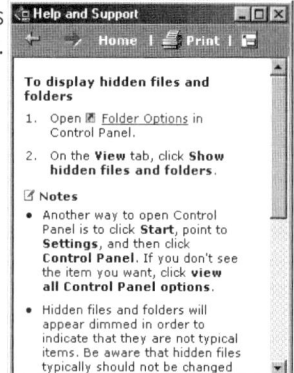

## Assisted support

If you can't find what you want in the Home or Index sections, go to this page to look for online support at Microsoft and MSN. The Microsoft link is direct to them; the MSN links first display a list of forums and message boards in the topic display area. Pick one of these and go online.

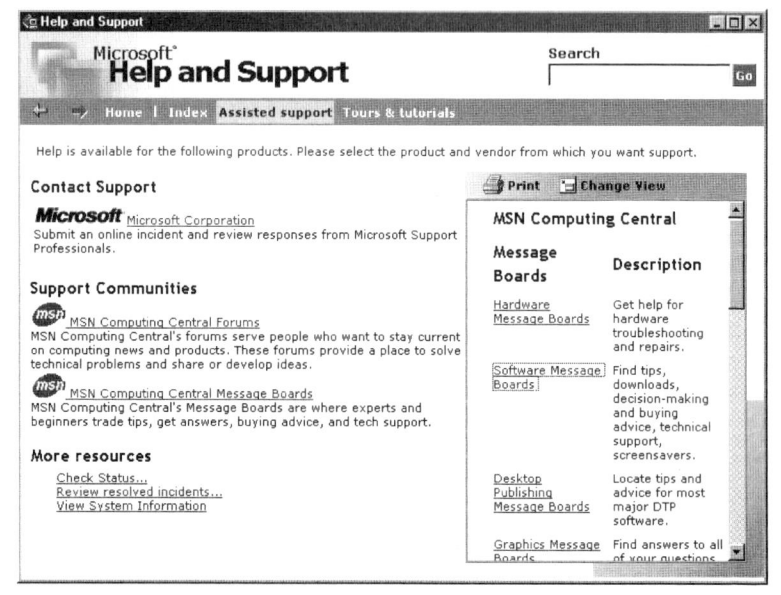

**Figure 4.6** It takes longer to get Help online, but there is far more available over a far wider range of topics – and you may be able to help others as well.

# HELP! 45

## Tours and tutorials

I hope this book does a good job of introducing the concepts and of guiding you into Windows, but it doesn't cover every aspect of this mammoth system. If you need a start on a new aspect of Windows, have a look at the **Tours and Tutorials**.

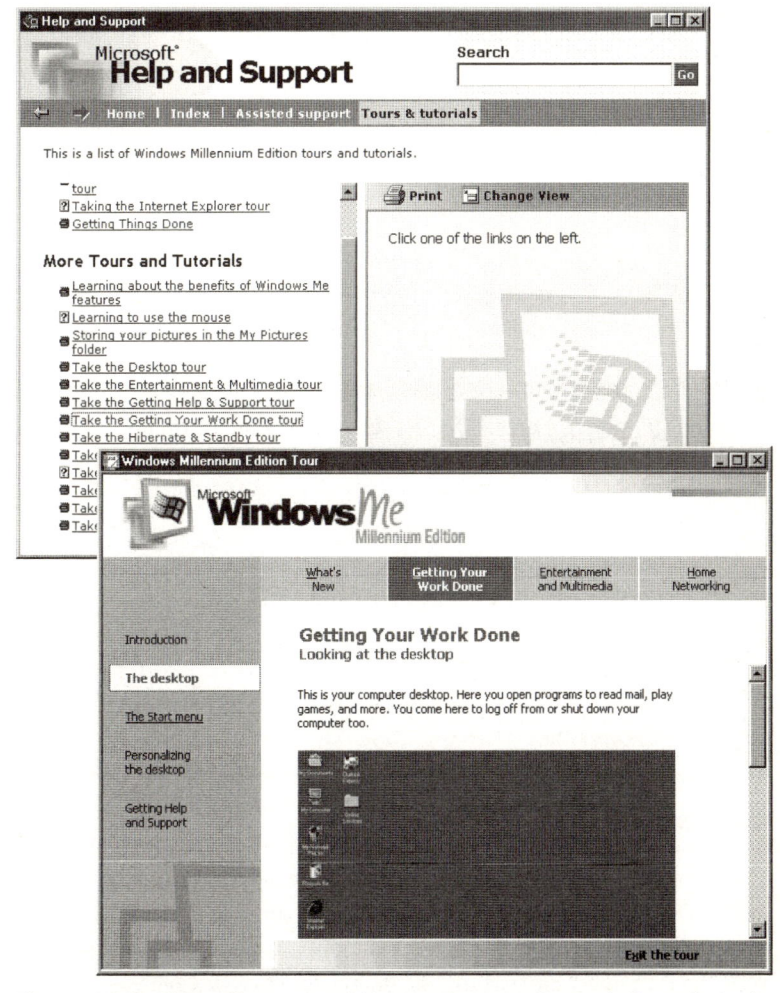

**Figure 4.7** Setting off on a tour! Have a browse through them to help familiarize yourself with what Windows Me has to offer.

## 4.2 Application Help

The utilities and applications that are supplied as part of Windows Me – and other Windows applications from Microsoft or any software producer – also have their own Help systems. These all use the same standard approach which looks different from, but behaves in much the same way as the Help and Support system of Windows Me.

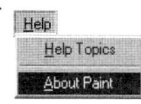

Look at the Menu bar in any application and you will see **Help** on the right. In the latest software, the first item on this menu will be **Help Topics**; in older software, the first will probably be **Contents** or **Contents and Index**. Whatever the label, the first item is the way into the Help system.

### Contents

A Help system can be thought of as a book, with a different topic on every page – though, unlike paper books, the pages vary in length. Related topics are arranged into chapters, and the whole book is extensively indexed. But this is a reference book. Don't attempt to read it all from start to finish, you'll just give yourself a headache.

The Help system normally opens at the **Contents** tab – if another tab is at the front, click on the **Contents** label to switch to it. Use this tab to get an overview of the available Help, and when you want to read around a topic. Initially, only the main section names will be visible.

- Beside each section name is a ● icon. Click on the section name or the icon to open the section.
- Some sections have subsections. Again, click on the name or ● to open one.
- When you see a list of topic pages, click on the name or ? icon to display a page in the right-hand panel of the window.
- Only one section is open at a time – the open one will close when you select another. If you want to close a section so that you can reach those that are off-screen, click the 📖 icon.
- As you browse through the system, the **Back** and **Forwards** buttons become active, allowing you to return to pages that you have opened earlier in that session.

# HELP!

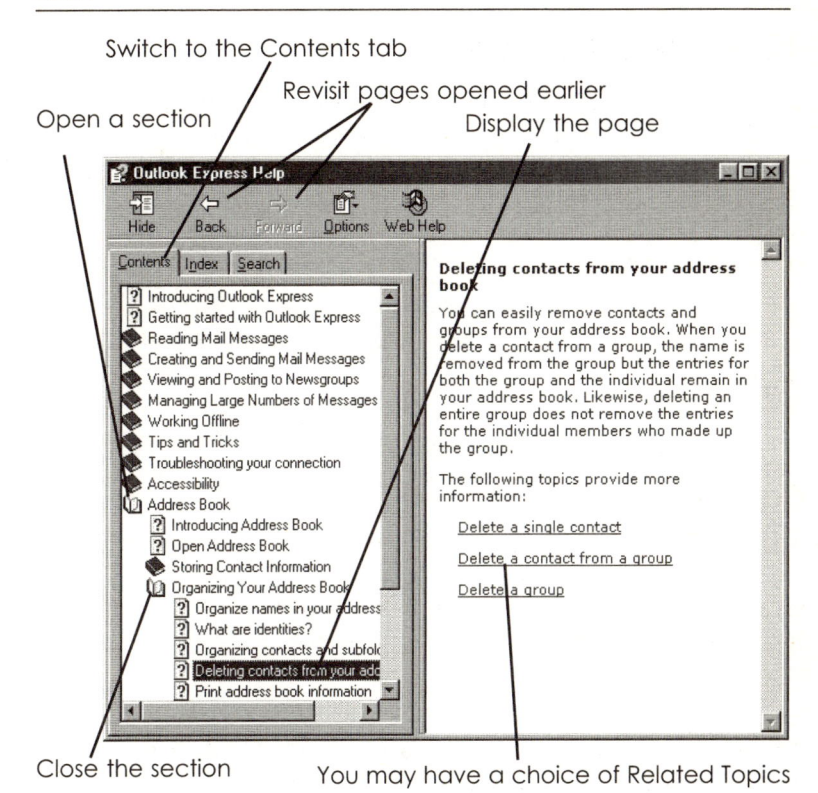

Switch to the Contents tab
Open a section
Revisit pages opened earlier
Display the page

Close the section
You may have a choice of Related Topics

**Figure 4.8** Outlook Express's Help system open at the **Contents** tab.

The Help pages contain descriptions of what things are and how they work, with instructions on how to perform tasks. The pages (both in Windows Me and in the latest applications) are written in HTML – HyperText Markup Language – the same coding system that is used for creating Web pages.

You will find that some text is underlined and hyperlinked – point to it and the cursor changes to 👆. Click and one of three things will happen:

- If the text is **Click here to...** a Wizard or application will start.
- If the text is **Related Topics**, either you will be shown a list of relevant pages from which you can pick one, or you will be taken directly to the related page if only one is available.
- If the text is a special term, a panel will appear giving a definition of the term. Click anywhere to close the panel.

## Index

The **Index** tab in application Help systems is very similar to that of Help and Support. Use it in just the same way.

❶ Start to type a keyword into the text box at the top. The list will scroll to bring into view the words that start with those letters.

❷ If the word you want is not yet visible, type more letters.

❸ Select an entry or sub-entry from the list and click `Display`.

❹ If the entry leads to several Help pages, you will see the **Topics Found** list – select one from here and click `Display`.

Type the first letter(s) of the word

Select an entry

Click Display

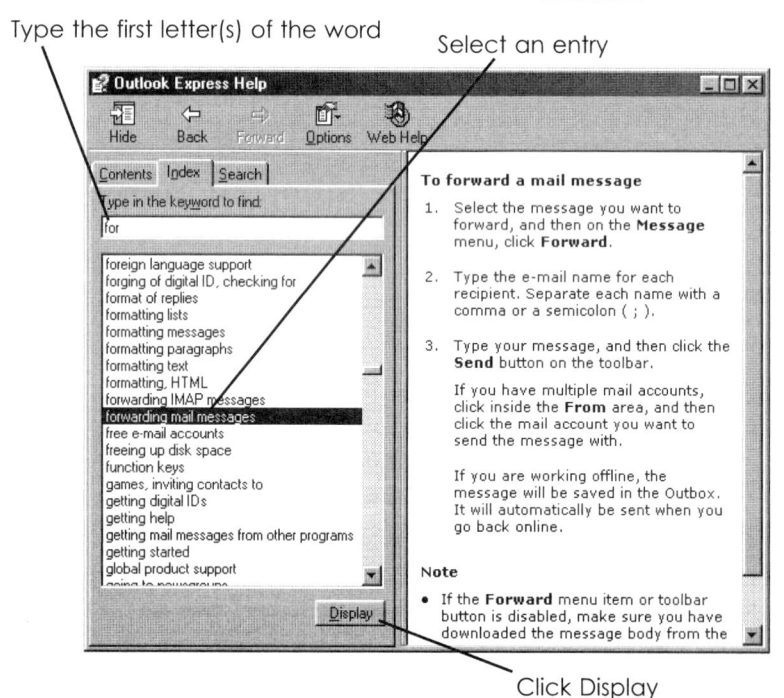

**Figure 4.9** Using the **Index** tab.

---

**CREATING THE INDEX**

The first time that you use the Index, you will have to wait for a moment while the system scans the Help pages to create it.

## Search

Like the Index, Search uses keywords to find pages – but there is a crucial difference between them. The Index is created from selected words, and the entries are grouped by topic. In contrast, the Search is based on a full-text search of all the Help pages. As a result, a Search will find all pages that contain any given word, while the Index will only find those that had merited an index entry. Depending upon how well the Help is indexed, a Seach can sometimes be far more productive than using the Index.

❶ Switch to the Search tab.
❷ Type one or more keywords into the text box.
❸ Press **Enter** or click  List Topics  .
❹ Select a Topic from the list and click  Display  .

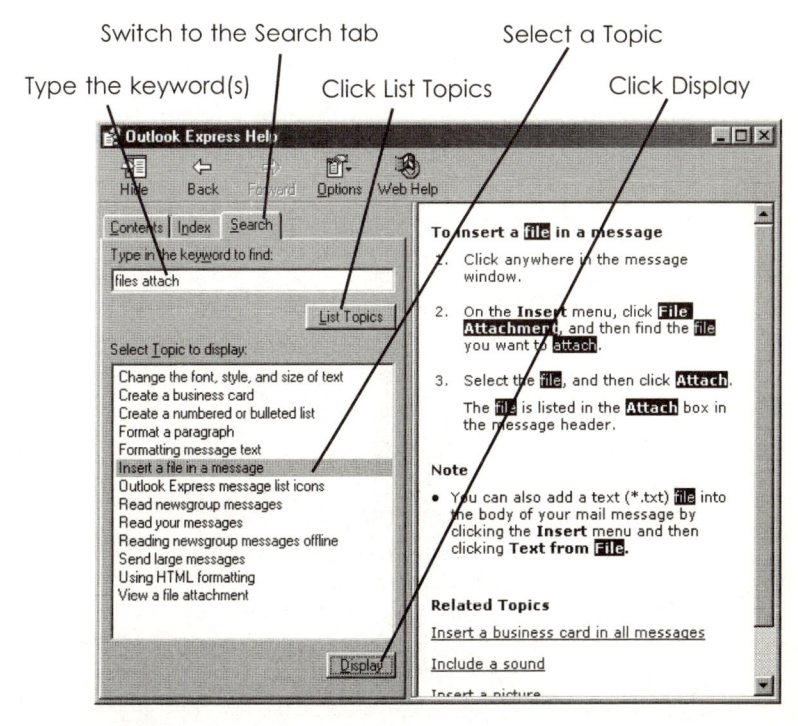

**Figure 4.10** Using the **Search** tab. The keywords are normally highlighted wherever they occur in the page.

## Tools and options

The Help system has a small set of tools and options, which should give you all the control you need – most of the time you will probably go into Help, find and read a page or two, and come straight out again.

Shuts the tab area, leaving just the page display – use it if you want to see more of the window beneath while you read the Help page. The icon then changes to Show – click this when you want to restore the tabs to view.

**Figure 4.11** If you want to see more of the screen beneath while you are reading the Help pages, hide the tabs, and resize the window.

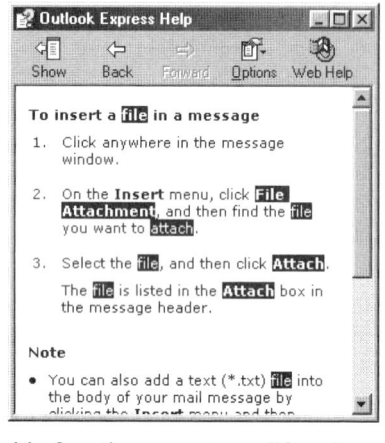

Reopens the Help page opened before the current one (if any) during the session.

Used after a **Back** move, to return to the next Help page in the sequence of those opened during the session.

Most of these duplicate the tools. Of the rest, these are worth noting:

**Refresh** If you click on an underlined term for the definition, or resize the window, the screen does not always redisplay correctly afterwards. Use Refresh to tidy it up.

**Print** Sends the current page to the printer.

**Search Highlight On/Off** Controls the highlighting of matching words in the pages found by a Search.

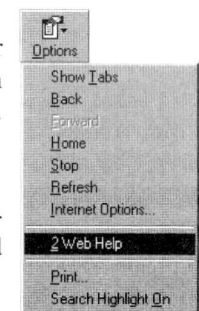

If you are online, this will connect to the Microsoft site where you can get Help with more advanced features or with technical problems. We will look at the Internet in Chapter 10.

## 4.3 Tips and prompts

### Tooltips

The icons on tool buttons are generally good *reminders* of the nature of the tool, but they are not always immediately obvious to the new user. Tooltips are little pop-up labels that tell you what icons stand for.

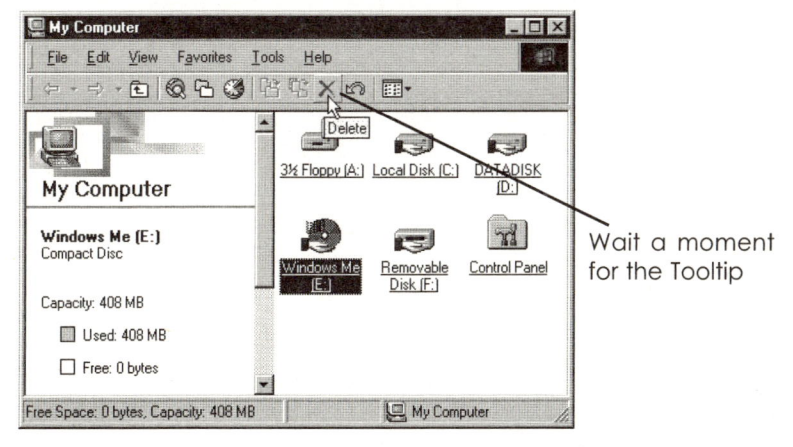

**Figure 4.12** If you don't know what an icon does, point to it and wait a second. A Tooltip will appear, giving its name. If you still need Help with it, at least you now know what to look up in the Index.

### Status bar prompts

The Status bar serves many purposes – it is through here that applications will communicate with you, so do keep an eye on it. One of the uses is to display a brief description of items as you point to them in the menus.

### Dialog box Help

If you look in the top right corner of dialog boxes and panels, you will normally see a [?] button. You can use this to get brief explanations of the options, buttons and other features in the dialog box.

The Status bar tells you about menu items

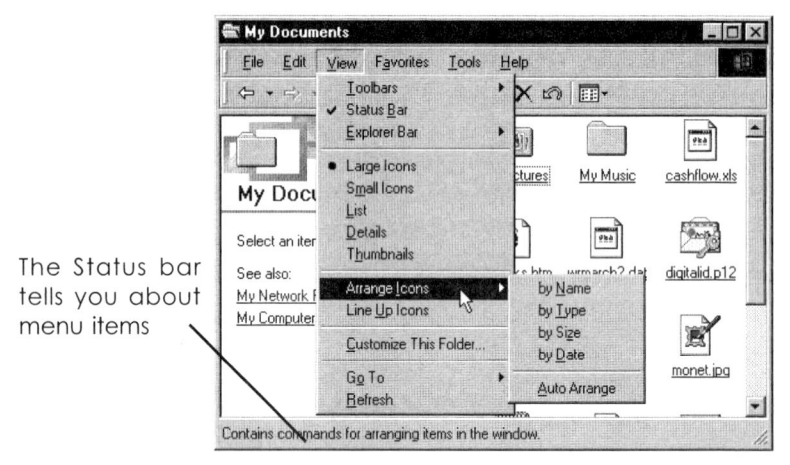

**Figure 4.13** When you point to an entry in the menu system, a brief description appears in the Status bar at the bottom of the window.

Here's how to get Help in a dialog box:
- ❶ Click [?]. The cursor changes to 🔍❓.
- ❷ Click on the item that you do not understand. A panel will open, displaying an explanation of the item.
- ❸ Click again – anywhere – to close the explanation panel.

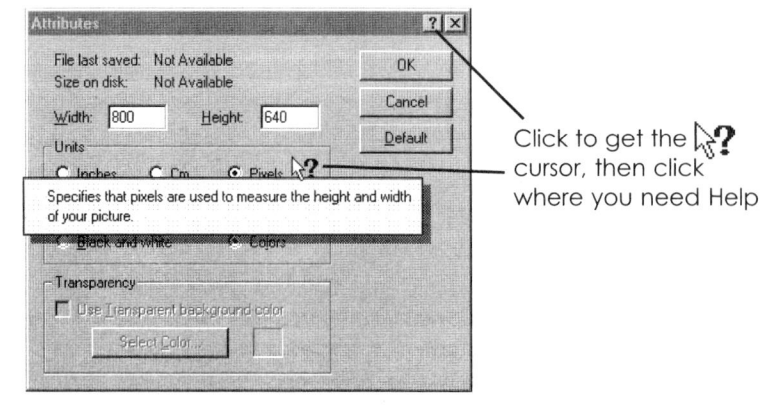

Click to get the 🔍❓ cursor, then click where you need Help

**Figure 4.14** When you first use a new dialog box, it's good to be able to get explanations of its options and features.

## 4.4 Wizards

The Wizards are not part of the Help system, but they play an important role in making Windows Me easy to use. As a general rule, if you have hardware or software to set up or reconfigure – especially if it is a lengthy or tricky operation – there will be a Wizard to help you through it.

All Wizards run in much the same way. You will see a series of panels. Each will ask you to set an option or provide some information, and will give you guidance on how you should respond.

At the bottom of the panel are three buttons:

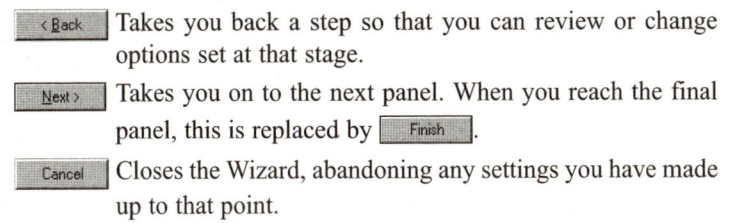

- **< Back**  Takes you back a step so that you can review or change options set at that stage.
- **Next >**  Takes you on to the next panel. When you reach the final panel, this is replaced by **Finish**.
- **Cancel**  Closes the Wizard, abandoning any settings you have made up to that point.

The Cancel button is more useful than you might think. There will be times when you get part way through a Wizard and realize that you do not have the information that you need to complete the operation.

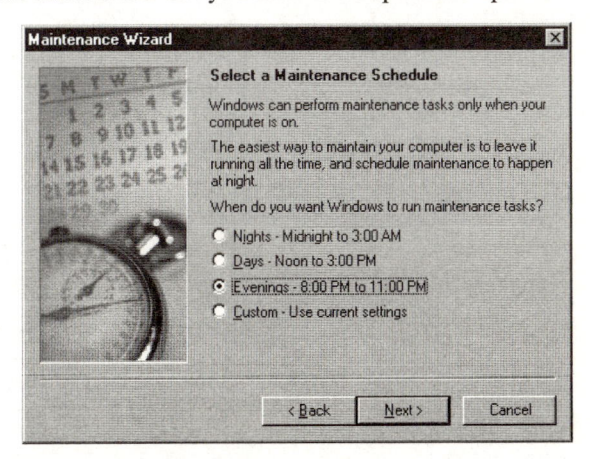

**Figure 4.15** A typical panel from a Wizard – this one will help you to organize the routine maintenance on your computer. (For more on this, see Chapter 12.)

## SUMMARY

Windows Me tries to be user-friendly and to provide help where it is needed.

- ✓ The Help command on the Start menu leads to the Help and Support system for Windows Me.
- ✓ Browse through Help and Support using the contents list in the Home section.
- ✓ To find Help and Support on a specific topic, use the Index section or run a Search.
- ✓ Additional Help is available online, through links in the Assisted Support area.
- ✓ The Tours and Tutorials provide an introduction to new topics.
- ✓ The Help systems in applications look different from Windows' Help and Support but are used in much the same way. Browse through the Contents or track down specific help through the Index or Search tabs.
- ✓ Tooltips and Status bar prompts can help you to get to grips with the tools and commands in a new application.
- ✓ The ? icon will give you explanations of the features of dialog boxes and panels.
- ✓ There are Wizards to help you with most configuration tasks.

# 5 PROGRAMS AND DOCUMENTS

## AIMS OF THIS CHAPTER

The whole purpose of Windows Me is, of course, to run applications and produce documents – almost everything in the system is concerned directly or indirectly with doing this. So, it's about time that we had a look at how to run applications, and how applications and documents are interrelated.

## 5.1 Definitions

Let's start with some definitions.

### Program

A program is a set of instructions, that make the computer perform a task. The task may be very simple, or highly complex. It is useful to divide programs into three types:

### Operating system level programs

These are run and controlled by Windows Me – which is itself a program (or rather a set of interlinked programs). You are only aware of them by their effect. They manage the screen, pick up your keystrokes and mouse movements, control the transfer of data to and from the disk drives, prepare documents for output to the printer, and similar chores. Those of us who cut our computing teeth on older operating systems sometimes regret that Windows takes such total control of these, but overall it must be admitted that Windows does a very good job of management.

### Utilities

These are the programs that you can use to manage your PC. Windows Explorer and My Computer, for example, allow you to organize your file storage (Chapter 7). There are programs in the Control Panel (Chapter 8) which you can use to customize the hardware and software, and another set that enable you to keep your disks in good order (Chapter 12).

### Applications

These are why you use computers. They include business applications such as word-processors, spreadsheets, databases and accounts packages; graphics software for creating and editing images; Web browsers and other tools for communicating and working cooperatively on the Internet and on local networks; multimedia viewers, players and editing software; games and much else. Most, though not all applications, will produce or display documents, and any given application can only handle documents of a certain type or range of types. We'll return to this after one last definition.

### Document

A document is an organized set of information produced by an application. It can be stored on disk as a file and – typically but not always – can be output onto paper, to be read or viewed away from the computer. The most obvious examples of documents are letters, essays and reports created on word-processors, but databases, spreadsheets and Web pages are also documents, as are images, sound and video files. When a document is saved, part of its name identifies the application that created it. This association with applications is central to the way that Windows Me handles documents. We will return to it in section 5.7.

## 5.2 Start → Programs

The simplest way to start an application or utility program is through the **Start** menu. Almost all of the programs currently on your computer, and of those that you install later, should have an entry in the **Programs** section of the menu.

---

**WHAT'S → THIS?**

→ is used to link the steps in a menu sequence, e.g. **Start → Programs** means 'select **Start** and from its menu pick **Progams**'.

---

# PROGRAMS AND DOCUMENTS

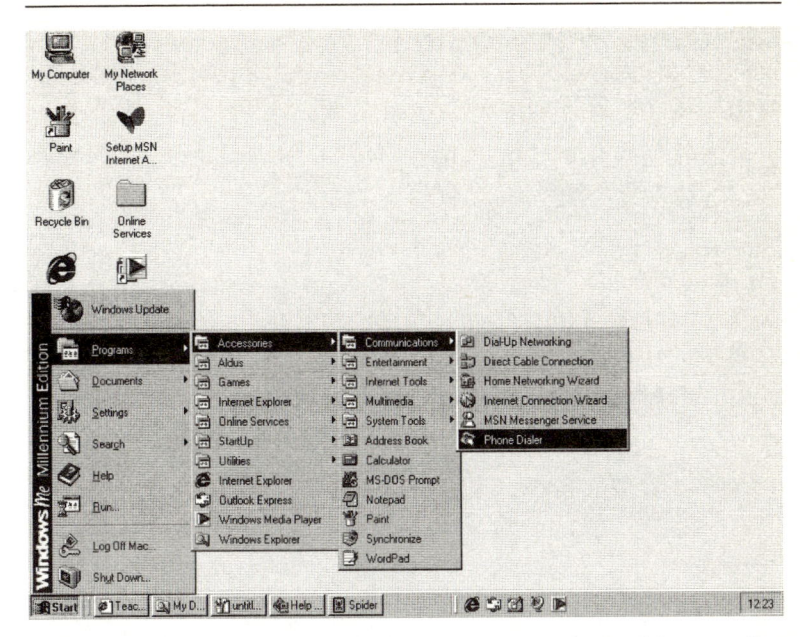

**Figure 5.1** Starting a program from the Start menu. In this case, the program, **Phone Dialer**, was on the third level of submenus. Notice **Windows Explorer** on the top level menu – you'll be needing that shortly! Notice also the Desktop Shortcuts in the background. These give quick access to regularly-used programs and folders.

A program may be on the first level of this menu, or may have been grouped onto a submenu – which may open up to a further level of submenus. The routines that install Windows Me and new software will create the Start menu entries and organize them into submenus, but if you do not like the structure, you can tailor it to suit yourself (see Chapter 9).

To start a program:

❶ Click **Start** or press ⊞ on your keyboard.
❷ Point to **Programs**.
❸ Click once on a program name.
*or*
❹ Point to a group name to open the next level of menu – and again if necessary – then select from there.

## 5.3 Other ways to start

### Explorer/My Computer

Windows Explorer and My Computer are the standard Windows Me file and folder management applications. The two do the same job in very similar ways, with very similar screen displays. We will be looking closely at these in Chapter 6. At this point it is worth noting that programs can be started from within them.

❶ Open the folder containing the program file.

❷ Click (or double-click) on the program name to start it.

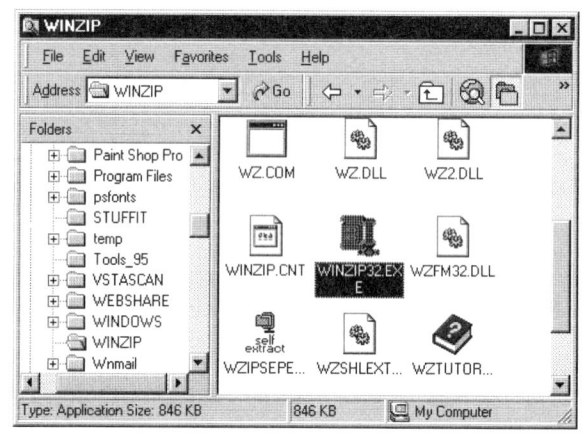

**Figure 5.2** Programs can be run from **Explorer** or **My Computer**, though it may sometimes take a while to find them!

---

**WHY START FROM EXPLORER OR MY COMPUTER?**

Not all programs have Start menu entries. For example, when you download software from the Internet, it is often in the form of a self-extracting Zip file – compressed and stored in an executable file (i.e. a program). When this is run, it extracts the software and installs it onto your system, normally creating Start menu entries so that you can run the new software. But, that initial downloaded file will not have a menu entry. To run it, you will have to find it on your disk and run it through Explorer or My Computer.

## Desktop Shortcuts

Shortcuts offer a quick route to regularly-used folders and programs. When you first start using Windows Me, you will find a dozen of these icons on the Desktop. Some, such as My Documents, lead to folders – click on these and My Computer will run, open at the selected folder. Others, such as the Internet Explorer icon, lead to applications – click on these to start the application.

Over time you may want to add more shortcuts to favourite applications. This can be done easily through either Explorer or My Computer (see Chapter 7).

## Taskbar toolbars

Initially, there is only one of these on the Taskbar, and that is the Quick Launch toolbar (page 5). It contains shortcuts to Internet Explorer, Outlook Express and Media Player, as well as **Show Desktop**, which sets all open windows to Minimize, clearing the Desktop. Other toolbars can be added – you can even create your own if you like this way of starting applications (see Chapter 9).

## Start → Run

The first item on the main part of the Start menu is **Run**. Click on this and a small panel opens. Here you can type a command line to start a program.

The command line must include the path – the route from the drive through the folders and subfolders to reach the one containing the program, e.g. \WINZIP\WINZIP32.EXE. If the program is not on the C: drive, the line must start with the drive letter (A: for the floppy and D: or E: for the CD-ROM).

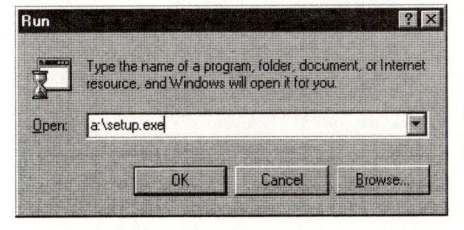

The **Run** panel being used to start an installation program from the A: drive.

There are two situations in which you may want to use the Run approach to starting a program:

- If you are installing new software from a floppy disk or CD-ROM, there will usually be an installation program (typically called SETUP.EXE). This can be started by typing the drive letter, then the path if necessary, followed by the program name, e.g. A:\SETUP.EXE.

  Remember that you can also use Explorer or My Computer to locate and start these installation programs.

- Some programs – particularly old MS-DOS ones – have start-up options which you can set by typing them into the command line. If you come across such a program, the start-up options will be explained in a README file. It is not something which will concern most people.

## 5.4 Starting from documents

Every type of document is – or can be – linked to an application (see *File Types* on page 87), so that any time you open a document, Windows will run the appropriate application for you. Those documents that you have been working on recently can be opened from the Documents folder on the Start menu:

❶ Click on **Start**.

❷ Point to **Documents**. Its submenu contains shortcuts to your most recently used documents.

❸ Select a document to run the linked application and open the document.

- Documents can also be opened from Windows Explorer or My Computer (see Chapter 7).

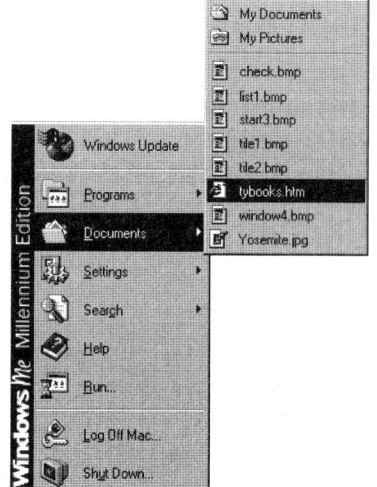

# PROGRAMS AND DOCUMENTS

> **DOCUMENTS FROM THE WEB**
>
> Internet Explorer also uses the File Types links – if it meets a file that it cannot handle, it opens the linked application to display the document (see Chapter 10).

## 5.5 Closing programs

When you have finished using an application, it must be closed down properly. Closing its window (page 36) will close the program, but you will also find a **Close** or **Exit** option on the **File** menu.

If you have created a new file or edited an old one, and not saved the changes, you will be prompted to save before the application closes.

* Select **Yes** to save the file.
* Select **No** to exit without saving.
* Select **Cancel** to return to the application.

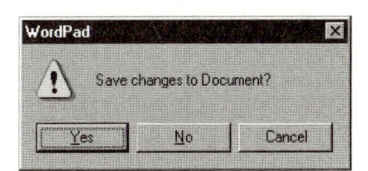

## 5.6 Coping with crashes

Windows Me is more reliable and robust than earlier versions of Windows, but software is rarely perfect. Some applications – and in particular some combinations of applications – are more likely than others to crash. If you are interested, crashes are normally caused by two programs trying to use the same area of memory, and you can go find a big technical book if you want to know more!

If you are lucky, you won't have crashes often. But just in case...

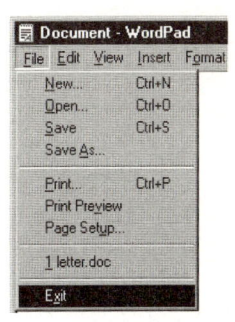

## Symptoms

One or more of:

- The busy symbol ⌛ appears and stays (but do wait twice as long as normal just in case it has a lot more to do than you thought).
- No response to key presses or mouse actions.
- The screen does not display properly – there might be part of a window or dialog box left behind and unmovable.

## Solution

- Hold down **Ctrl** and **Alt**, and press **Delete**. The **Close Programs** dialog box will appear, and the program that has crashed will be at the top of the list – with 'not responding' after the name.

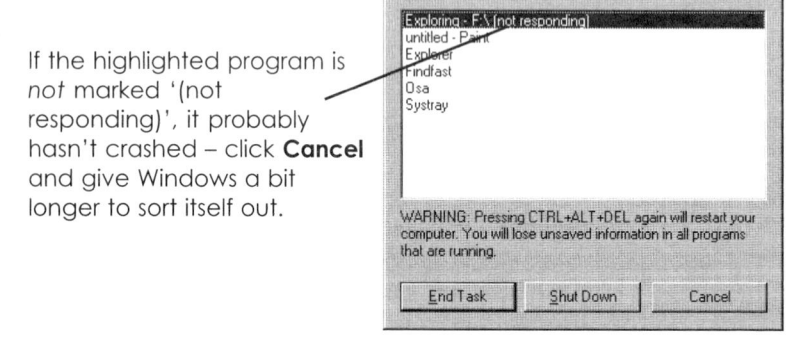

If the highlighted program is *not* marked '(not responding)', it probably hasn't crashed – click **Cancel** and give Windows a bit longer to sort itself out.

**Figure 5.3** The **Close Programs** dialog box.

- If it is an application that is not responding, click **End Task** – you will be asked to confirm that you really want to close it down. The system should work properly once it is out of the way.
- If Explorer or Systray is 'not responding', click **Shut Down**. These are core programs – Windows cannot function unless they are both working properly.

> **NEED MORE RAM?**
>
> If your system is light on memory and you are running several big applications, switching between them can be very slow as Windows parks the data from one into temporary storage on disk then reloads the data from the other – it might appear to have crashed. You can work with 32Mb, but 64Mb is a more realistic minimum if you want to run, say, two Office applications and a few smaller programs at the same time.

## 5.7 Filenames and extensions

When documents are saved onto disk, they are given a name which has two parts. The first part identifies that particular document, and can be more or less anything you want (see *Rules for filenames*, below). The second part is a three-letter extension which identifies the type of document. This is normally set by the application in which the document is created, and it is through this extension that Windows can link documents and applications. (We'll look at how to create these links on page 87.)

Here are some extensions that you are likely to meet:

| | |
|---|---|
| .TXT | Simple text, e.g. from NotePad |
| .DOC | Word document |
| .HTM | Web page – can be created by many applications |
| .BMP | bitmap image, e.g. from Paint |
| .GIF | a standard format for image on Web pages |
| .JPG | an alternative format for Web page images |
| .WAV | audio file in Wave format |
| .EXE | an executable program – not a document! |

### Rules for filenames

The first part of the name can be as long as you like (up to 250 characters!) and can consist of any combination of letters, numbers, spaces and underlines, but no other symbols. It's common sense to make sure that the name means something to you, so that you can easily identify the file when you come back to it later – and the shorter the name, the smaller the chance of making a mistake if you have to type it again.

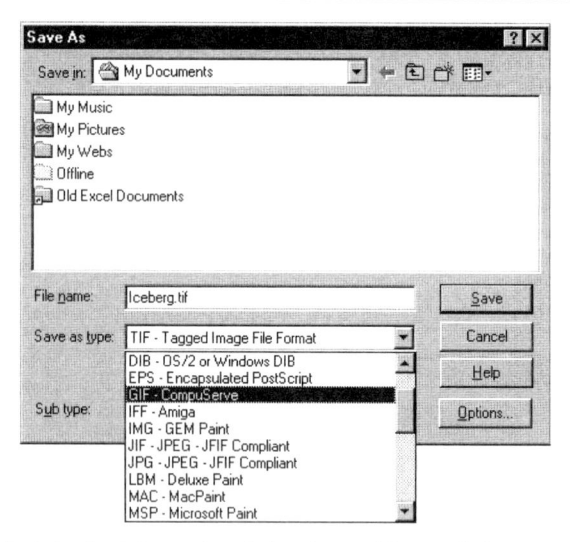

**Figure 5.4** A typical **Save As** dialog box. This one is from a graphics package, and can save in several standard formats. All applications have their own 'native' format, and many can also import or export documents in other formats for use with other applications.

---

### STANDARD FORMATS

Life would be easier if there was only one standard format for each type of document, but instead there are loads of them, especially for word-processing and graphics. You might wonder why. According to the old joke, computer people love standards – which is why they have so many.

In fact, there are several reasons. When a software house develops a new application, or a new version of an existing one, it will normally use a different document format – partly to handle its special features, and partly to distinguish it from its rivals. Some formats are developed to meet particular needs. With graphics documents, for instance, there is a trade-off between file size and image quality, and formats have been developed across the range.

The extension must match the application. As a general rule, when you save a file for the first time, simply give the identifying name and let the application set the extension. If the application can output documents in different formats, and you know that you need a particular format, select it from the **Save as type** list. After the first save, the filename is set, though the file could be later saved under a different name and in a different format. You might, for example, have written a report in Word, but want to give a copy to a colleague who used WordPerfect.

## SUMMARY

- ✓ There are three main types of programs: those run by the operating system, utilities for managing your computer, and applications for doing useful work or having fun!
- ✓ The data files produced by or displayed by applications are known as documents.
- ✓ Programs can be set running from the Start menu, Desktop Shortcuts, the Taskbar, the Run dialog box or from within Explorer or My Computer.
- ✓ Opening a document in the Start Documents menu or in Explorer or My Computer will run its associated application.
- ✓ Programs should be closed down properly when you have finished using them.
- ✓ If a program crashes and hangs the system, the **Ctrl + Alt + Delete** key combination will open the Close Programs dialog box. You should be able to close the offending program from here.
- ✓ Documents are given filenames when they are saved onto disk. These have two parts: the first part is simply an identifying name and can be more or less anything you like; the second part describes the format of the file and is usually set by the application in which it was created.

# 6 BASIC TECHNIQUES

## AIMS OF THIS CHAPTER

One of the great attractions of Windows is consistency. Every Windows application will have a similar basic layout and tackle the same jobs in much the same way. As a result, once you have learnt how to use one Windows application, you are well on the way to knowing how to use any other. This chapter looks at some of the basic techniques for working with Windows – selecting objects, moving objects on screen and copying through the Clipboard and through 'scraps'.

## 6.1 Selection techniques

Before you can do any work on an object or a set of objects – e.g. format a block of text, copy part of an image, move a group of files from one folder to another – you must select it.

### Text

Use WordPad, NotePad or any word-processor to try out these techniques. They can also be used with text objects in graphics packages and even with small items of text such as filenames.

**With the mouse:**
 ❶ Point to the start of the text.
 ❷ Hold down the left mouse button and drag across the screen.
 ❸ The selected text will be highlighted.

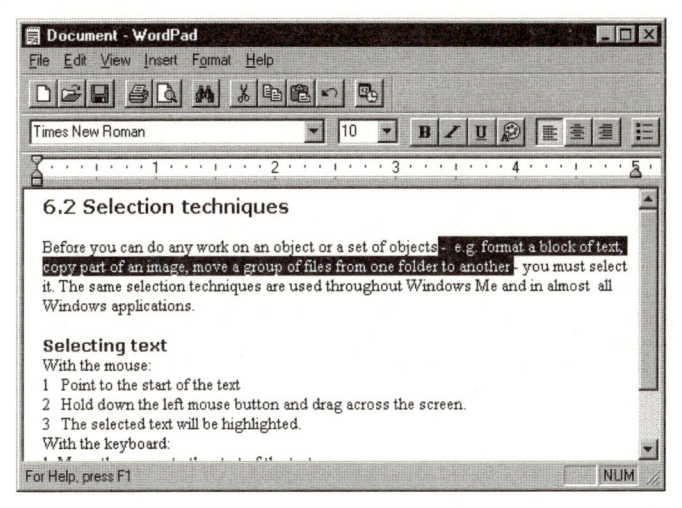

**Figure 6.1** Once the text has been selected, it can be formatted, deleted, copied or moved.

### With the keyboard:
- ❶ Move the cursor to the start of the text.
- ❷ Hold down the **Shift** key.
- ❸ Use the arrow keys to highlight the text you want.

## Graphics

The same techniques are used for images in graphics applications, and for icons on the Desktop, files in My Computer and other screen objects.

### Single object:
- ♦ Point to it. If this does not highlight it, click on it.

### Adjacent objects:
- ❶ Imagine a rectangle that will enclose the objects.
- ❷ Point to one corner of this rectangle.
- ❸ Hold down the left mouse button and drag across to the opposite corner – an outline will appear as you do this.

*or*

- ❹ Select the object at one corner.
- ❺ Hold down **Shift** and select the object at the opposite corner.

## Scattered objects:

① Highlight the first object.
② Hold down the **Ctrl** key and highlight each object in turn.
③ If you select an object by mistake, point to (or click on) it again to remove the highlighting.

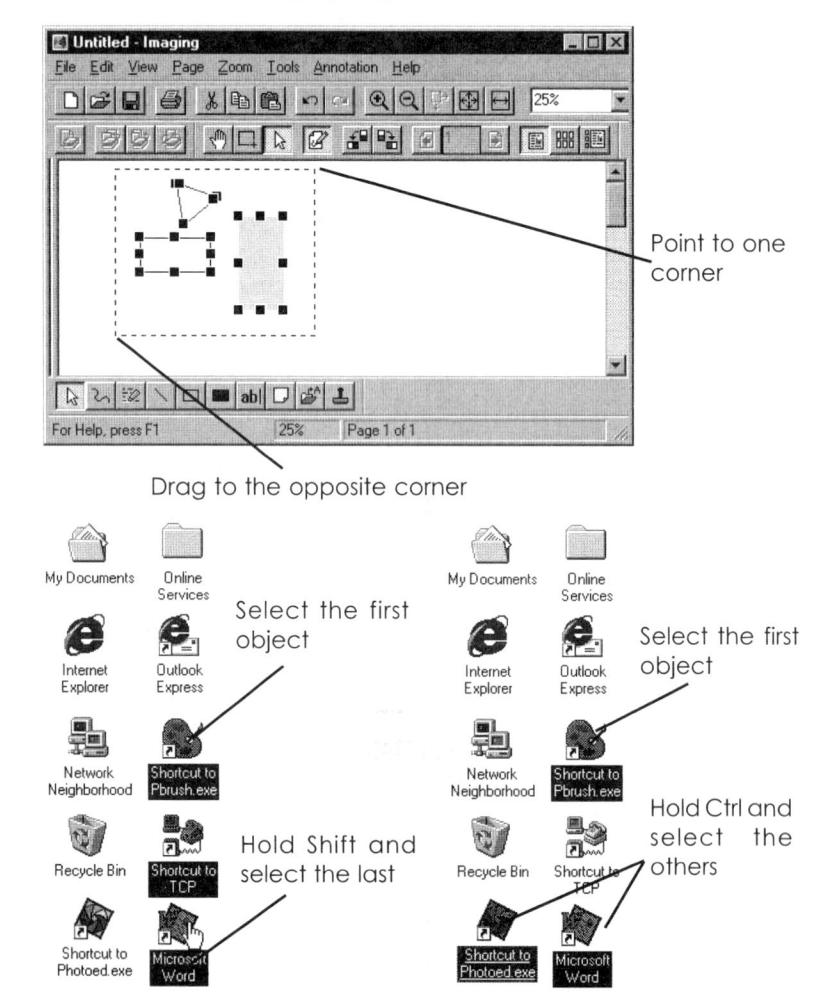

**Figure 6.2** Selecting images and other objects.

BASIC TECHNIQUES 69

> **DELETING OBJECTS**
>
> All applications have a Delete command (usually on the Edit menu), but selected objects can also be deleted by pressing [Delete] or [←]. Use these with care!!

## 6.2 Cut, Copy and Paste

If you look at the Edit menu of any Windows application, you will find the commands **Cut**, **Copy** and **Paste**. You will also find them on the short menu that opens when you right-click on a selected object. These are used for copying and moving data within and between applications.

- **Copy** copies a selected block of text, picture, file or other object into a special part of memory called the *Clipboard*.
- **Cut** deletes selected data from the original application, but places a copy into the Clipboard.
- **Paste** copies the data from the Clipboard into a different place in the same application, or into a different application – as long as this can handle data in that format.

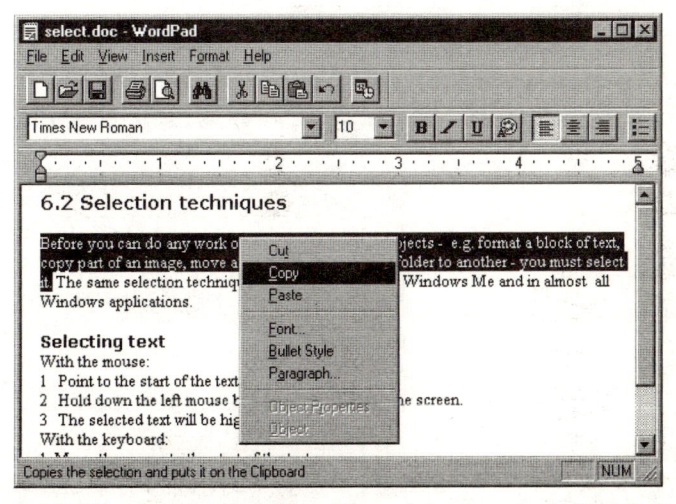

**Figure 6.3** The short menu offers the quickest route to the Cut and Paste commands. If the Clipboard is empty, Paste will be 'greyed out' or omitted from the menu.

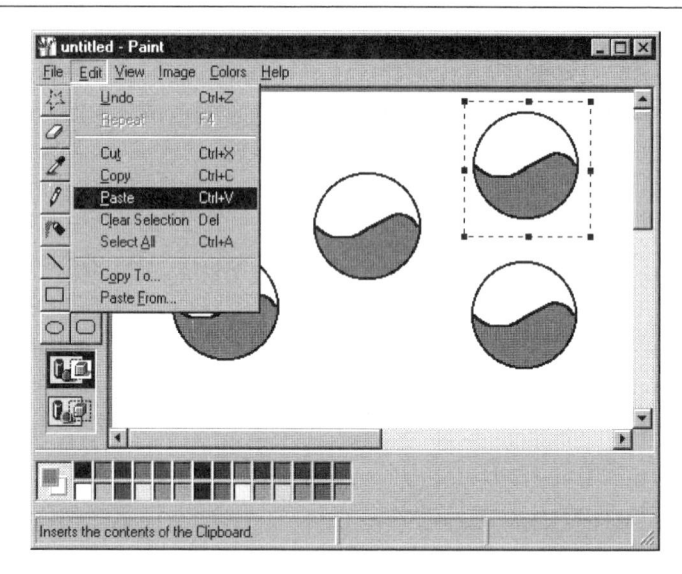

**Figure 6.4** Pasting a copied image in Paint. Selected graphics usually have an enclosing frame with 'handles' at the corners and mid-sides. You can drag within the frame to move the object, or on the handles to resize it.

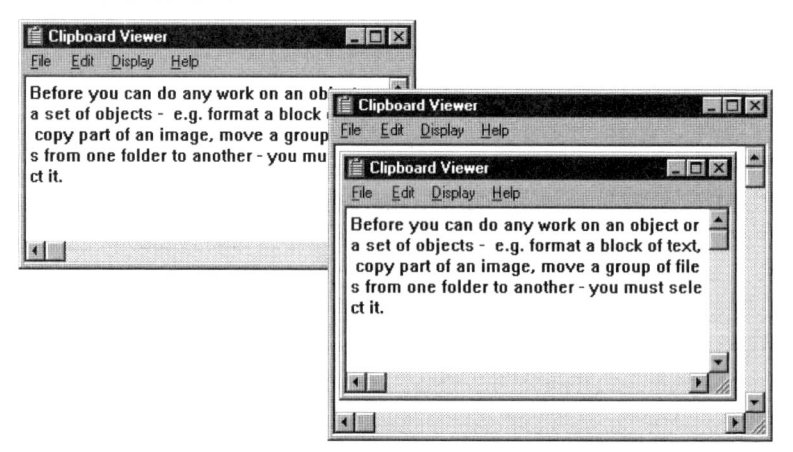

**Figure 6.5** Two shots of the Clipboard Viewer. The first is after copying some text; the second is after capturing the screenshot of the Viewer – which is stored in the Clipboard! The Clipboard can hold data in any format, and the Viewer can display all major Windows formats.

**BASIC TECHNIQUES** 71

The data normally remains in the Clipboard until new data is copied or cut into it, or until Windows is shut down. (Some applications have a **Clear Clipboard** command.) If you want to see what's in the Clipboard – just for interest, as this serves few practical purposes – you can use the Clipboard Viewer. It should be on the **Programs → Accessories → Systems Tools** menu. (This is an optional utility and may not have been installed.)

## 6.3 Drag and drop

This is an alternative to Cut and Paste for moving objects within an application or between compatible applications. It is also the simplest way to rearrange files and folders, as you will see in the next chapter.

The technique is simple to explain:

- ❶ Select the block of text or the object(s).
- ❷ Point anywhere within the highlighted text or in the frame enclosing other objects.
- ❸ Hold down the mouse button and drag the object across the screen or, with text, move the cursor (which is now ▨).
- ❹ Release the button to drop the object into its new position.

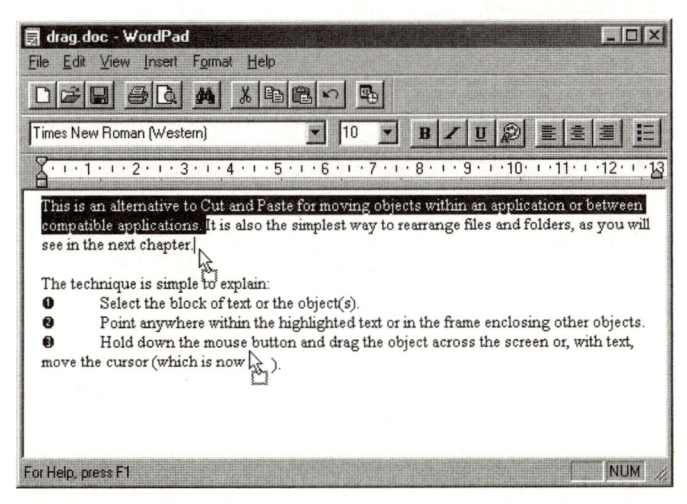

**Figure 6.6** Dragging text in a word-processor (WordPad). The target position for the text is marked by the thin bar to the left of the arrow.

**Figure 6.7** You can drag a document from My Computer or Windows Explorer and drop it into a suitable application – this is sometimes quicker than opening files from within the application.

In practice, accurate positioning depends upon good mouse control. And one of the best ways to improve your mouse control is to play the games. The card games use drag-and-drop for moving cards; Minesweeper helps to build speed and accuracy. (Remember this when you need an excuse.)

## 6.4 Scraps

A 'scrap' is a special sort of file parked on the Desktop. It is typically a fragment of a word-processor document – though it could be the whole of one. Scraps can be used as highly visible reminders of urgent jobs, or to hold blocks of text that you will reuse in other files, or simply as temporary storage.

What distinguishes a scrap from an ordinary file are the ways that it is created and used.

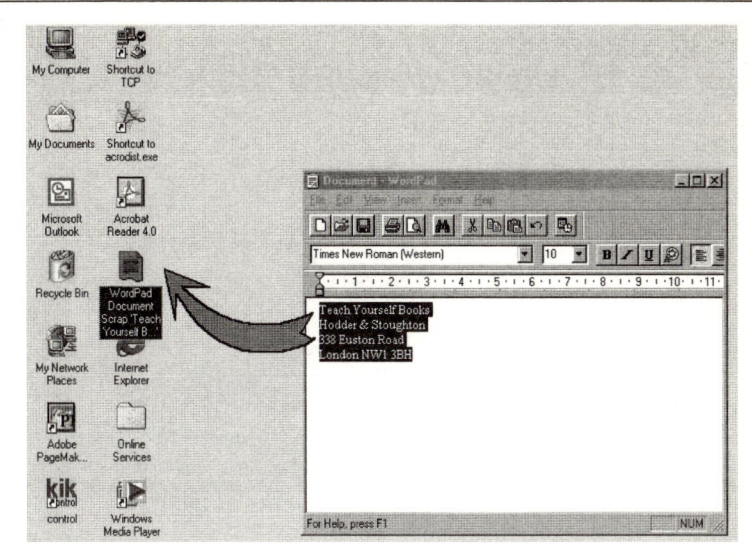

**Figure 6.8** Creating a scrap. To reuse it, drag it back into the application.

❶ Set the word-processor window into Restore mode so that some of the Desktop is visible.
❷ Select the text.
❸ Drag the selection and drop it on the Desktop.
❹ To reuse the scrap, either drag it into the application window,
*or*
❺ Double-click on it to open the application and load in the scrap document.

## SUMMARY

- ✓ Text can be selected with the mouse or the keyboard.
- ✓ Graphics and other objects are selected by dragging an outline around them, or by using the mouse in conjunction with Shift or Ctrl.
- ✓ Selected data can be cut or copied to the Clipboard, then pasted into the same or a different application.
- ✓ Use the Clipboard Viewer to see what's in the Clipboard.
- ✓ Text and some objects can be moved by drag and drop.
- ✓ Text can be stored on the Desktop as scraps.

# 7 FILES AND FOLDERS

> ### AIMS OF THIS CHAPTER
>
> To be able to use your computer efficiently, you must know how to manage your files – how to find, copy, move, rename and delete them – and how to organize the folders on your disks. In Windows Me, these jobs can be done through either Windows Explorer or My Computer – the two are almost identical. In this chapter we will have a look at these and see how they can be used for file and folder management. We will also look at creating links between documents and applications, and at the Recycle Bin – a neat device which makes it much less likely that you will delete files by accident.

## 7.1 Disks and folders

A floppy disk holds 1.4 Mb of data – enough for a few decent-sized documents. A typical hard drive has 10 Gigabytes of storage – over 6,000 times! Obviously, with this much storage space, it must be organized if you are ever to find anything. The organization comes through *folders*. A folder is an elastic-sided division of the disk. It can contain any number of files and subfolders – which can contain other subfolders, and so on *ad infinitum*. The structure is often described as a tree. The *root* is at the drive level. The main folders branch off from here, and each may have a complex set of branches leading from it. At the simplest, a C: drive might contain three folders – *My Documents*, *Program Files* (with subfolders for each application) and *Windows* (which has subfolders for the sets of programs and files that make up the Windows Me system). You can create new folders, rename, delete or move them to produce your own folder structure.

> **FLOPPY FOLDERS**
>
> You can also create folders on a floppy disk, if you want to keep several distinct sets of files on one disk.

## 7.2 My Computer

My Computer, Windows Explorer and Internet Explorer are all aspects of the same program. They look a little different – at least in their default settings – and have slightly different selections of tools, but are otherwise the same. The simple proof of this is that you can change any one into the other. Click on an Internet link or type an Internet address into My Computer or Windows Explorer and it will become Internet Explorer. Start to browse your hard disk from Internet Explorer and it will become Windows Explorer.

My Computer can only be started from the Desktop icon. It is Windows Explorer at its simplest, with the display set to do no more than show the contents of one drive or folder. It is convenient if you just want to work in one folder – to see or delete its contents.

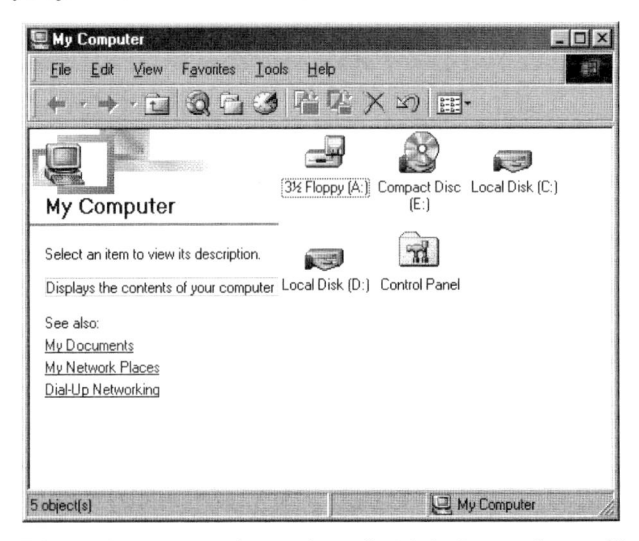

**Figure 7.1 My Computer**, shown here in Web Page view, with large icons and the Address and Links toolbars turned off.

# FILES AND FOLDERS

If you set My Computer so that it opens a new window for every folder (one of the *Folder Options*, see page 84), it can also be used for reorganizing your file storage.

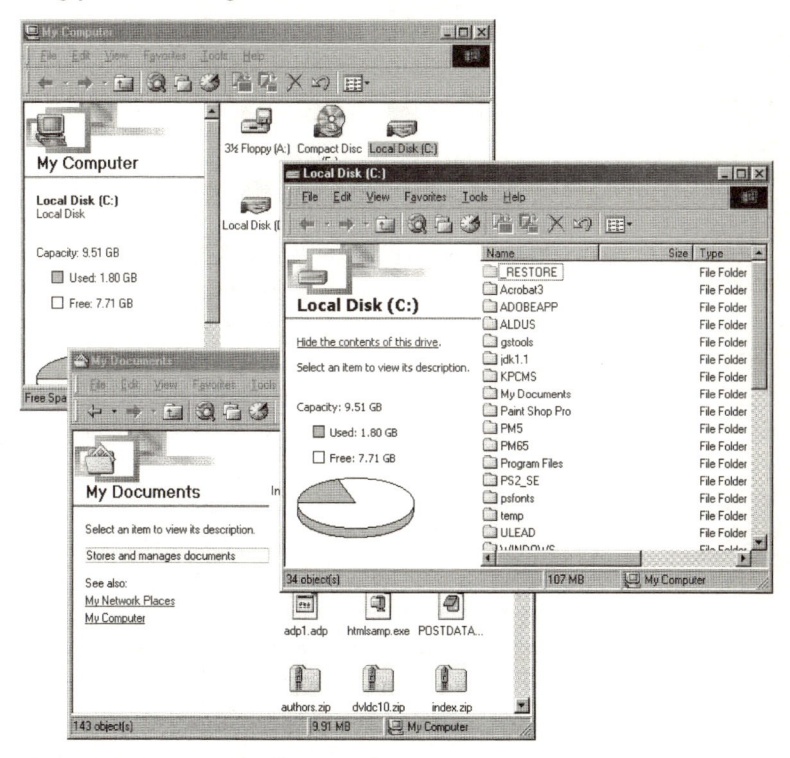

**Figure 7.2** Run My Computer in multiple windows if you want to move files between the folders.

## 7.3 Windows Explorer

Windows Explorer is the key tool for managing your files and folders. Get to know this program! Compared to My Computer, it gives you easier ways to switch from one folder to another, and to move files between folders.

- To run it, click **Start** and point to **Programs** then to Accessories. Find Windows Explorer and click once to run it.

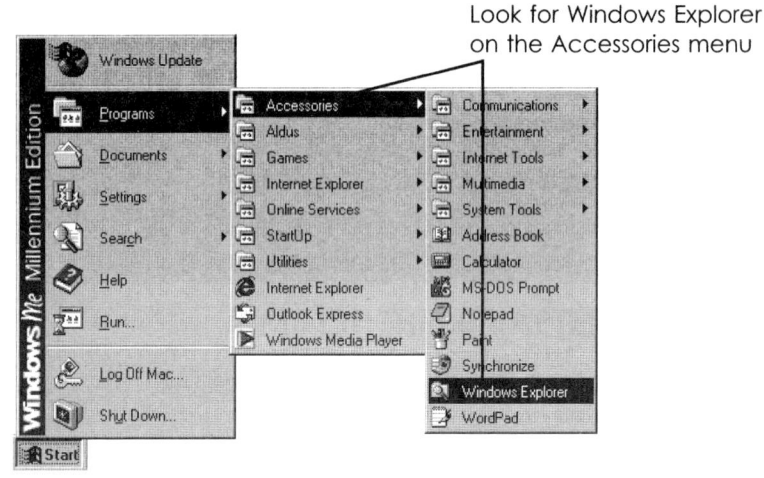

**Figure 7.3** Windows Explorer should be on the Start → Programs → Accessories submenu. If you use it a lot, you may prefer to move it onto the main Programs menu.

When Explorer opens, it will display the contents of your C: drive – the main (and perhaps the only) hard disk. The window has two panels.

The left panel (the **Explorer Bar**) normally shows **Folders**, but can be used for other things or closed if not wanted (see page 81). In the folder display, ⊞ to the left shows that a folder has subfolders. Click this to open up the branch. The icon changes to ⊟ and clicking this will close the branch.

When a folder is selected, its files and subfolders are listed in the main pane. Files can be listed by name, type, date or size, and displayed as thumbnails or large or small icons, with or without details (see page 80).

The **Status bar** at the bottom shows the number of objects in the folder and the amount of memory they use, or the size of a selected file.

### The controls

These are at the top of the window. The **Menu bar** is always visible. As with any Windows application, the full command set can be reached through the menu system, but those that you will use most often can be accessed faster through toolbar buttons or keyboard shortcuts.

*The available menu options vary when a file, folder or drive is selected.*

# FILES AND FOLDERS

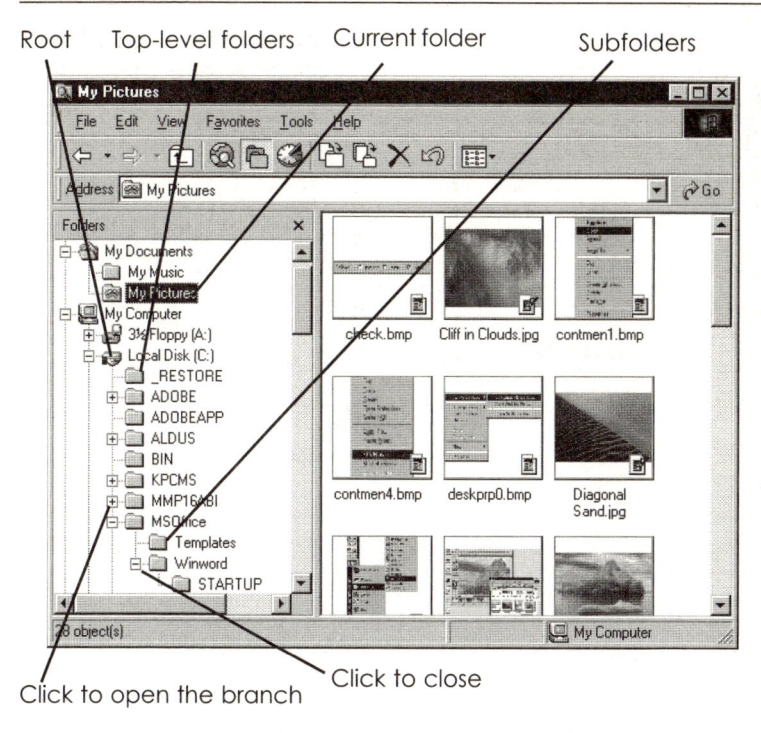

Root  Top-level folders  Current folder  Subfolders

Click to open the branch — Click to close

**Figure 7.4 Windows Explorer**, showing the main features. Yours may well look different as there are many combinations of display options.

There are four toolbars, all of which are optional – turn them on or off through the **View** menu.

The **Standard toolbar** (Figure 7.6) contains buttons for all essential jobs.

The **Address Bar** shows the current selected folder, and can be useful for navigating around the system.

**Links** are shortcuts to places on the Internet – yes, you can go there from within Explorer (see Chapter 10).

**Radio** holds the controls and links to Internet radio stations (see page 153).

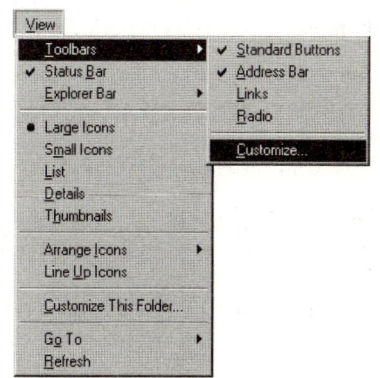

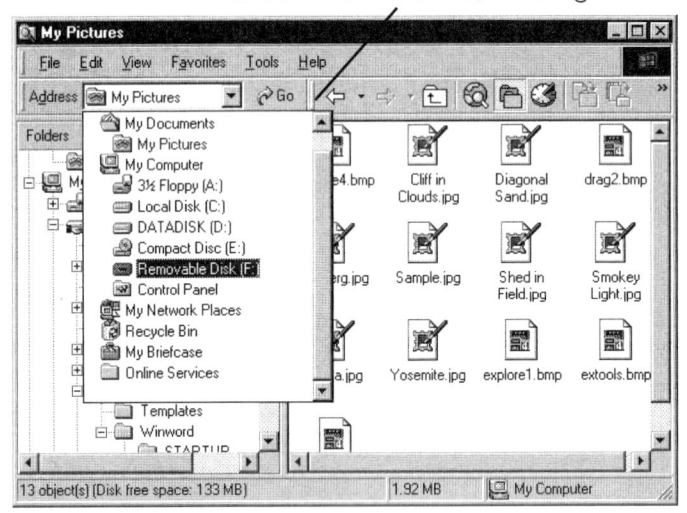

**Figure 7.5** The **Address Bar** offers a quick way to get around – useful if you have opened up several levels of branches, producing a very long Folders display.

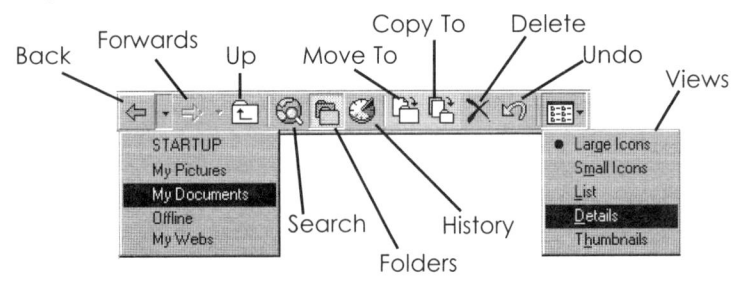

**Figure 7.6** The **Standard toolbar**. Drop-down lists from the Back and Forwards buttons provide an easy way to move between folders that you have selected earlier in the same session.

## The Standard buttons

(with **menu commands**)

- Back (**Go ➜ Back**) and Forward (**Go ➜ Forward**) When you select a folder, it is added to their drop-down lists – you must go Back before you can go Forward.

FILES AND FOLDERS

- Up (**Go → Up one level**) takes you up to the next level folder, or from a folder to the drive, or a drive up to My Computer.
- Move To (**Edit → Move To Folder…**) – moves the selected file to a folder picked from a list at the next stage.
- Copy To (**Edit → Copy To Folder…**) – copies the selected file to another folder.
- Delete (**File → Delete**) – deletes the selected file or folder, placing it in the Recycle Bin (page 98).
- Undo (**Edit → Undo**) – undoes the previous action, if possible. In practice, about the only things that can be undone are some of the view options.
- Views – leads to a drop-down list containing the main options from the View menu.

## 7.4 View options

### Explorer Bar

If you click on View to open the menu, point to Explorer Bar and wait a moment, this submenu will open.

**Search** helps you to find files and folders on your system. Internet searches can also be run from here. This is the same Search as the one on the Start menu. We'll come back to it later (page 99).

**Favorites** open up your list of favourite places – normally Web sites. We'll deal with this when we look at Internet Explorer.

**History** stores links to the sites and folders that you have visited recently – this is also more important in Internet Explorer, so we'll leave this until Chapter 10.

**Folders** is the default, displaying the folder structure.

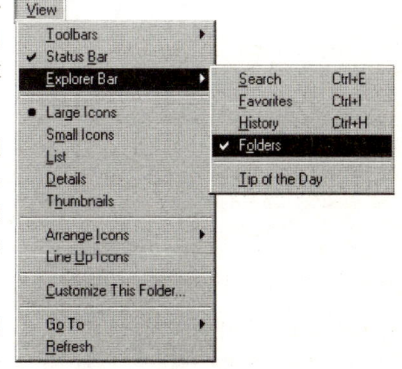

Obviously, only one of these can occupy the Explorer Bar at any one time.

Not so obvious, but worth noting, is the fact that you can turn them all off and free up the full window for the file display. Deselect (click to clear the tick) the option in the View menu or click the **X** in the top right corner of the Explorer Bar.

The **Tip of the Day** opens a new pane at the bottom right of the window and displays a helpful hint. You may find this useful at first.

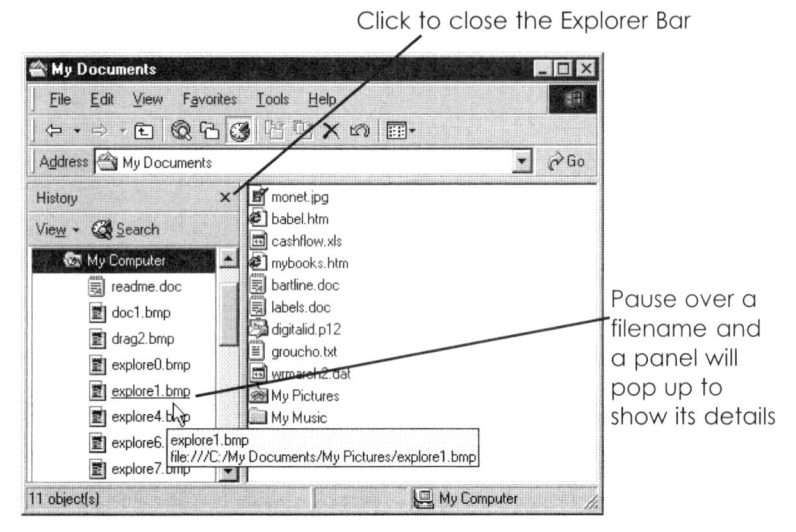

**Figure 7.7** The **Explorer Bar** being used to display History – this can be the easiest way to find files that you have worked on recently.

## 7.5 Displaying and sorting files

Files and folders can be shown as **Large icons**, **Small icons**, **List**, **Details** or **Thumbnails** – make your choice from the **View** menu or from the drop-down list on the **View** button.

**Large icons** aren't just easier to see, they are also larger targets if you are less than accurate with the mouse!

**Small icons** and **List** differ only in the order – listing either across or down the screen. Both are good for selecting sets of files (see page 92).

# FILES AND FOLDERS

**Details** gives a column display under the headings Name, Size, Type and Modified. Click on a heading to sort the files in ascending order by that feature. Click a second time to sort them in descending order. This display is useful for tracking down files that you were working on at a certain date (but have forgotten the names), or for finding old or large files if you need to create some space.

**Thumbnails** shows – if possible – a miniature image of each file. It is, of course, best for use with images, but it can be handy for Web pages and some formatted documents.

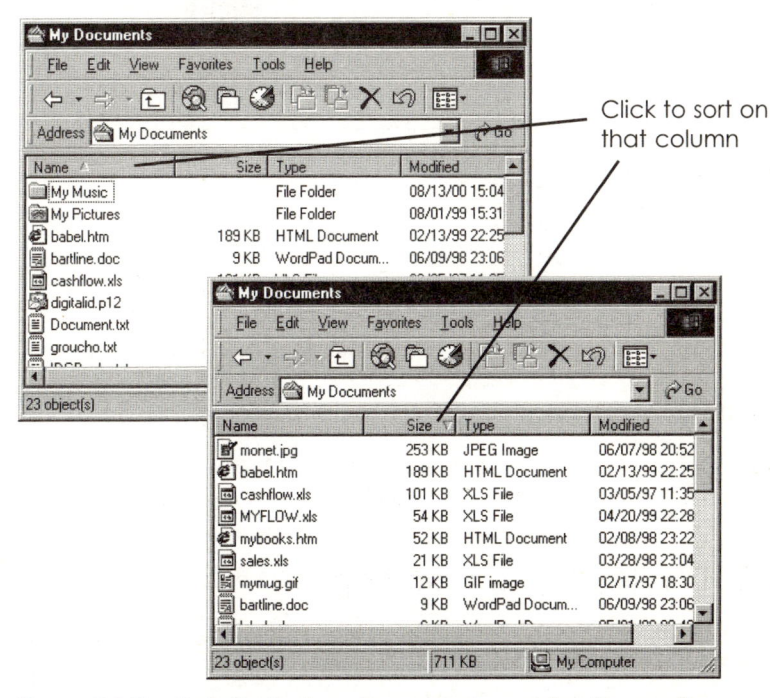

Click to sort on that column

**Figure 7.8** The **Details** display allows you to sort the files easily.

---

**ARRANGE ICONS**

The **View → Arrange Icons** menu command can be used to sort the files by **Name**, **Type**, **Size** or **Date** in any mode, whether or not the details are displayed on screen.

**Figure 7.9** The **Thumbnails View** is excellent for finding images and some types of formatted files – but you don't get many to a screenful. The Explorer Bar has been closed here to free up some more space.

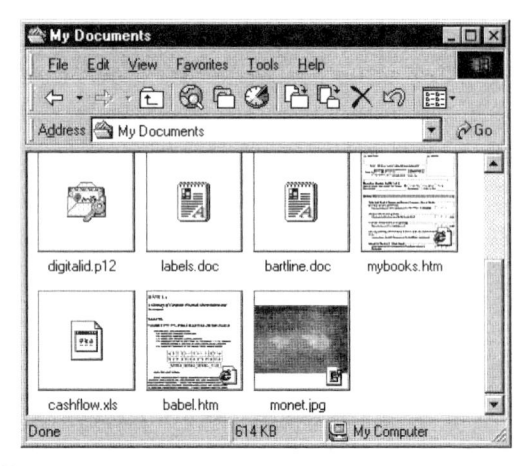

## 7.6 Folder Options

We looked at the **Folder Options** panel earlier when we were customizing the Desktop (page 18). Time now for another look, as these settings are crucial to how you view and manage your files and folders. To reach it, open the **Tools** menu and select **Folder Options**.

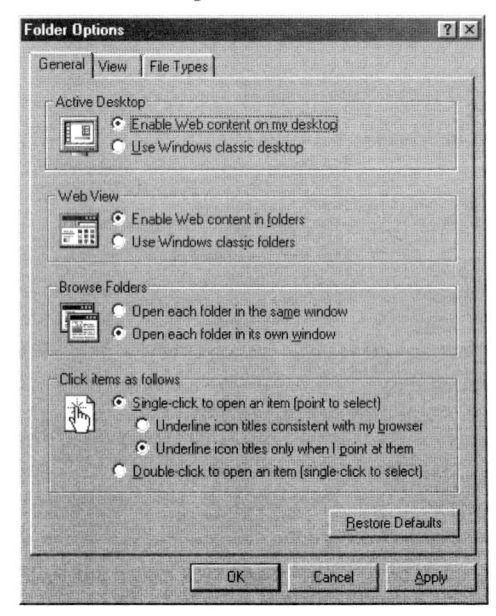

**Figure 7.10** The **General** tab of **Folder Options**. The settings shown here produce Web-style display and behaviour.

On the **General** tab under **Web View**, **Enable Web content in folders** if you want a 'richer' experience, with decorated folders and automatic previews of files. **Use Windows classic folders** for a simpler file display.

The Browse Folders option is mainly aimed at My Computer. Opening each folder in its own window is useful for moving files from one to another, but can produce a cluttered screen. When you actually open a folder, you can switch to the opposite by holding down **Control**. If you have selected **Open each folder in the same window**, hold down **Control** when opening to have the folder open in a new window.

The **Click items as follows** settings apply to all files and folders, whether on the Desktop or in My Computer/Windows Explorer.

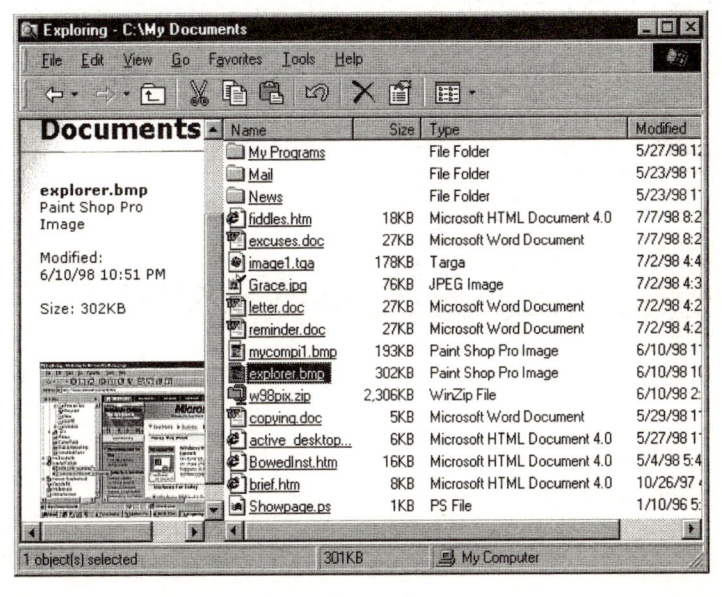

**Figure 7.11** In **Web page view**, the area to the left is used to display details, and sometimes a preview of the selected document.

## Folder views

Some of the options here really are just fine-tuning, and you can come back and play with these when you want to see what they do. The more significant ones are covered here.

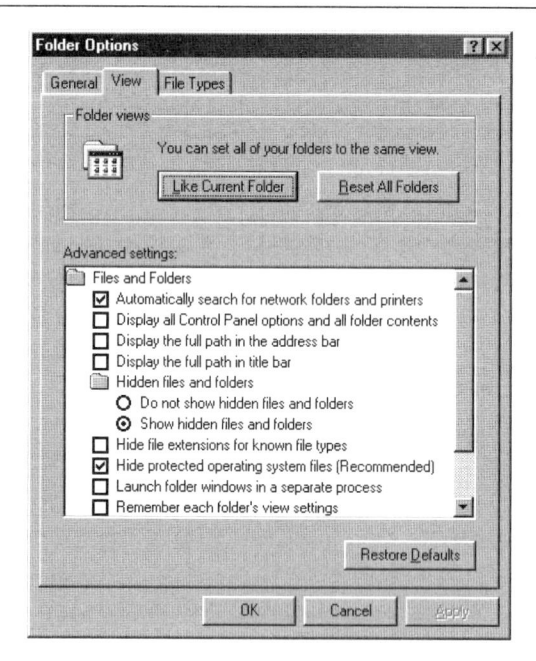

**Figure 7.12** The **View** tab of **Folder Options**. Most are best left at their default settings.

Click **Like Current Folder** if you want the current settings – principally the choice of **View** – to be applied to all folders. If you have got into a bit of a mess with your options (easily done!), click **Reset All Folders** to go back to the original settings.

### Advanced Settings

Most of these should be left at their defaults until you have been using Windows Me for a good while. A couple are worth checking now.

**Hidden files** – Windows Me 'hides' essential files, to prevent accidental deletion. They can be shown if you want to see them, or these and system files – also crucial – can be hidden. For safety, hide them.

**Remember each folder's view settings** will retain the separate options from one session to the next. The settings can be different for each folder – which makes sense. You may well want more detail in folders that contain documents than in those that contain program or system files.

## 7.7 File Types

Documents can be associated with applications, so that picking a document from the **Documents** list on the **Start** menu or out of a folder will start up its application and open the document within it.

The **File Types** tab of **Folder Options** lists all the 'registered' file types – the ones associated with applications. There should be lots there already as Windows Me sets up associations between a whole host of documents and applications when it first starts, and most applications will add their own types to the list as they are installed.

Select any one of them from the list, and in the bottom part of the panel you will see the **Extension**(s) that mark this type, the MIME type (used when documents are sent by e-mail) and the application that the document **Opens with**.

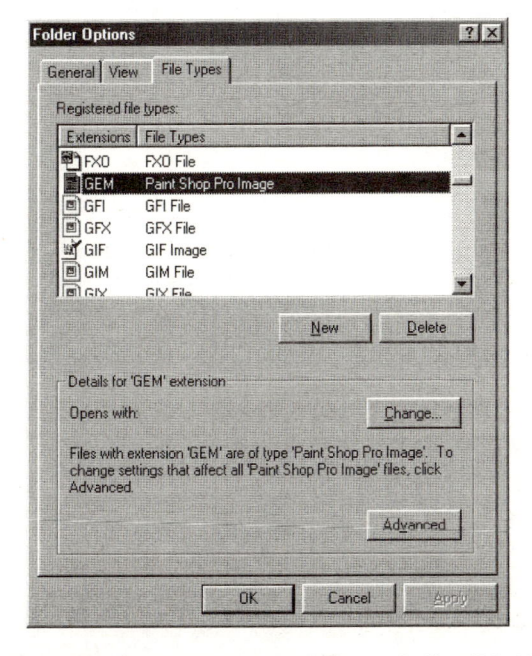

**Figure 7.13** The **File Types** tab – scroll through the list. You will be amazed at how many types your system knows about already!

## New File Types

Not all applications come equipped with the installation routines to set up associations for you – older software, and shareware downloaded from the Internet tend not to. If you want to be really thorough about it, you can go through all your applications, making a note of the file types that they can handle, then go through the File Types list and check that all are included. If any have been overlooked, you can create the association here, by clicking the **New Type** button. It's not a particularly difficult process – but it takes time, and there is an easier way to do things.

❶ Close the **Folder Options** panel and forget about file types for now.

❷ When, at some point in the future, you try to open a document of an unregistered type, you will be presented with the **Open With** panel.

❸ Scroll through the list of applications and select the right one for the type. If you cannot see it in the list, but know that it is on your system, click the **Other...** button and track down the program file.

❹ If you want to give a description (to appear in the **File Types** list), do so, but this is not essential.

❺ Click **OK**.

♦ Now try to open the document and the associated application should run.

If you do not want to set up a permanent link with an application, clear this box and the document will be opened with the chosen program on this occasion only.

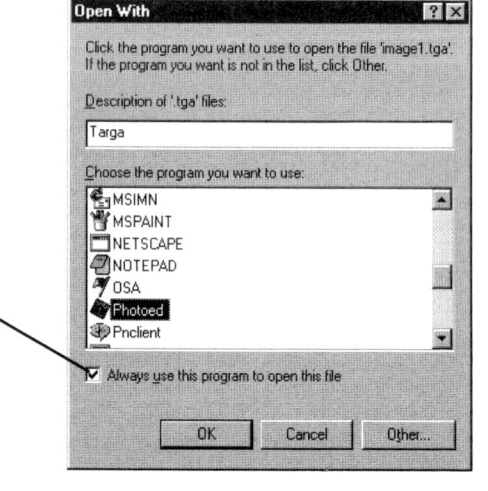

## 7.8 Organizing folders

Windows Me sets up one folder for your files, called *My Documents*. This is unlikely to be enough for very long. You need to create more folders if:

- you will be storing more than a few dozen documents – it's hard to find stuff in crowded folders;
- more than one person uses the PC – everyone should have their own storage space;
- your documents fall into distinct categories – personal, hobbies, different areas of work, etc.

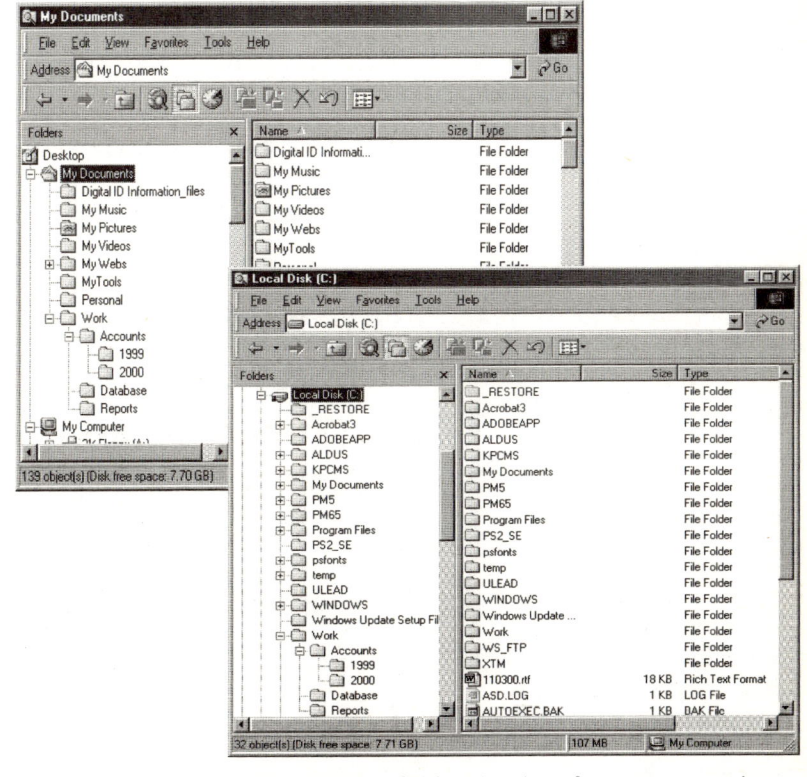

**Figure 7.14** Two approaches to a folder structure for someone who uses the PC for work and personal use. In the top one, the new folders have been created with *My Documents*; in the lower, the folders are all at the main level. Either works just as well.

> **MIXED CONTENTS**
>
> Putting documents of different types in one folder is not as confusing as it might seem. It might look untidy when you view it through Explorer – though sorting by Type will help to clarify. In practice, you will mainly access your documents through applications, and when you open a file there, the **Open File** dialog boxes will normally only list those of the right type.

## Creating folders

A new folder can be created at any time, and at any point in the folder structure. Here's how:

❶ In Explorer, select the folder which will contain the new one, or select the drive letter for a new top-level folder.

❷ Open the **File** menu, point to **New** then select **Folder**.

❸ Replace *New Folder* with a meaningful name.

♦ If you decide the folder is in the wrong place, select it and drag it into place in the All Folders list.

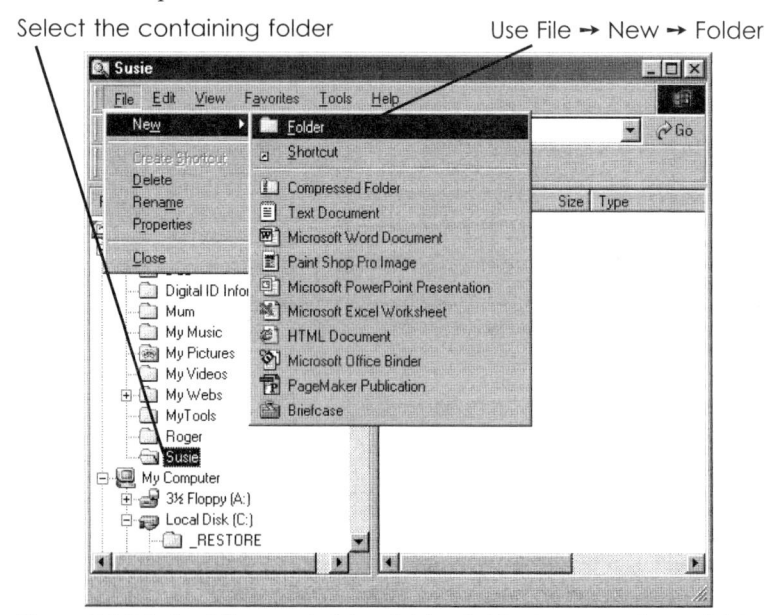

**Figure 7.15** Select the containing folder first before creating a folder.

# FILES AND FOLDERS

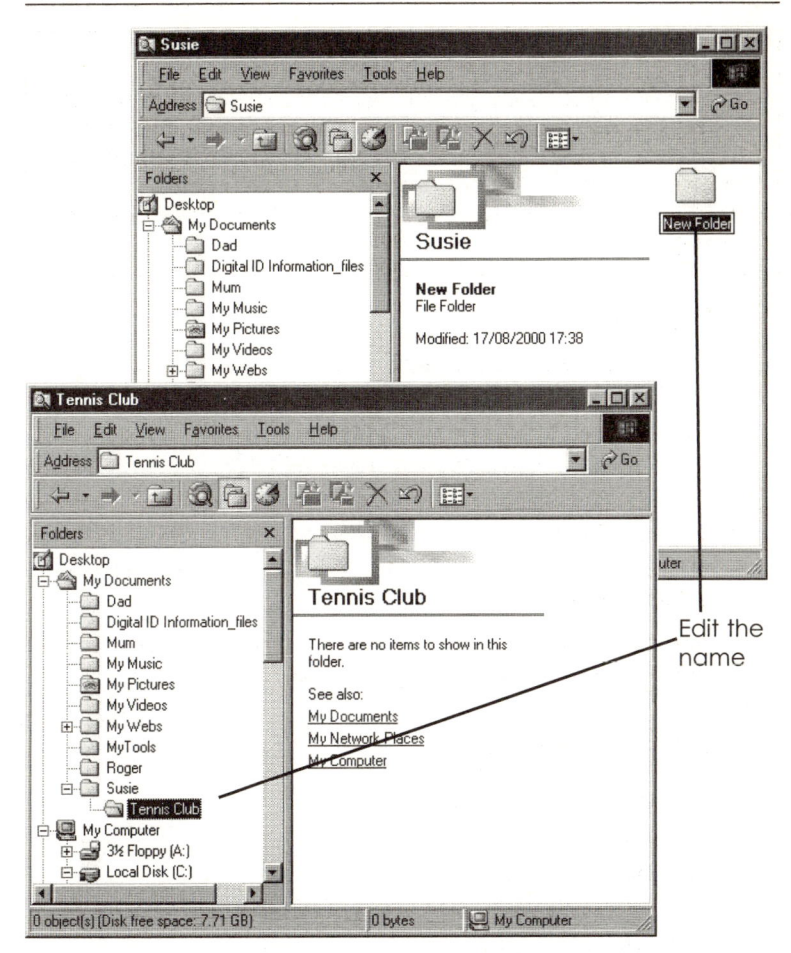

**Figure 7.16** The new folder will need renaming.

Edit the name

---

## FOLDERS ARE FILES

We think of folders as containers, but to the PC they are files, with lists of the names and disk locations of other files. They are special – you cannot read them, and the system interprets them to create the folder displays – but they can be renamed, copied and deleted just the same as document files.

**Figure 7.17** Folders can be dragged to rearrange the structure – here *Homework* is being moved into *Roger*'s folder.

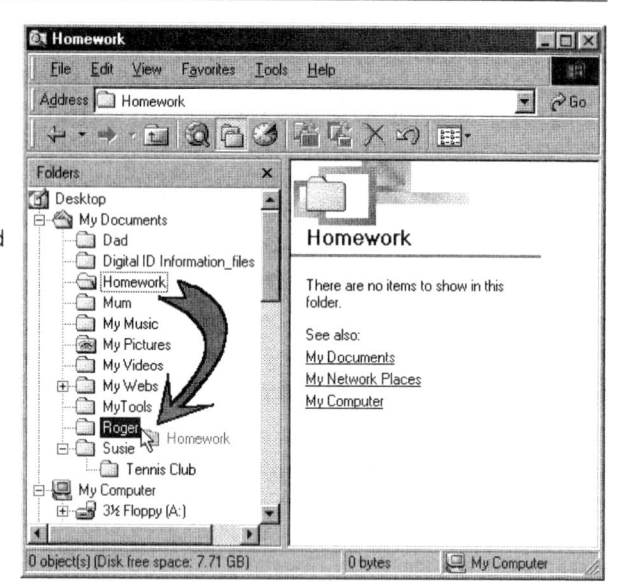

## 7.9 Creating shortcuts

A Desktop shortcut offers the simplest and quickest way to start an application or open a folder – as long as you can see the Desktop! You can create new shortcuts in several ways. This is probably the easiest.

### Application shortcuts

① Open the application's folder in Explorer or My Computer.
② Locate the program file. If you are not sure whether it is the right one, click (or double-click) on it. If the application runs, it's the right file.
③ Drag the file onto the Desktop.
④ Edit the name to remove 'Shortcut to...', if you like.

### Shortcuts to folders

① Select the folder in Explorer or My Computer.
② Hold the right mouse button down and drag the icon onto the Desktop.
③ Select **Create Shortcut(s) Here**.

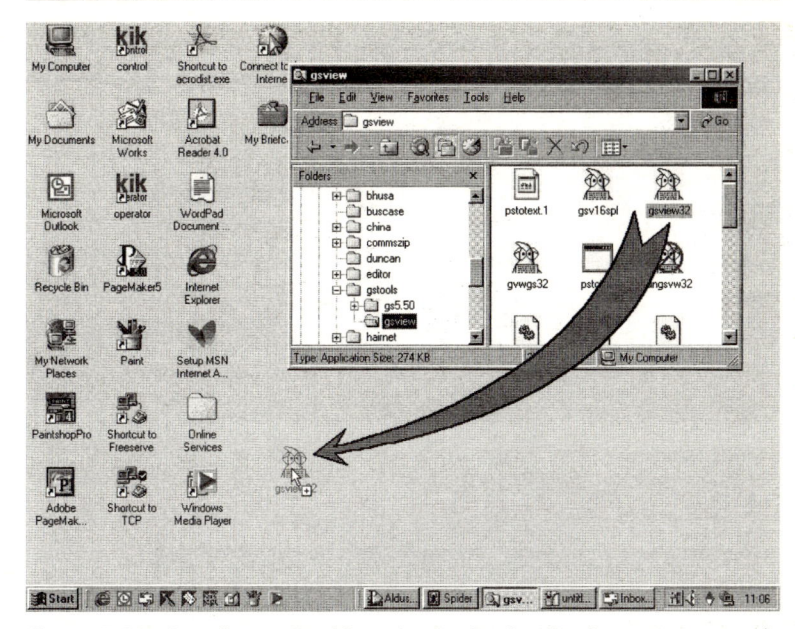

**Figure 7.18** Creating a **Desktop shortcut** using Explorer.

## 7.10 File management

As a general rule application files – the ones that make up the software – should be left well alone. Start messing with these and your programs may well not work. Document files are a different matter. They need to be managed actively or your folders will become cluttered, making it hard to find files.

### Selecting files

Before you can do anything with your files, you must select them.

- *To select a single file*, point to it (if you use the Web Page mode), or click once on it (in Classic mode).
- *To select a set of adjacent files*, click on the window to the right of the top one and drag an outline over the set;
- *or* select the first, hold down the **Shift** key, and select the last.
- *To select scattered files*, select the first, hold down the **Control** key and select the rest in turn.

Drag an outline or hold down **Shift** to select a set

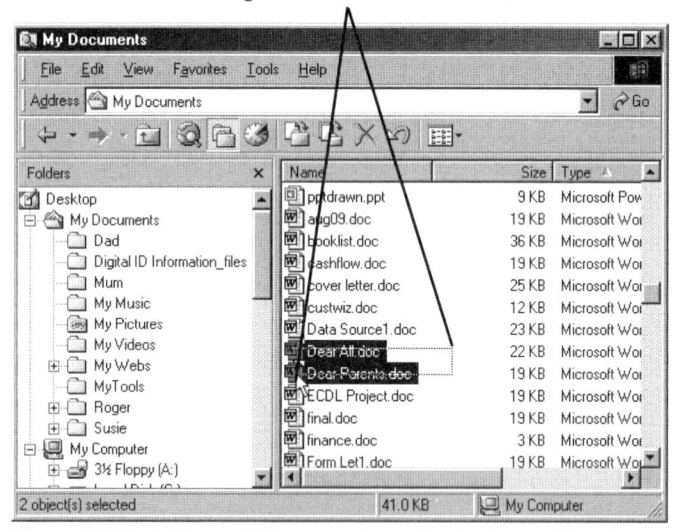

**Figure 7.19** Adjacent files can be selected as a block.

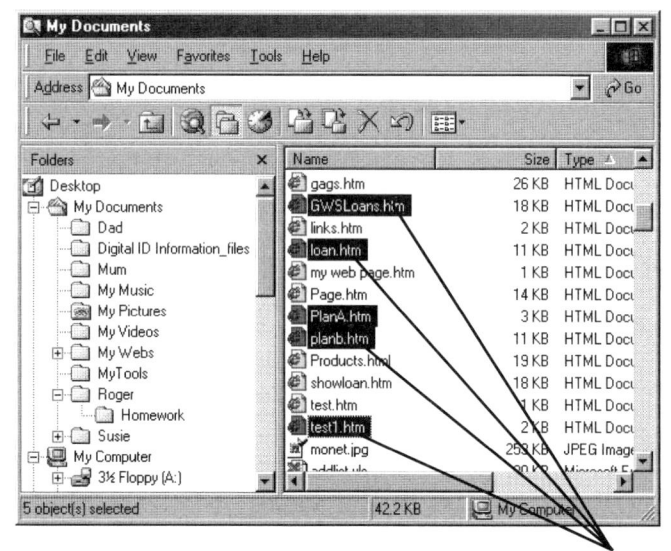

Hold **Control** to select scattered files

**Figure 7.20** Scattered files can also be selected together – it's fiddly, but still simpler than repeating operations on individual files.

FILES AND FOLDERS 95

## Moving and copying files

Files are easily moved or copied. The technique is similar for both.
- ❶ Select the file(s).
- ❷ Scroll through the **All Folders** display and/or open subfolders, if necessary, until you can see the target folder.
- ❸ Drag the file(s) across the screen until the target folder is highlighted, then drop it there.
- ◆ If the original and target folders are both on the same disk, this will move the selected file(s).
- ◆ If the folders are on different disks, or your target is a floppy disk, this will copy the file(s).

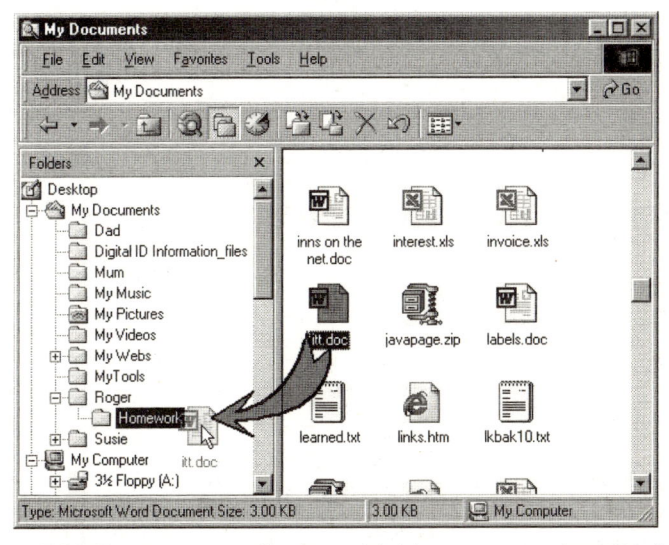

**Figure 7.21** If you can see the target folder, you can drag files into it.

If you want to move a file from one disk to another, or copy within the same disk, hold down the right mouse button while you drag. When you release the button, select **Move** or **Copy** from the short menu.

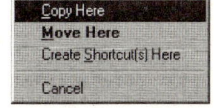

Dragging is simplest in Explorer. If you are using My Computer, you can open multiple windows and drag across the screen between them.

## Copy To and Move To Folder

If your mouse control is a bit iffy, things can go astray when dragging files and folders. A slower, but more reliable alternative is to use the Copy To and Move To Folder commands.

❶ Select the file(s).

❷ To move a file, click 🗒, or use the **Edit → Move to Folder...** command.

*or*

❷ To copy, click 🗒 or use **Edit → Copy to Folder...**

❸ The **Browse For Folder** dialog box will open. Work your way down through the folder structure and select the target folder, then click OK.

♦ If you copy a file into the same folder, it will be renamed '*Copy of...*' (the original filename).

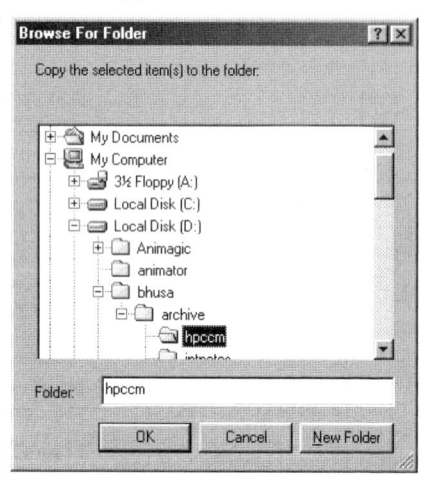

## Renaming files

If you want to edit or retype a file's name, select the file and press **F2** on your keyboard, or use **Rename** from the **File** or shortcut menu. Change the name as required and press **Enter** to fix the new name.

♦ If you are working in Classic mode (where you click to select), a second click on the filename will switch into edit mode.

---

**EXTENSIONS**

When renaming files, do not change their extensions! If you do, you will lose the document–application link (page 88).

---

# FILES AND FOLDERS

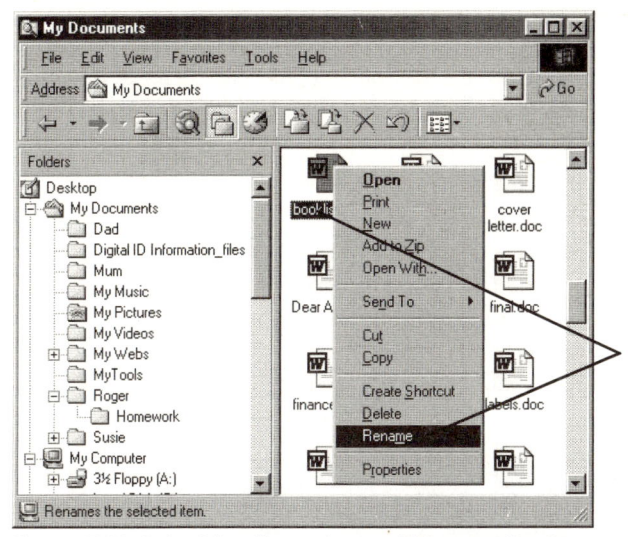

**Figure 7.22** Select the file and press [F2] or use the Rename command.

## Sending files elsewhere

The **Send To** command on the **File** menu or the shortcut menu offers a simple way to copy a file to a floppy disk or to your Mail system for sending by e-mail, or to start uploading a Web page to your Web space.

Just select the destination to begin!

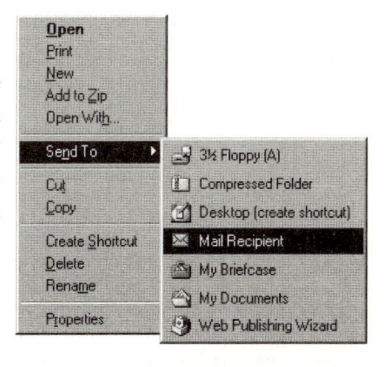

## Deleting files

If a file is no longer needed, select it and press **Delete** on your keyboard or use the **File →Delete** command. If you delete a folder, all its files are also deleted.

Windows Me makes it very difficult to delete files by accident! First, you have to confirm – or cancel – the deletion at the prompt. Second, nothing is permanently deleted at this stage. Instead, the file or folder is transferred to the Recycle Bin. Let's have a look at that now.

## 7.11 The Recycle Bin

The true value of the Recycle Bin is only appreciated by those of us who have used systems which lack this refinement, and have spent hours – or sometimes days – replacing files deleted in error! In practice, you will rarely need this, but when you do, you will be glad that it is there!

Recycle Bin

If you find that you need a deleted file, it can be restored easily.

- ❶ Open the Recycle Bin, from the Desktop icon or from Windows Explorer (at the end of the All Folders list).
- ❷ Select the file.
- ❸ Open the **File** menu, or right-click for the shortcut menu and select **Restore**.
- ♦ If the file's folder has also been deleted, it will be re-created first, so that the file can go back where it came from.

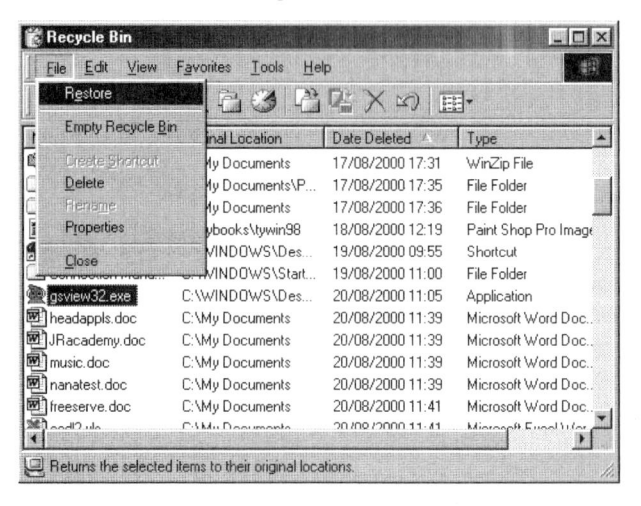

**Figure 7.23** Files deleted in error can be restored from the Bin.

One of the main reasons for deleting files is to free up disk space, but as long as they are in the Recycle Bin, they are still on the disk. So, make a habit of emptying the bin regularly. There is an **Empty...** option on the Bin's right-click menu, but this should only be used when you are absolutely sure that there is nothing in it that you might want to restore.

# FILES AND FOLDERS

- Play safe! Open the Bin and check its contents carefully, restoring any accidental deletions, before using the **File → Empty Recycle Bin** command.
- The default settings allows the Recycle Bin to use up to 10% of the drive's capacity, which should work well. If you want to change this, right-click on the Bin's icon to open its Properties panel and set the level there.

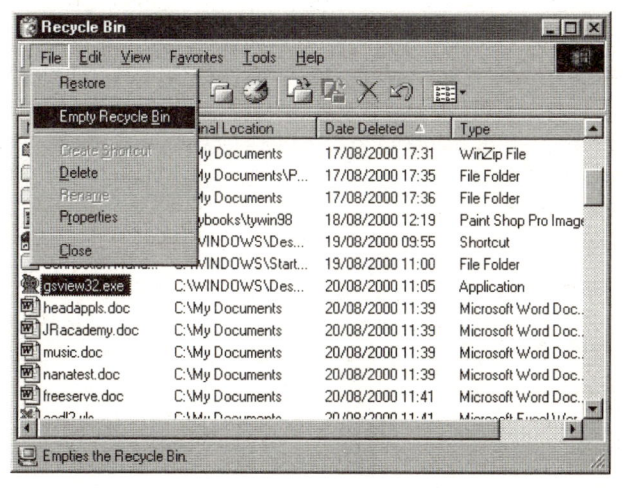

**Figure 7.24** The Bin should be emptied regularly to free up disk space.

## 7.12 Search

Windows Me has several Search utilities, but the one we are interested in here is **File or Folders**, which can track down lost files for you, hunting for them by name, location, contents, date, type and/or size. If you organize your folders properly, and always store files in the right places, you'll never need this utility. However, if you are like me, you will appreciate it.

- In Explorer, click the Search icon.

*or*

- click **Start**, point to **Search** and select **For Files or Folders**.

A simple search can be by all or part of the filename or for some text within a file – or a combination of the two. Suppose, for example, you were trying to find a letter to Mr Ree but could not remember what you called it or where you stored it. You at least know that it contained his name and that it was a Word document – and so would have the .doc extension. You could simply give 'Mr Ree' as the Containing text, and the search would find it, but if you also gave 'doc' in the filename slot, it would speed things up, as the search would then only have to read through document files (plus any others that happened to have 'doc' somewhere in their names) and could ignore all the rest.

If you can specify which drives or folders to start looking in, that will speed the search up further. And note that the search will normally look into all the subfolders below the start point.

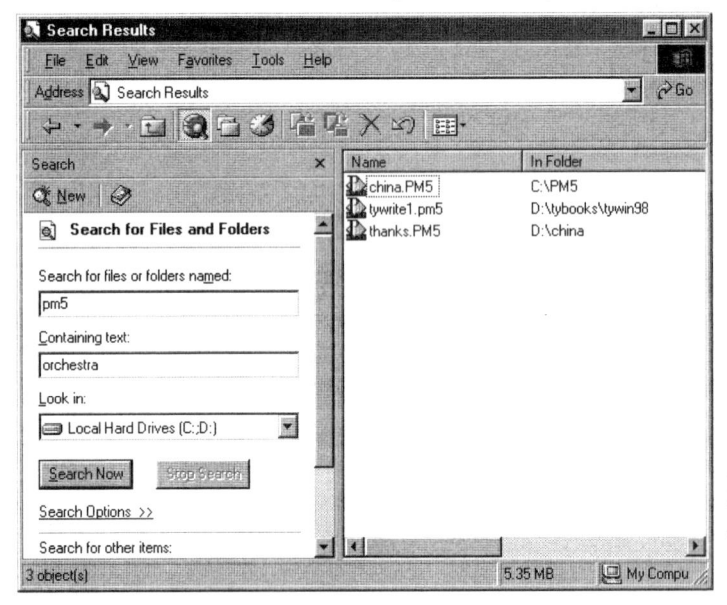

**Figure 7.25** Using the **Search** routine to track a PageMaker (pm5) file I did for the youth orchestra's summer tour.

### Search Options

Clicking **Search Options>>**, opens a panel where you can define a search by specifying the **Date**, **Type**, **Size** or other **Advanced options**.

# FILES AND FOLDERS

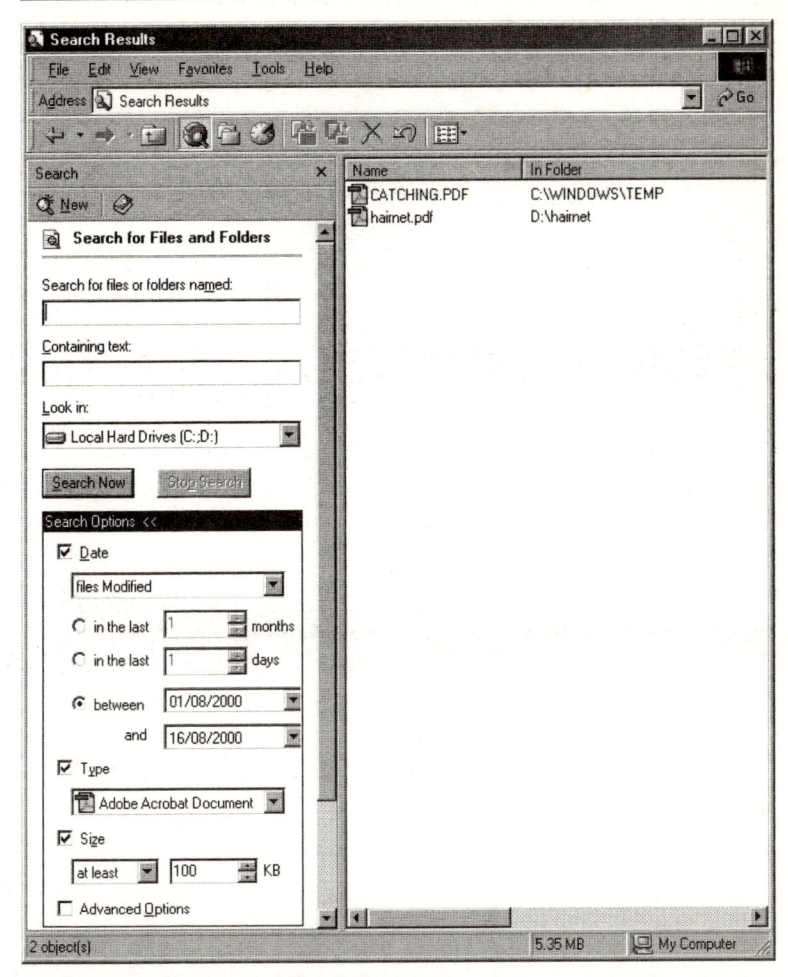

**Figure 7.26** Setting **Search** options. If you know when a file was created, modified or last accessed, you can set the date limits. The little drop-down calendar provides a very neat way to set dates! The Type can be picked from the (long!!) drop-down list. Specifying the size might be useful sometimes. The Advanced options are rarely much use. They simply let you turn off the subfolder search or turn on case sensitivity.

## SUMMARY

- ✓ Folders on hard (and floppy) disks create organized storage for your files.
- ✓ My Computer is a simpler version of Windows Explorer.
- ✓ Windows Explorer is the main utility for managing files and folders. It has a comprehensive set of tools.
- ✓ The View options and Folder options allow you to set up the Explorer display to suit yourself.
- ✓ The simplest way to create a new File Types association is to select the appropriate application when Windows asks you what it should open a document with.
- ✓ Files can be displayed as large or small icons or thumbnails, or in a detailed list. They can be sorted into name, size, type or date order.
- ✓ You should create folders for each area of your computer work, and for each person who uses the machine. Folders can be created within other folders if needed.
- ✓ Desktop shortcuts can be created by dragging file or folder icons from Explorer or My Computer onto the Desktop.
- ✓ Files can be moved, copied, renamed or deleted.
- ✓ To select sets of files, drag an outline with the mouse, or use the mouse in combination with Shift or Ctrl.
- ✓ When renaming files, do not change the extensions, as these identify the type of document.
- ✓ The Send command offers a simple way to copy a file to a floppy disk, or to e-mail it to someone.
- ✓ When a file is deleted, it is transferred to the Recycle Bin. If necessary, files can be restored from the Bin.
- ✓ The Search routine allows you to track down files through their name (or part of it!), location, date, type or size.

# 8 THE CONTROL PANEL

## AIMS OF THIS CHAPTER

Windows' plug and play facility for new hardware, and the installation routines for new software, help to ensure that your system is properly configured. However, there are some things which Windows cannot do for you as they depend upon your preferences. The Control Panel has around 30 components – the actual number depends upon your system – which you can use to customize your setup to suit yourself. In this chapter we will be looking at eight of the key components. Even if you are happy with the way that your system is running – or if you are hesitant about making changes that you might regret – do have a look at these. All the panels have a **Cancel** button!

## 8.1 Using the Panel

Open the Control Panel by clicking on the **Start** button, pointing to **Settings** and selecting it from there.

If you are running your folders in Web mode, only the six most commonly-used components will be visible at first – click the **view all Control Panel options** link to see the rest.

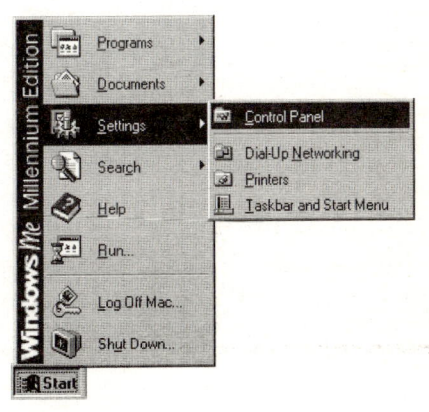

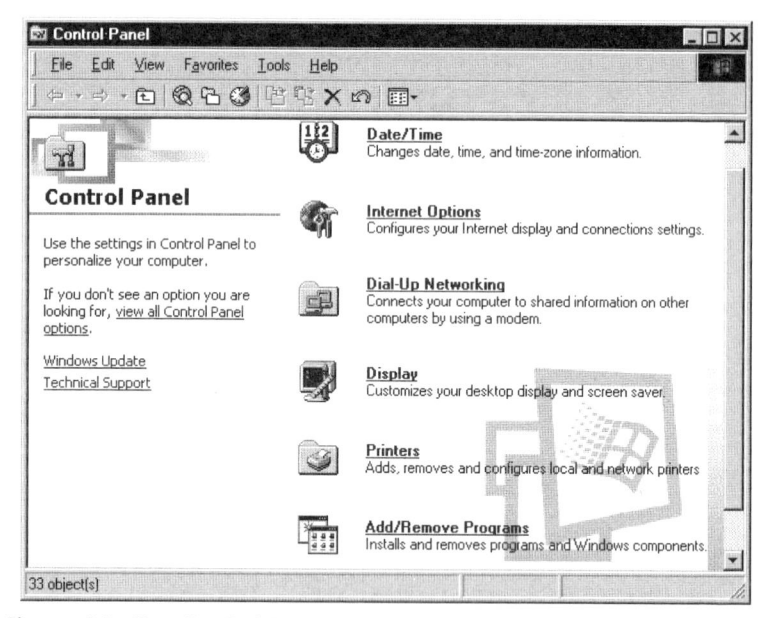

**Figure 8.1** The **Control Panel**, seen here when first opened in Web mode. The options displayed are the ones that you are most likely to need to adjust. Display was covered in Chapter 2; Internet Options and Dial-Up Networking we will leave until Chapter 10; Printers until Chapter 13. In this chapter the focus is on the options that configure your system for day-to-day use.

Run a component by clicking (or double-clicking) on its icon. This will open the appropriate **Properties** panel. View and edit its settings, clicking **OK** at the end to fix the new settings, or **Cancel** to abandon your changes.

Repeat with other components as required – the Control Panel remains open until you close it with **File → Close** or by clicking ⊠.

## 8.2 Accessibility

The options here are designed to make life easier for people with disabilities, but are worth investigating by anyone who is less than comfortable with the keyboard or mouse.

# THE CONTROL PANEL

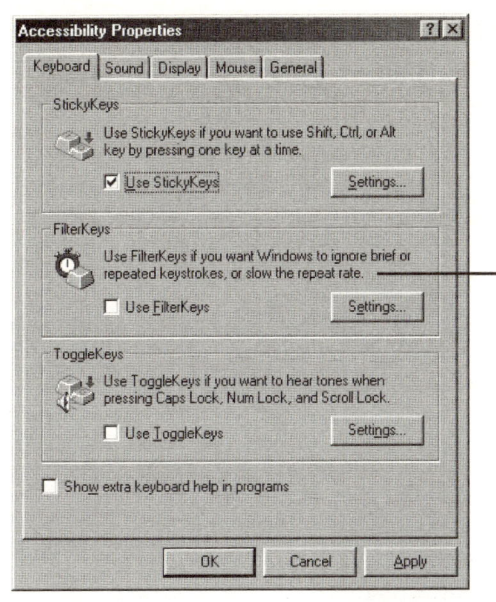

Set the keyboard options through the **Keyboard Properties** panel (page 113) before tweaking with **FilterKeys**

The panels that open from the **Settings** buttons vary, of course, but all have a **Keyboard shortcut** option. If used, the feature can be turned on and off – either to suit different users, or to suit the way you are working at that time.

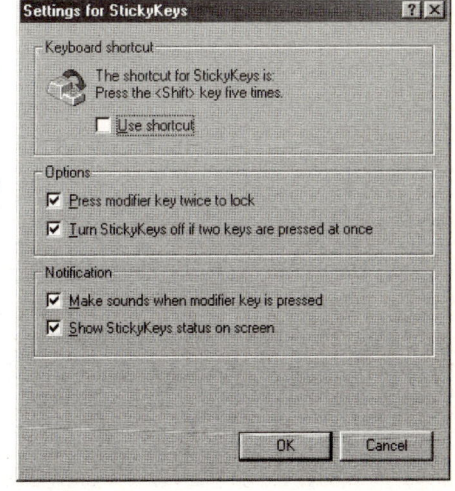

**Figure 8.2** The **Accessibility** options can make your system easier to use, see and hear.

### Keyboard

**StickyKeys** allow you to get the **Shift**, **Ctrl** and **Alt** key combinations by pressing them in sequence rather than simultaneously.

**FilterKeys** control the point at which a keystroke is picked up, or is repeated, and the repeat rate. Most of these settings can also be controlled through the Keyboard component (page106). If you still find that the keys are not responding as you would like after you have set the options there, come back and check out FilterKeys.

**ToggleKeys** will alert you when the Caps Lock, Num Lock or Scroll Lock keys are pressed. This is handy if, like me, you sometimes hit Caps Lock when aiming for Tab, and then type merrily on in CAPITALS!

### Sound

The main option on this tab turns on visual clues to replace, or emphasize sound prompts.

### Display

The high contrast display options, which are also available through the Display Properties panel (Chapter 2), can be turned on here.

### Mouse

The **MouseKeys** option allows you to use the Number pad keys to make mouse actions. The central key (5) does the left click; minus and 5 do the right-click; the number keys (7, 8, 9, 4, 6, 1, 2, 3) move the mouse.

### General

If you have set up an accessibility option so that it can be toggled on and off as required, go to this tab to define when to turn options off, and how to notify you of their status. If you have a device plugged into your serial port, to use in place of the standard keyboard or mouse, it can be set up through this tab.

## 8.3 Add/Remove Programs

Any software that is written to the Windows 95, 98 or Me specifications will be registered with the system when it is installed, so that it can be uninstalled, or the installation adjusted later through this panel.

# THE CONTROL PANEL

**Figure 8.3** All properly written Windows software can be uninstalled, or its components varied through this tab.

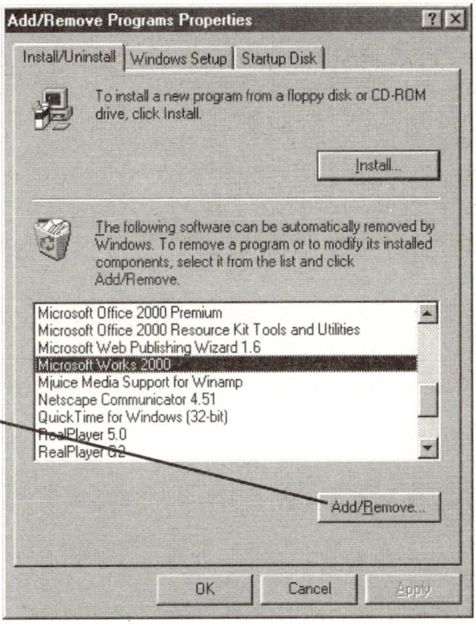

Clicking **Add/Remove** will take you to a routine to select components to add or remove from a suite, or uninstall simpler one-part software

## Install/Uninstall

New software can be installed through this tab, but can equally well be installed by running the 'install' or 'setup' program directly. It is not normally worth running Add/Remove Programs to do the job.

The main value of Install/Uninstall is in clearing unwanted software off your system, and in adding or removing components from software suites, such as Microsoft Office. If you simply delete a program's folder in Windows Explorer, it may remove all or most of the software's files – though there may be others scattered elsewhere in your disks – but it will not remove the entry in the Start menu, or the File Types associations. A proper uninstall will (normally) do a full clean-out from your system.

## Windows Setup

Windows Me is a huge package with a vast set of utilities and accessories – most people will use only a limited number of these and no one will use all of them. If you installed Me over an earlier version of Windows, you will have made some choices of which components to include. If Windows Me was installed when you acquired the PC, the selection will have

☑ all components selected under this heading

☑ some components selected

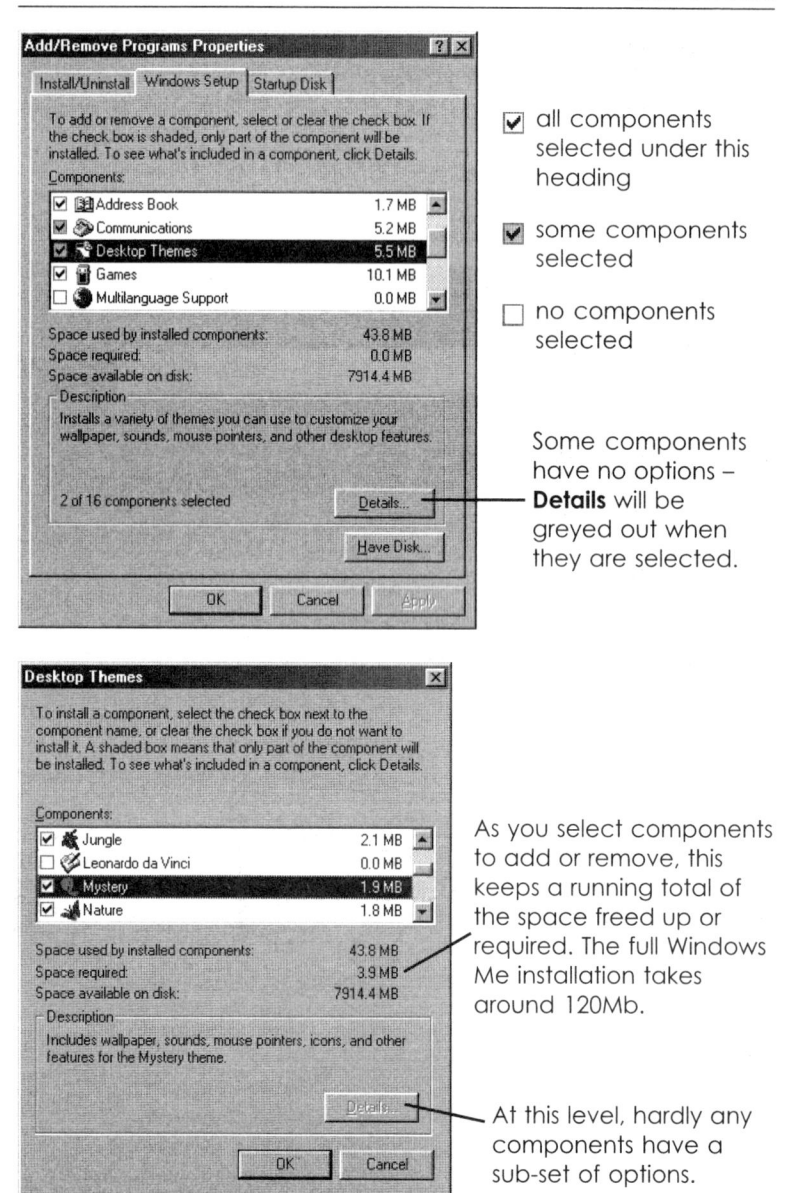

☐ no components selected

Some components have no options – **Details** will be greyed out when they are selected.

As you select components to add or remove, this keeps a running total of the space freed up or required. The full Windows Me installation takes around 120Mb.

At this level, hardly any components have a sub-set of options.

**Figure 8.4** Adjusting the Windows Setup.

THE CONTROL PANEL                                                                 109

been made for you. Either way, it is quite likely that you will decide, after having used Windows Me for a while, that some components are a waste of space, but that there are others that you need.

- ❶ Find your Windows CD and switch to the **Windows Setup** panel.
- ❷ Select a **Component** heading from the list and click the **Details** button.
- ❸ At the next panel, tick the checkbox to add a component, or clear it to remove an existing one, then click **OK**.
- ❹ Click **OK** on the main panel when you have done, and wait while Windows adds or removes components. You may have to restart the PC for some changes to take effect.

## 8.4 Date/Time

Even if you do not display the Clock on the Taskbar (see page 120), you should still make sure that the clock/calendar is correctly set if you want the date and time details to be right on your saved documents.

PCs are good time-keepers – Windows Me even adjusts for Summer Time automatically – as long as they are set correctly at the start. Open the Date/Time Properties panel and check yours.

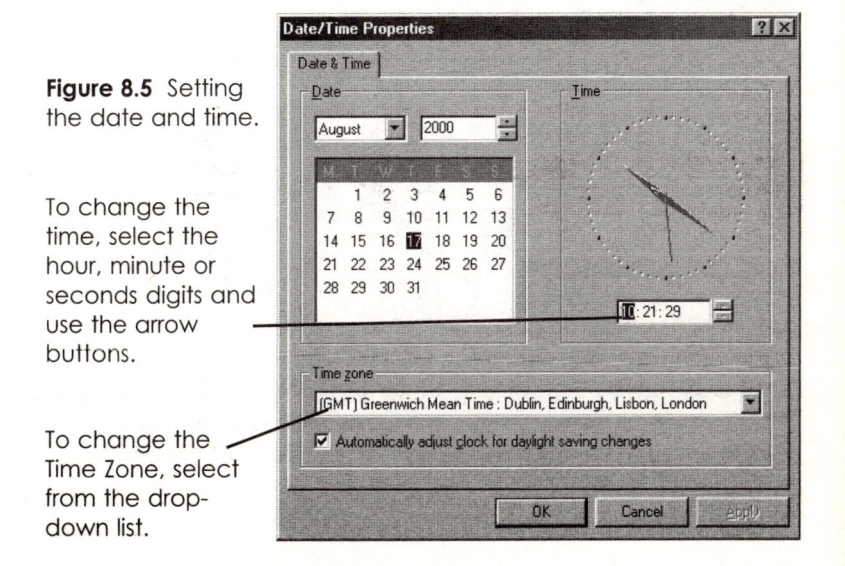

**Figure 8.5** Setting the date and time.

To change the time, select the hour, minute or seconds digits and use the arrow buttons.

To change the Time Zone, select from the drop-down list.

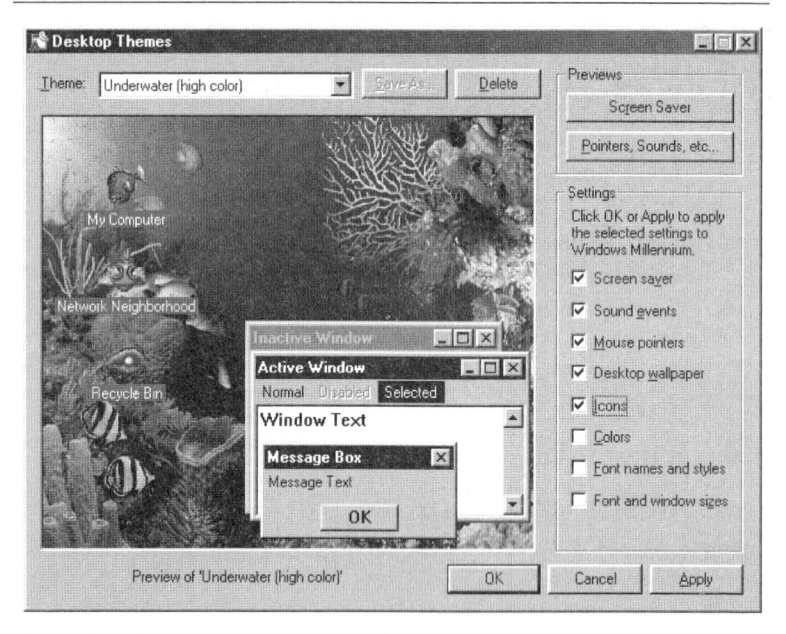

**Figure 8.6** If you use all aspects of a theme, your Desktop will have a more consistent appearance but may not be as clear as you might like! It is just as well that the icons here are labelled.

## 8.5 Desktop Themes

These are purely decorative, but can be fun. A theme will give a consistent look to your Desktop, its icons and screen saver, as well as mouse pointers, sounds and the fonts used in Windows – though you don't have to apply all aspects of the theme. Themes are installed onto the disk through the Windows Setup routine. This lets you select which one to use.

- ❶ Select the theme from the drop-down list at the top.
- ❷ Preview the screen saver, mouse pointers and sounds.
- ❸ Clear the checkboxes for any parts that you do not want.
- ❹ Click **Apply** if you want to see the theme in place before finally committing yourself – if you don't like it, start again.
- ❺ Click **OK**.

**THE CONTROL PANEL** 111

## 8.6 Fonts

A font is a typeface design, identified by a name. Within one font you will get type in a range of sizes (some are more variable than others), and the appearance may be varied by the use of bold, italic or other styles.

Fonts can be divided into three categories:

- **Serif** – like this (Times New Roman), marked by little tails at the ends of strokes. The tails (serifs) make the text easier to read, which is why serif fonts are normally chosen for large blocks of text.
- **Sans serif** – like this (Arial), with simpler lines. Sans fonts are typically used for headings and captions.
- Display – *decorative* fonts of all kinds. These are mainly used for headlines, posters, adverts, party invitations and special effects.

There are thousands of fonts in the world, and a couple of dozen of the best of these are supplied with Windows Me. You will get more with any

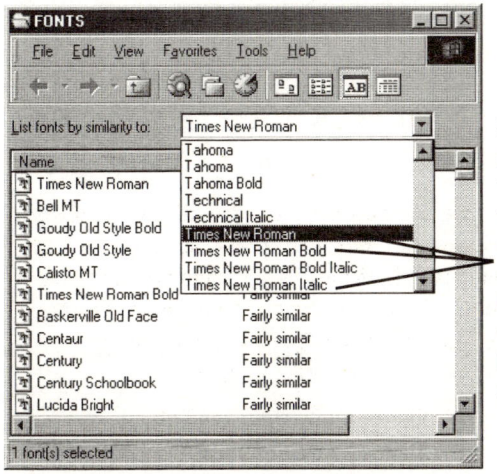

Some fonts have Bold, Italic and Bold Italic variations. Within a word-processor you will normally only see the main name in the font list – the Bold or Italic versions are then used if these effects are selected later.

**Figure 8.7** The Fonts folder, here using the *List by similarity* view. Choose a font from the drop-down list, and the whole set is then listed in order of closeness of match. This view is useful for weeding out excess fonts – to remove an unwanted font, select it then use **Delete** on the **File** menu.

word-processing and page layout software that you install, and you can buy CDs full of fonts.

You do not need a huge number. Professional designers normally work to the 'three-font' rule: no more than three fonts on any one page – one serif, one sans serif and one display – using different sizes and styles for variety and emphasis. It may well be a different set of three fonts for each project, but three or four serif and sans fonts and a dozen or so display fonts should be enough for most purposes. The more you have, the longer it will take to scroll through the font list whenever you are formatting text!

Do include Times New Roman and Arial in your selection. These two are used far more often than any others, simply because they are clear, attractive and highly readable. They are also – along with Courier New – the standard fonts for Web pages.

## Viewing fonts

If you want to see what a font looks like, just click on it. A viewer will open, showing samples of the characters in a range of sizes. If the font is to be used for extensive work, and it is especially important that it looks

True Type fonts are virtually identical on screen and paper. If they are not True Type, they are more likely to vary. In any case, a test print is often worth having.

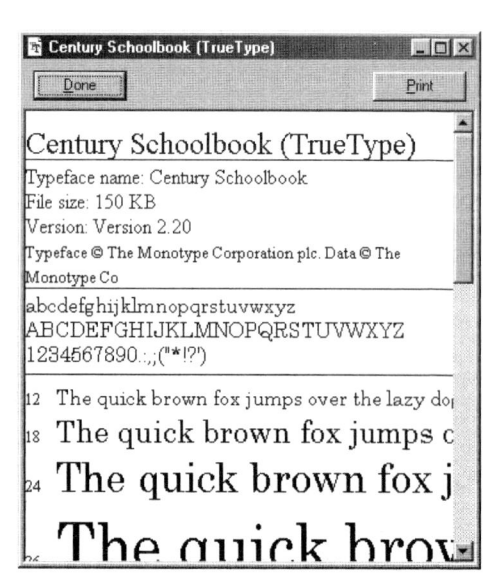

**Figure 8.8** The font viewer in use.

# THE CONTROL PANEL

just right, click the **Print** button to get a printed copy – there are often subtle differences between the screen display and printed output.

Click **Done** or ☒ to close the viewer, or select another font – a second copy of the viewer will open – if you want to compare them side by side.

## Installing fonts

If you have bought fonts on disk or CD-ROM, or have downloaded them from the Internet, they must be installed properly before they can be used.

❶ Open the **File** menu and select **Install New Font**.
❷ At the **Add Fonts** panel, select the drive and folder.
❸ Select the fonts from the list, holding down **Ctrl** while you click if you want to pick several.

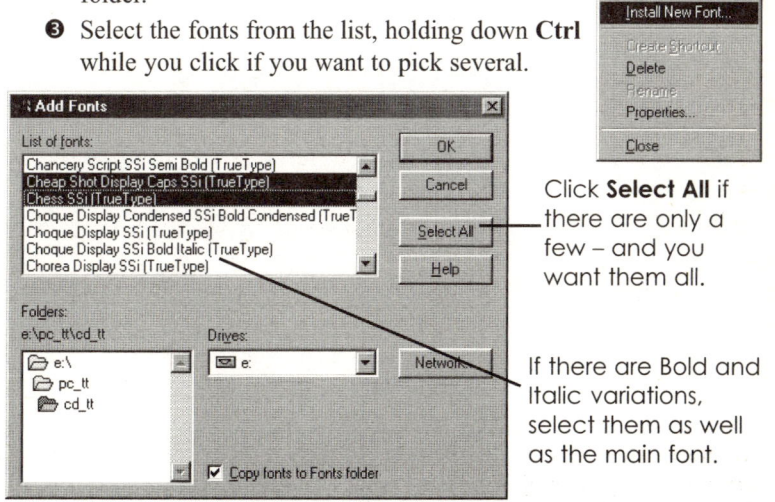

Click **Select All** if there are only a few – and you want them all.

If there are Bold and Italic variations, select them as well as the main font.

❹ If the font file is already on your hard disk, clear the **Copy fonts to Fonts folder** checkbox. There is no point in duplicating storage.
❺ Click **OK**.

## 8.7 Keyboard

How long your fingers linger on the keys affects the way that keystrokes are repeated. You normally want keystrokes to be picked up separately, but will sometimes want them to repeat – perhaps to create a line of ******.

If you sometimes write in a different language, use the **Language** tab to set up the keyboard to toggle between two character sets.

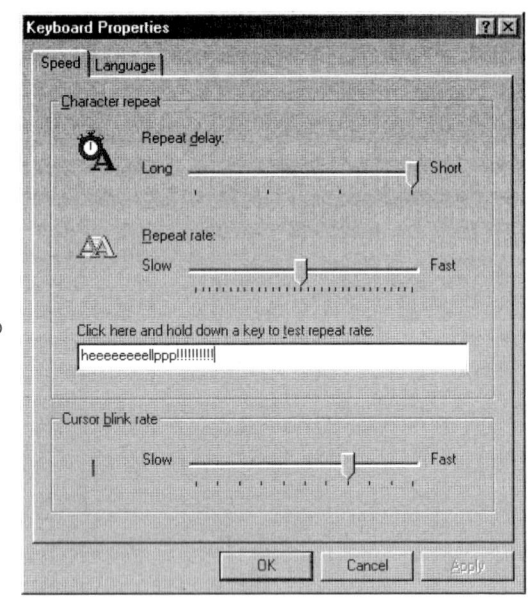

**Figure 8.9** Use the **Keyboard** panel to set the speed to suit you.

- The **Repeat delay** is how long to wait before starting to repeat – if you are heavy-fingered, set this to *Long*.
- The **Repeat rate** is how fast the characters are produced. This should match your reaction times.

Test the settings by typing in the test area, before you click **OK**.

## 8.8 Mouse

### Buttons

The only crucial setting here is the **Double-click** speed. Test the current setting by double-clicking on the jack-in-the-box, and use the slider to adjust the response if necessary.

You can switch the buttons over if you are left-handed, but it is better to get used to the standard layout, unless you only ever use the one PC. (Switching to the left-handed layout will also thoroughly confuse anyone else who tries to use the machine!)

# THE CONTROL PANEL

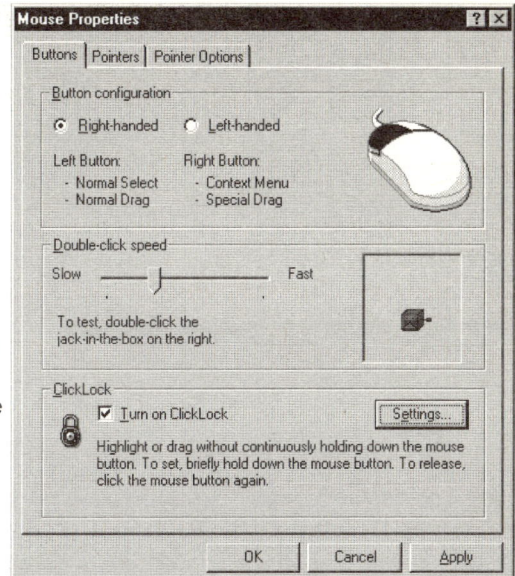

When the double-click speed is set correctly, you should be able to get the jack in and out of the box effortlessly.

**Figure 8.10** The **Buttons** tab of the **Mouse** panel.

## Pointers

The options here are almost entirely decorative, though obviously anything which makes is easier for you to see what you are doing must be beneficial. There are a dozen or so pointers, each related to a different mouse action. If you do not like some or all of the current set, select them one at a time and click **Browse**. You can then pick a new one from the pointers folder.

## Motion

The **Pointer speed** pane controls how far and how fast the pointer moves in relation to the mouse movement. To test this out, move the mouse and watch the pointer. If you don't feel comfortably in control of it, drag the slider towards Slow. If it's taking too long to get around the screen, set it faster. Click **Apply** and test again. Click **OK** when it feels right.

The **Pointer trail** option is only really relevant for laptop users. Pointers do not show up well on LCD screens, particularly when they are in motion. Turning on the trail makes them much easier to see.

View the animated cursors in the Preview pane

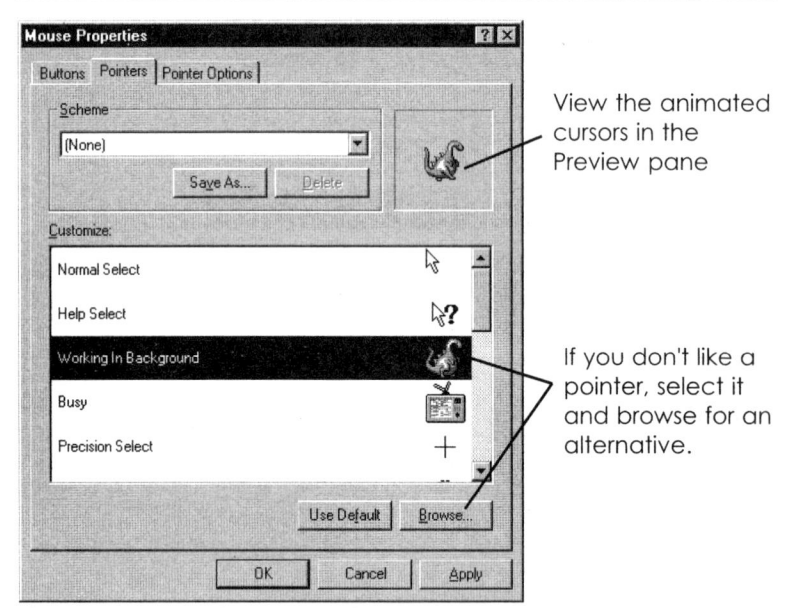

If you don't like a pointer, select it and browse for an alternative.

**Figure 8.11** The **Pointers** tab of the **Mouse** panel.

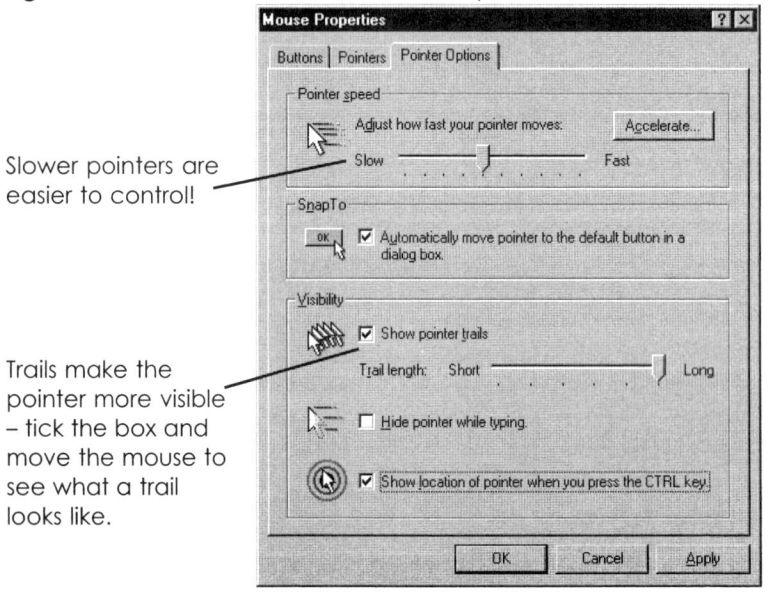

Slower pointers are easier to control!

Trails make the pointer more visible – tick the box and move the mouse to see what a trail looks like.

**Figure 8.12** The **Pointer Options** tab lets you control the pointer.

# 8.9 Sounds

Windows can attach sounds to certain events so that you get, for example, a fanfare at start up and a warning noise when you are about to do something you may later regret. Some of these are just for fun, others can be

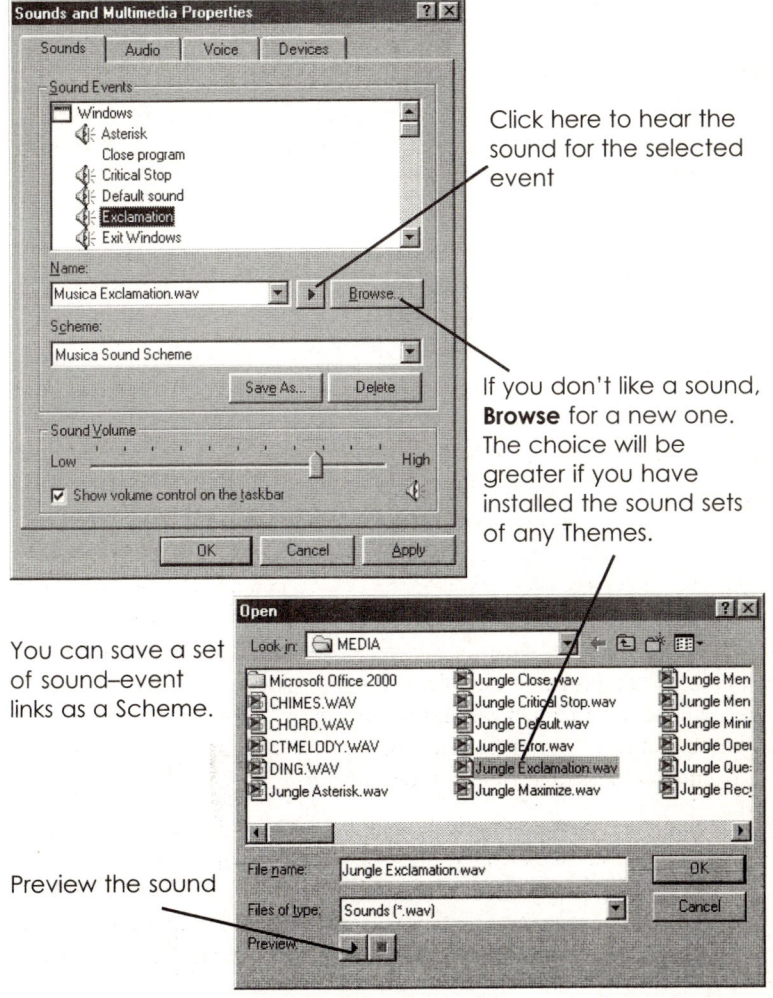

Click here to hear the sound for the selected event

If you don't like a sound, **Browse** for a new one. The choice will be greater if you have installed the sound sets of any Themes.

You can save a set of sound–event links as a Scheme.

Preview the sound

**Figure 8.13** Selecting a new sound to attach to an event. If you do not want a sound, select *None* in the **Name** box of the Sounds panel.

very useful. If you tend to watch the keyboard, rather than the screen, when you are typing, then an audible warning will alert you to a situation before it becomes a problem.

The Sounds Properties panel is where you decide which events are to be accompanied by a sound, and which sounds to use.

## SUMMARY

- ✓ You can configure your system to suit your way of working through the components of the Control Panel.
- ✓ The Accessibility options can make the keyboard easier to use and the screen easier to see.
- ✓ Use Add/Remove Programs to add or remove the components of application suites and of Windows.
- ✓ If you PC displays the wrong date or time, adjust it through the Date/Time panel.
- ✓ The Desktop Themes are mainly for fun – and why not?
- ✓ Use the Fonts folder to view fonts, remove unwanted ones and install new ones.
- ✓ Test and adjust the response rate of the keyboard through the Keyboard panel.
- ✓ Use the Mouse panel to set the double-click response and the speed at which the mouse moves the pointer. New pointer icons can be selected here.
- ✓ Sounds can be attached to events to alert you to them.

### OTHER CONTROL PANEL COMPONENTS

Other key components have been or will be dealt with in other chapters, where they are directly related to the aspect of Windows being covered. For **Display**, see Chapter 2; **Internet**, Chapter 10; **Printers**, Chapter 13; **Network**, Chapter 14. The **System** properties, though crucial to the correct running of your PC, are best left to Windows – look, but don't touch!

# 9 | TASKBAR AND START MENU SETTINGS

## AIMS OF THIS CHAPTER

By now you should be familiar with using the Taskbar and Start menu in your Windows sessions. Here we will look at ways in which you can customize the Taskbar and reorganize the Start menu. The techniques are simple and worth learning – these are two elements of the Windows system that you use regularly, so you should have them set up to your way of working.

## 9.1 Taskbar options

The Properties panel for the Taskbar and Start Menu can be opened either from the **Start ➜ Settings** submenu, or by right-clicking the Taskbar and selecting **Properties**.

The Taskbar tab has five on/off options. You can see the effects, as you set them, in the preview pane.

- **Always on top** – if set, the Taskbar overlaps any windows that reach the bottom of the screen.
- **Auto hide** – if set, the Taskbar slides off-screen when not in use. Pointing off the screen makes it pop-up again.

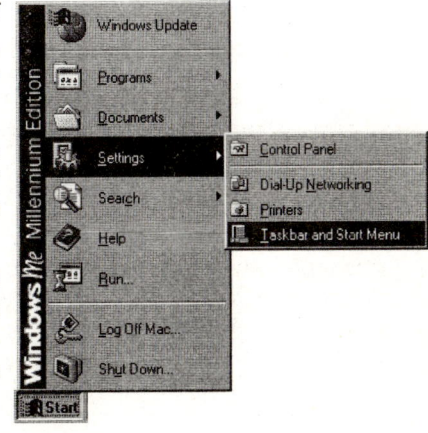

**Figure 9.1** Setting the Taskbar options. If you have a small screen, either turn off **Always on top** or turn on **Auto hide** to maximize your working area.

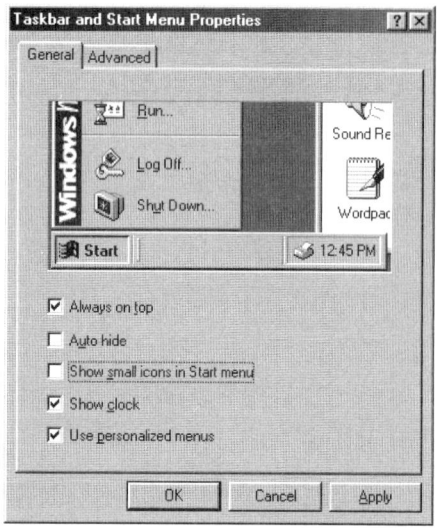

- **Show small icons in Start menu** – turn this off for more visible icons.
- **Show clock** – displays the clock in the far right of the Taskbar. Note that if you point to the clock, the date will pop up.
- **Use personalized menus** – sets Windows to monitor your use of menu items. Those that are not used regularly get missed off the main display, but can be seen by clicking the double arrow at the bottom of the menus. It takes a while for this to kick in!

## 9.2 Toolbars

In its initial settings, the Taskbar will have one toolbar on it – **Quick Launch** (see page 5). More can be added if you want to be able to start more applications from the Taskbar. There are four ready-made toolbars.

- **Address** – enter an Internet address here, and Internet Explorer will start and try to connect to it.
- **Links** – carries a set of buttons with Internet addresses, clicking one starts Internet Explorer to make the connection.
- **Desktop** – contains copies of the icons present on the Desktop.
- **Quick Launch** – for starting the main Internet applications.

# TASKBAR AND START MENU SETTINGS

Right-click on any blank area of the Taskbar to open the short menu

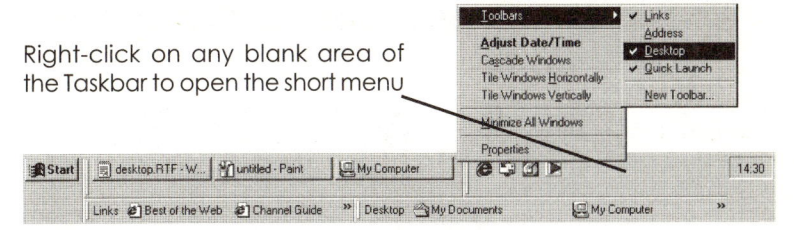

**Figure 9.2** The Taskbar with the Links and Desktop toolbars. Click the arrowheads on the right to display rest of the items on the toolbars.

## Toolbar options

The short menu that can be opened from a toolbar contains the usual Taskbar items, plus a small set of options that control the appearance of the toolbar.

**View** – **Large** or **Small** sets the icon size.

**Show Text** – adds labels.

**Refresh** – simply redraws the toolbar.

**Open** – opens the toolbar's folder so that you can add or remove shortcuts.

**Show Title** – displays the toolbar's title.

## Creating new toolbars

If you like working from the Taskbar, you can set up one or more toolbars containing shortcuts to your favourite applications, folders – or Internet links (see Chapter 10):

1. Create a folder, within My Documents, and name it 'My Tools' or something similar.
2. Set up shortcuts to the chosen applications or folders – hold the right button down as you drag the icons into this folder, and select the **Create Shortcut Here** option.
3. If you are going to show text labels on the toolbar, edit the names so that they are as brief as possible or you will have trouble displaying them all.

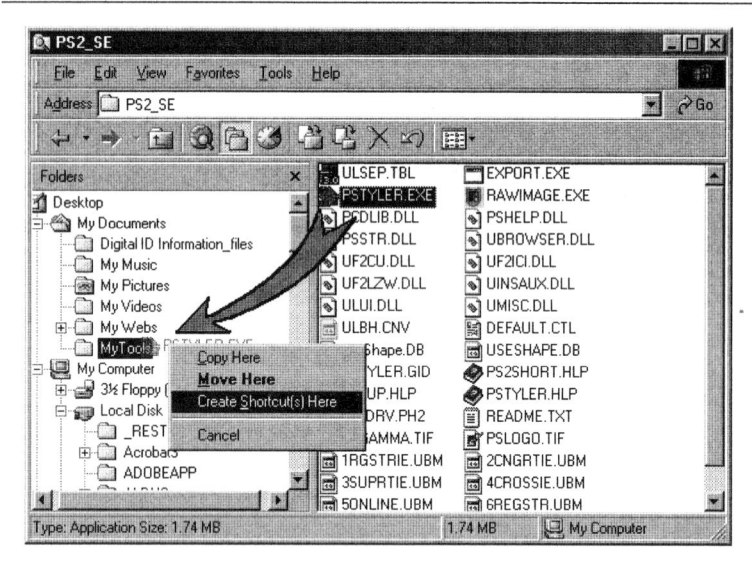

**Figure 9.3** Creating a shortcut for the new toolbar. If you want to copy existing shortcuts from the Start menu, you will find them in C:\WINDOWS\Start Menu.

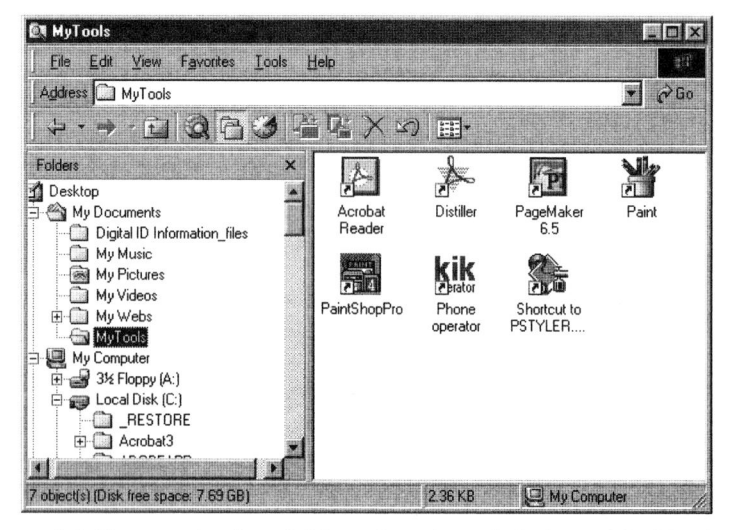

**Figure 9.4** The new toolbar folder, almost ready to be added to the Taskbar – the PhotoStyler shortcut name needs editing.

# TASKBAR AND START MENU SETTINGS

❹ When you have assembled your shortcuts, right-click on the **Taskbar**, point to **Toolbars** and select **New Toolbar...**

❺ Work through the folder display to find the one containing your shortcuts.

❻ Click **OK**.

**Figure 9.5** Adding the new toolbar. You could create several toolbars, one for each of the PC's users, or to suit the different kinds of work that you do on the machine.

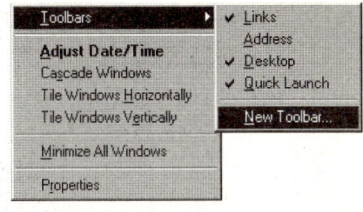

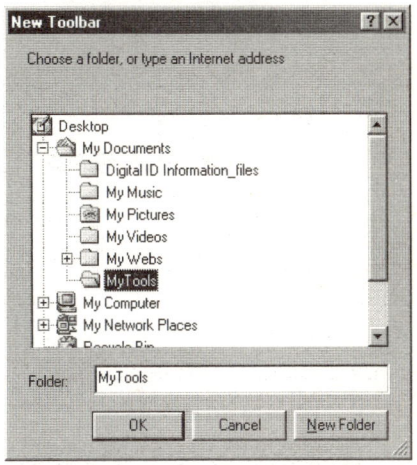

## 9.3 Moving and resizing

The Taskbar is normally a thin bar across the bottom of the screen, and this works very well when it is used only for the Quick Launch toolbar and a few application buttons. Add more toolbars and it is going to get crowded and difficult to use. There are two possible solutions:

- Make the Taskbar deeper by dragging its top edge upwards. The toolbars can be rearranged within this area by dragging on their handles. Move them up or down between the lines, or drag sideways to adjust their relative sizes.

Drag the edge to change the depth

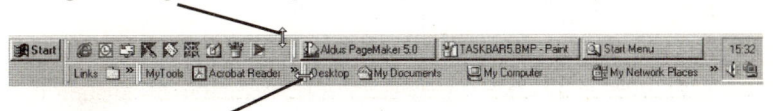

Drag on a handle to move a toolbar or to make it wider/narrower

- Move the Taskbar to one or other side of the screen. By default it will be wide enough to show the Text labels on the icons. You will probably need to adjust the layout by dragging on the handles between the sections, and may want to make the bar slimmer – drag its edge inwards.

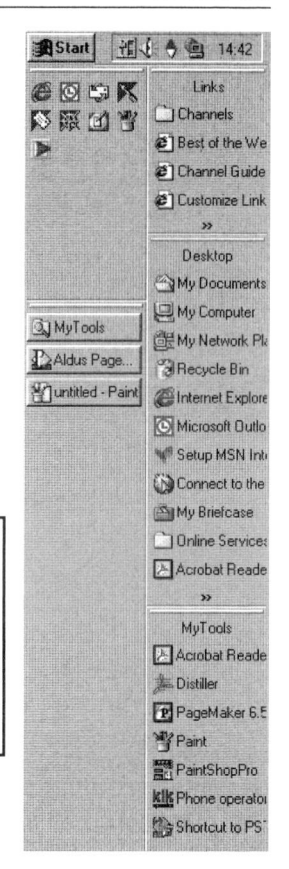

> **DO YOU NEED LABELS?**
>
> If the icons are clear enough, the toolbar titles and shortcut labels are not really necessary. Turning them off will save a lot of space, allowing you to pack more into a slim Taskbar.

## 9.4 The Start Menu

If you switch to the **Advanced** tab of the **Taskbar and Start Menu Properties** panel, you can control which items appear on your menu system, and where they appear.

### Adding

This is the fiddliest of these three jobs, but fortunately not one that you will have to do very often – with modern software, the installation routines normally add the Start menu entries for you.

# TASKBAR AND START MENU SETTINGS

[Screenshot of Taskbar and Start Menu Properties dialog, Advanced tab]

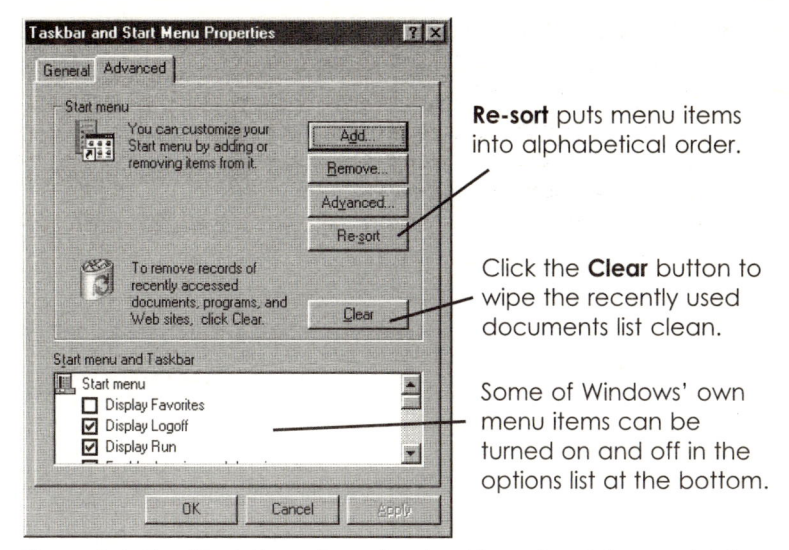

**Re-sort** puts menu items into alphabetical order.

Click the **Clear** button to wipe the recently used documents list clean.

Some of Windows' own menu items can be turned on and off in the options list at the bottom.

**Figure 9.6** The Start Menu is customized from the **Advanced** tab.

- Before you start, locate the application's main file, using Explorer or My Computer. It will be easier to find it through one of these than at the Browse dialog box in step 2.
- ❶ Click **Add**. This will start a wizard to guide you through the process.
- ❷ At the **Create Shortcut** stage, click **Browse** and locate the program file. Click **OK**, then click **Next** at the wizard panel.
- ❸ Select the Start menu folder – opening them as necessary to reach subfolders (submenus) – and click **Next**.
- ❹ Finally, type a name for the menu item and click **Finish**.

## Removing

Start menus can get cluttered and messy. Some installation routines don't just put in entries for the applications, they also create shortcuts to the 'Readme' file (that you will read once, if at all) and to the Help pages (that you normally only open from within the application). Some uninstall routines fail to remove the entries from the Start menu when the program files are deleted. Some software creates duplicate entries in the main menu and in submenus.

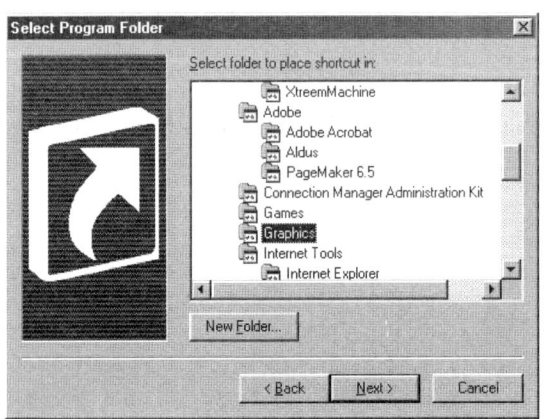

If you know the folder and filename, you can type it in, but browsing is usually simpler.

The menus are presented as folders – open them as needed to reach the right place.

**Figure 9.7** The main stages of the Add routine. If you make a mistake at any point, click **Back** to redo a stage.

Removing entries is very simple.
- ❶ At the Start Menu Programs tab, click **Remove**.
- ❷ Open up the folders to display the unwanted entries.
- ❸ Select a folder or menu item and click **Remove**.
- ❹ Repeat as necessary.
- ❺ Click **Close**.

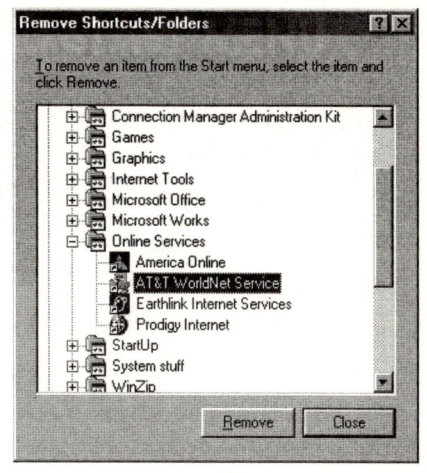

## Reorganizing the menus

The Start menu system is stored as a set of folders and subfolders in the *C:\Windows\Start Menu* folder. You can open it in Explorer or My Computer, though it is probably simpler to click the **Advanced** button on the **Start Menu Programs** tab. This opens a limited version of Explorer. You cannot move up out of the Start Menu folder, but all the normal file management techniques for moving, deleting and renaming files and folders work here.

If you have installed so many applications that your Start menu has become overcrowded, create 'group' folders and move the entries and folders of related applications into these. A short main menu that leads to two or three levels of submenus is much easier to work with than one huge menu!

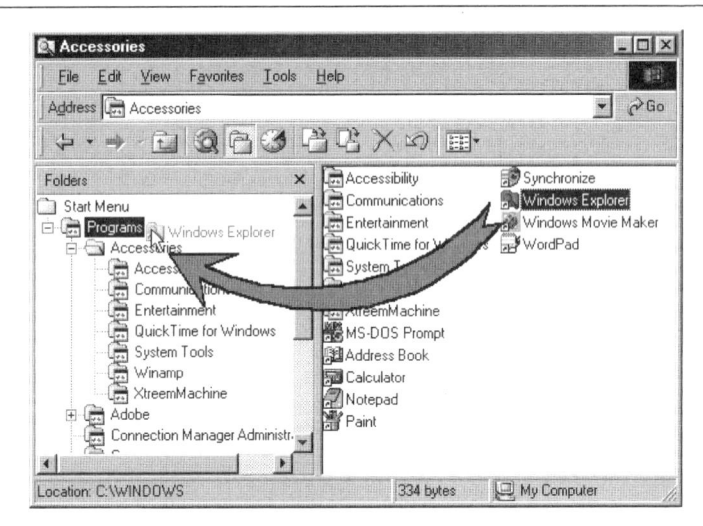

**Figure 9.8** The **Advanced** button lets you explore the Start menu. In the example, Windows Explorer is being moved to the main Programs menu – such a useful program should be easy to get to.

## SUMMARY

- ✓ Taskbar can be displayed on top of all other windows, behind them, or tucked off screen when not in use.
- ✓ Ready-made toolbars can be added to the Taskbar.
- ✓ You can create your own folders of shortcuts and turn them into Taskbar toolbars.
- ✓ You can adjust the depth and position of the Taskbar, and move the toolbars within it.
- ✓ Entries can be added to or removed from the Start menu.
- ✓ The menu structure can be reorganized using the normal file management techniques.

# 10 INTERNET EXPLORER

## AIMS OF THIS CHAPTER

This chapter concentrates on the practical aspects of getting online through Windows Me, and on setting up and using Internet Explorer. We will have a brief look at some of the facilities that can be reached through the Internet, but there isn't room in this book to tackle this huge area properly. If you want to know more about the Internet, try *Teach Yourself The Internet*.

## 10.1 What is the Internet?

The Internet is a world-wide communications network, linking thousands of computer networks, through a mixture of private and public phone lines and microwave links. Its component networks are run by government agencies, universities and commercial organizations, working co-operatively and loosely controlled by the Internet Society. These organizations bring many millions of people onto the Internet, and millions more link in their home computers through one or other of the many service providers.

At the time of writing, Autumn 2000, there are well over 25 million host computers supplying services and information over the Net, and the number of users is estimated to be upwards of 250 million. In the UK alone, there are over 400,000 host computers on the Internet, and around half of the population has access either from home, or through their work or through their school or university.

The Internet can be accessed and used in a number of ways. For most people, the most important aspects of the Internet are the World Wide

Web, electronic mail and newsgroups. Once you get into it, you will soon discover that there are other ways to use the Internet and you might want to investigate some of these over time.

## The World Wide Web

This is probably the most exciting and useful aspect of the Internet for most users. It consists of hundreds of millions of *pages* of information, stored on host computers throughout the world. The pages contain text, graphics, video clips, sounds and – most importantly – *hyperlinks* to other pages. Clicking on a hyperlink will take you to another page, which may be in the same computer, or in one a thousand miles away.

Some Web pages are excellent sources of information in their own right, some are treasure troves of links to other valuable pages; and some are pure trivia. You have to be selective, and you have to keep an eye on the phone bill, for Web browsing is a fascinating, but time-consuming activity.

To access the Web you need a browser – such as Internet Explorer – which can display the text and images, and interpret the links that will take you from one page to another.

### Finding stuff

Despite the massive quantity of information that is available on the Web, finding the things that interest you is not usually that difficult. There are several *directories*, which hold large sets of organized links to Web pages – and to other parts of the Internet. Yahoo! (page 147) is probably the best known of these, and is an excellent place at which to start researching a subject. There are also *search engines* where you can hunt for pages that contain given words. They are most useful when you are looking for information on a very specific topic as they can pick out the relevant pages from the millions on the Web. The Search button in Internet Explorer will link you to Excite's search engines (see page 145).

### On-line sales and services

The World Wide Web is becoming a good place to do business. New companies have been started to sell goods over the Web (books, CDs, fancy gifts, and computer hardware and software seem to do best at present) and an increasing number of existing shops and other firms are now marketing their goods and services online. Fraud is a problem on the

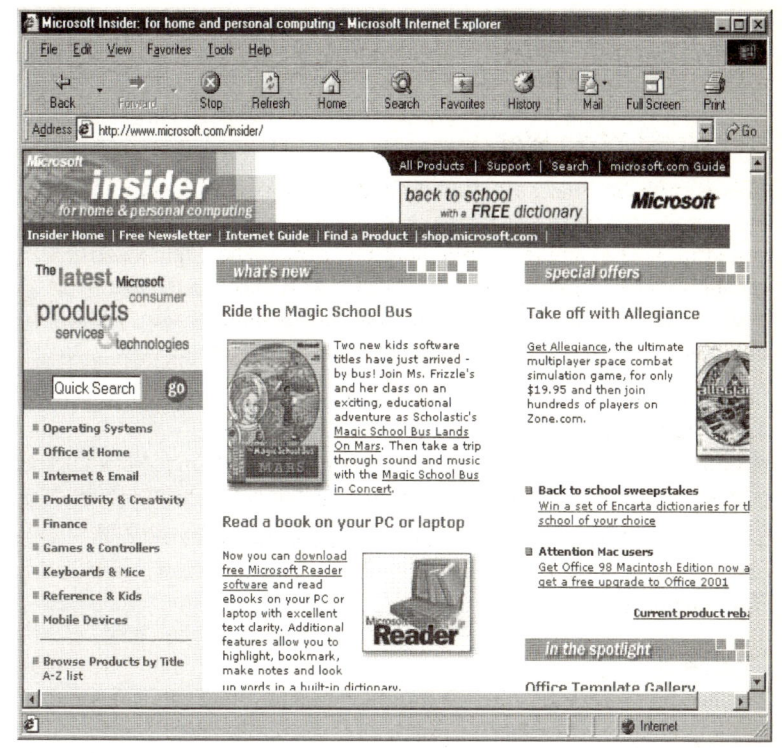

**Figure 10.1** Microsoft runs an extensive Web site – a great source of information and software, with links to many resources beyond its site.

Internet, but probably no more so than it is in any area where business is done. You can shop and deal as safely over the Internet as you can by mail order or in the high street. It's largely a matter of choosing your firms wisely and avoiding too-good-to-be-true bargains.

### Your own Home Page

Almost all Internet service providers offer their subscribers the opportunity to have their own home pages. Some people use the pages as notice boards for their local sports or hobby clubs; some run fan clubs on theirs; some will pull together information and links on a subject, making their home pages into valuable resources for others who share their interests.

If you want to create your own home page, you should have some understanding of *HTML* (HyperText Markup Language) – the coding system behind Web pages. It is not difficult to learn, and you don't need to learn much of it if you use FrontPage Express, or other HTML editor. This will handle the nitty-gritty of the HTML system and let you get on with the job of designing the layout and producing the content.

## E-mail

Electronic mail is probably the most widely used of all the Internet facilities – after the novelty of browsing the Web has worn thin, you will still be logging on regularly to collect and send e-mail! E-mail is mainly used for sending plain text messages, but you can also send formatted text, and attach graphics, sounds and other data files to your messages.

Most e-mail is one-to-one communication, but there are also mail lists that circulate messages to their members. Each of the many hundreds of lists covers a specialist interest, and almost all are open to anyone to join.

## Newsgroups

These are a development of mail lists, and have much in common with them. There are thousands of newsgroups (over 20,000 at the last count), covering an amazing range of interests, activities and obsessions, from the mundane to the bizarre. Some newsgroups are very active, with hundreds of new articles every day; others have much lighter traffic. Some groups clearly have members with too much free time and free access to the Internet; in others, the articles are typically brief but relevant and interesting. Some groups are moderated – i.e. they have someone to edit submissions and filter out the irrelevant ones. Unmoderated groups on topics that attract obsessives can produce vast quantities of articles that are of little interest to anyone but their authors.

You may not have access to all the Internet's newsgroups. You can only reach those that are handled by the news server at your service provider, and some providers are more selective than others. Some may even offer you the option of accessing only those that are suitable for family audiences – an option worth considering if children use your Internet connection.

## 10.2 Getting online

Windows Me has all the software that you need to access the Internet. To actually get online from home, you will also need:

- a modem – to convert computer signals into a form that can be sent down the phone lines. If your PC is not already equipped with one, a modem is easily added. Expect to pay around £100 for a fast (56K) modem, or half as much for a 28.8K modem. (The Internet's connections are often so busy that faster modems rarely get the chance to run at full speed!)
- a phone socket within reach of your computer.
- an account with an ISP (Internet Service Provider). This gives you access to the Internet and an e-mail address.

If you have just bought a new Windows Me PC, it will almost certainly have a built-in modem and the software to connect you to an ISP. Unless there are special reasons otherwise, you may as well use the recommended ISP for your first ventures into the Internet. It is not difficult to change ISPs – the biggest bother is letting all your contacts know your new e-mail address!

### Internet Connection Wizard

This can be used to find a service provider or to set up a connection to an existing provider. As with all wizards, work through it stage by stage, supplying information or making choices in response to prompts.

- If you are in doubt about anything, accept the default settings.
- Don't touch the **Advanced Settings** unless the provider tells you exactly what to do! Most should work with the defaults.
- If you think you have made a mistake at any stage, click the **Back** button to check and correct earlier entries – or if it's a really crucial mistake, click **Cancel** and start again!
- If you are going to use this to find a provider, you will need persistence and patience. It can take many attempts before you get through to Microsoft's online referral service, where the list of providers is kept!
- If you have already set up an account with a provider, make sure that you have at hand any information they sent to you – including their phone number, mail and news servers' names,

your user details. This is normally all that's needed, but some providers may give you technical details. Have them ready.
- You will be offered the chance to set up your mail, news and Internet directory service. Mail and news are worth doing. The directory service could well be left until later.

You should find the Connection Wizard in the **Programs** ➙ **Accessories** ➙ **Communications** submenu of the **Start** menu.

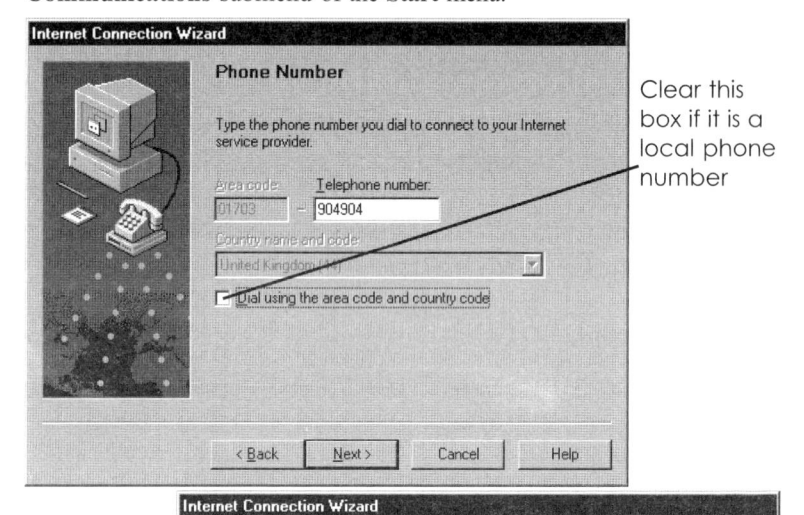

**Figure 10.2** Two stages (of many) from the Connection Wizard.

> **TROUBLE CONNECTING?**
>
> If you have any difficulties in establishing a working connection with your provider, look for the Modem Troubleshooter in the Help pages. It will show you what to check, and what to try to solve the problem. If that fails, ring your provider's technical support line – patience is a virtue with most of these.

## 10.3 Internet Explorer

You can access the Internet from many places in the Windows Me system, but the main tool for this job is Internet Explorer. It is very similar to Windows Explorer or My Computer – especially when using Web page view. In fact, if you use the Favorites, Links buttons or Address box to connect to an Internet site through either Windows Explorer or My Computer, they will effectively turn into Internet Explorer.

- Microsoft would like you to view the Internet as an extension of your Desktop. If you connect through an ISDN line, or better still a fast, high-capacity leased line that is permanently open, then this may be a viable view. If you connect by dialling in to a service provider, the transition from Desktop to Internet will rarely be smooth.

For the rest of this chapter, I'll concentrate on Internet Explorer, but it's worth bearing in mind that this is not the only route into the Net.

Internet Explorer is designed for fast, easy navigation, both on and offline. When you browse a page, its files are stored in a temporary folder on your hard disk. When you return to the same page, its files are then loaded from the disk, rather than downloaded from the Internet. This makes browsing far, far quicker! We all have our own favourite places that we use to start searching for stuff, and when following up links you will often find pages with several good leads, and you will want to return to these to pick up new trails. These stored files also allow you to 'revisit' sites when you are offline, but it should be noted that this does not always work. Some pages insist on downloading new files – typically adverts – each time they are opened, and will not display without them.

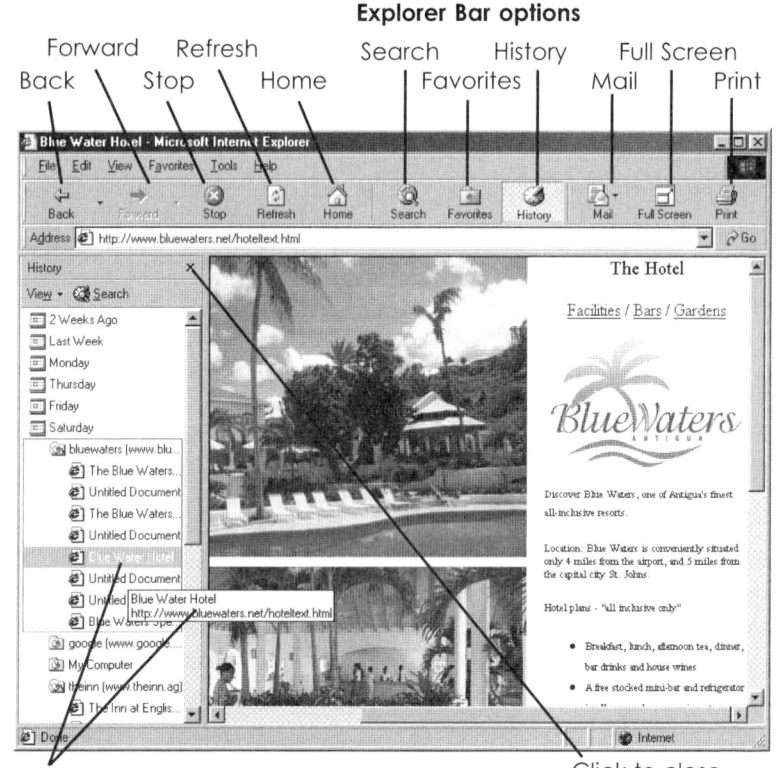

**Explorer Bar options**

Figure 10.3 The Internet Explorer display. The Explorer bar panel on the left can be opened to display the History list (pages visited recently), Favorites or an online Search facility.

## The Internet Explorer window

- The **Standard**, **Address, Links** and **Radio toolbars** can be turned on or off – the Address (page 146) is more useful here than it is in Windows Explorer.
- The **Explorer Bar** can display Search (page 145), Favorites (page 149) or History (page 148).
- For maximum viewing area when browsing, switching to **Full Screen View** will turn off all the features of the window, except the Standard toolbar.

### The Standard toolbar

These buttons contain almost all of the controls that you need when you are online.

- **Back** and **Forward** move between the pages already visited during the session.
- **Stop** – use it when you realize at the start of a long download that you don't really want to see that page.
- **Refresh** redraws the current page.
- **Home** goes to your start page – your jumping off point into the Web. This can be your own home page or any other.
- The **Explorer bar** buttons open the bar to run a Search, or browse the Favorites or the History folders.
- **Full Screen** toggles between Full Screen and normal view.
- **Mail** starts or switches to your mail software (normally Outlook Express) for reading or sending e-mail or newsgroups (see Chapter 11).
- **Print** prints the current page (text and graphics).

### Menu commands

Most of the ones that you will use regularly are duplicated by the Toolbar buttons, and are better handled through them. However, there are some very useful commands that can only be reached through the menus:

- **File → New → Window** opens a second browser window, so that you can keep one page at hand while you follow up other leads.
- **File → Work Offline** should be turned on when using Explorer offline.
- **Edit → Find** will search for words in the current page.
- **View → Text size** lets you set the size of the text (headlines are scaled to match).

**File → Open**, **Tools → Internet Options** and the **Add** and **Organize Favorites** commands are also important. We will return to them in the next few pages.

## 10.4 Internet Options

These options can be set or changed at any time on or offline (though the odd couple only take effect after you restart the PC). A few should be set before you start to use Explorer in earnest, others are best left until you have been using it for a while and have a clearer idea of what settings best suit your preferred way of working.

- Use **Tools** → **Internet Options** to open the panel, and click on the tab names to move between the sets of options.
- If you set options that change the appearance of the screen, click **Apply** to see how they look.
- Only click **OK** when you have finished with all the tabs.

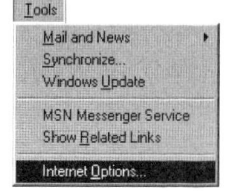

### General

The **Home page** defines where Explorer goes when it is first started. This could be a personalized start page at Microsoft (or other content provider – many offer this facility), your own home page, or a blank page if each session is a new voyage. An address can be typed in here, but it is simpler to wait until you are online at the right place, then just come back to this tab and click **Use Current**.

In **Temporary Internet files**, click **Settings** to define Explorer how should handle page files.

- In the **Check for newer version of stored pages**, select *Every visit to the page*, if the pages you use a lot change frequently.
- The **Amount of disk space to use** depends upon how much browsing you do, how often you return to pages and how much space you have. When the space is used up, older files are wiped to make way for new ones. A typical page of text and graphics might add up to 50Kb – say 20 pages per Mb. How many pages do you want in store – remembering that, if you update pages when you revisit, those that you use regularly will be relatively new files.
- If you have more spare space on a second hard disk, click **Move Folder** and set up the temporary storage space there.

# INTERNET EXPLORER

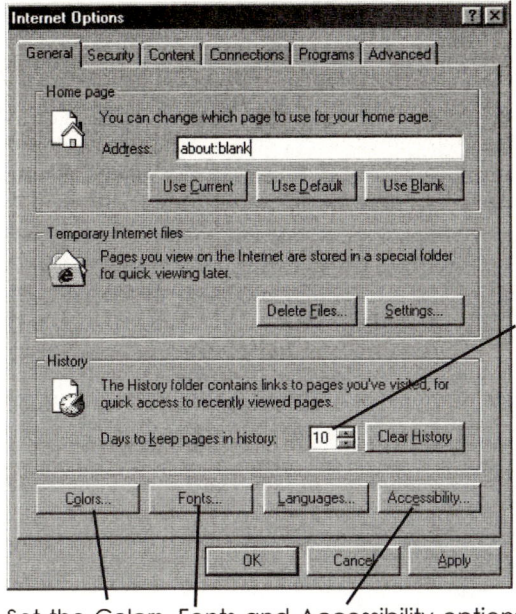

The History records your movements, to allow easier revisiting – how long do you want to keep it?

Set the Colors, Fonts and Accessibility options if you need a high visibility display.

If you tend to visit pages that have a lot of graphics or information, and you want to be able to study these later, offline, set a high disk space level.

**Figure 10.4** Setting the **General** options.

## Security

The Internet is basically a safe place – as long as you take a few sensible precautions. If you spend most of your time at major commercial and other well-established sites, and at ones they recommend, security should not be a major concern. If you browse more widely, you may bump up against the mischievous and the unscrupulous. The main dangers are these:

- **Viruses** – You can only get these by running executable files (programs) or macros in documents. You cannot pick up a virus simply by browsing a page or reading e-mail or news articles. A virus-checker will give you an extra level of protection.
- **Active content** – Web designers may use small programs (applets), written in Java, Javascript or ActiveX to enhance their pages – though many are just decorative. The languages are designed to be secure – the programs should not be able to access your system – but hackers do find loopholes.
- **Privacy intrusions** – Every time you fill in a form online, run a search or make a choice, you send some information about yourself along with the intended data. Some sites may attempt to store and misuse this information.
- **Cookies** – A cookie is a short file, written by a site onto your hard disk. They are normally used to store your personal preferences at that site – so that when you revisit you don't have to set preferences again – or simply to log your visit. You don't have to accept cookies. To disable them, or to get a prompt before accepting them, go to the Custom Level panel.

### Zones and security levels

If you have a **local intranet** (Web site within the organization and only open to its members), this zone can be set to *Low* security.

The **Internet zone** covers all unclassified sites (initially everywhere) and should be set to *High* or *Medium* security.

Sites that you know and trust can be added to the **Trusted sites zone**, and its level set to *Low*.

If your Internet zone setting is at Medium, any sites that you are wary of – but still want to revisit – should be added to the **Restricted sites zone**, and its level set to *High*.

# INTERNET EXPLORER

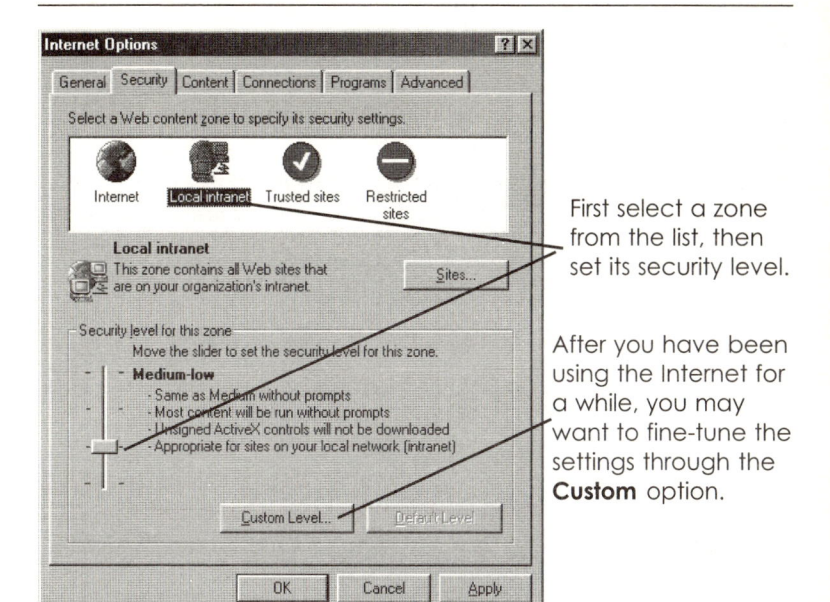

First select a zone from the list, then set its security level.

After you have been using the Internet for a while, you may want to fine-tune the settings through the **Custom** option.

**Figure 10.5** The **Security** tab – when in doubt, play safe!

If you **disable** cookies, some sites will not let you in. **Prompt** is a compormise, but some sites set an awful lot of cookies – and the constants prompts get tedious. If you want to control who stores what on your hard disks, these are prices you have to pay!

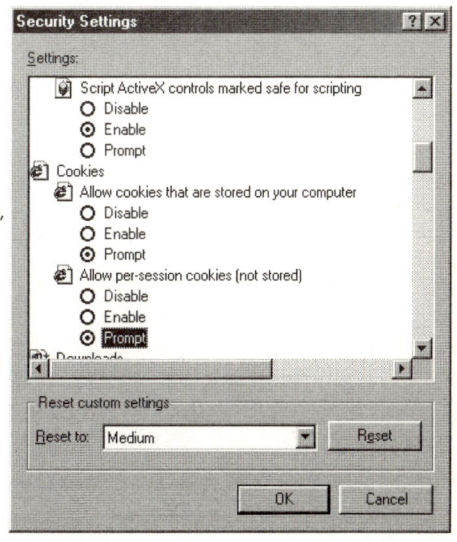

**Figure 10.6** Using the Security Setting dialog box to control cookies.

## Content Advisor and safe surfing

If children can get online from your PC, you may want to enable the Content Advisor to set limits to the types of material that they can access through the Internet.

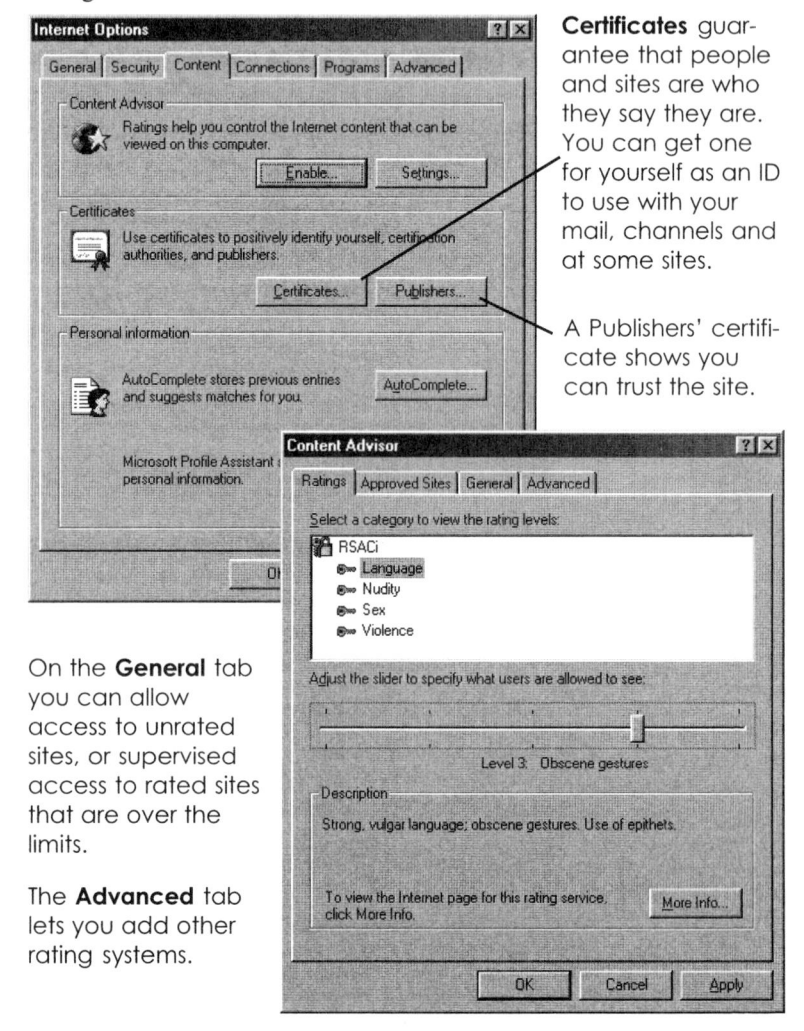

**Certificates** guarantee that people and sites are who they say they are. You can get one for yourself as an ID to use with your mail, channels and at some sites.

A Publishers' certificate shows you can trust the site.

On the **General** tab you can allow access to unrated sites, or supervised access to rated sites that are over the limits.

The **Advanced** tab lets you add other rating systems.

**Figure 10.7** The **Content** tab. Turn on **Content Advisor** if you are going to let children have unsupervised access to the Internet.

The Content Advisor allows you to restrict unsupervised access to those sites which have been rated by the Recreational Software Advisory Council for the Internet (RASCi). This rates sites an a scale of 1 to 5 for language, nudity, sex and violence. You set the limits of what may be accessed from your machine.

Many perfectly acceptable sites do not have a rating, simply because they have not applied for one, but this is not a major problem. It just means that the kids will have to ask someone who knows the password to override the restrictions when they find somewhere good but unrated. And if you want to browse unrestricted, you can disable the advisor.

---

**SAFER SURFING**

If you are concerned about people reaching the murkier corners of the Internet, Content Advisor is only the first line of defence. For more about child safety, browse over to http://www.safekids.com.

---

## Advanced

Most of the **Advanced** options should be left well alone until you really know what you are doing, but there are a couple that you might want to look at now.

In the **Multimedia** section, turn off the **Play** options for faster browsing. Turning **Show Pictures** off will also improve downloading times, but pictures often carry essential information and hyperlinks. With **Show Pictures** off, you can download an individual picture by clicking on the 🖼 which appears in its place.

If you don't want to accept **Cookies**, you can disable them. Should you find that there are some sites that you can only use properly if you accept cookies – there are plenty of clubs and user groups that use them as IDs – then switch to '**Prompt before accepting**'. It will slow things down but leave you in control.

In the **Java** section, the **Java JIT compiler** should be enabled if you want to run any Java applets that you meet.

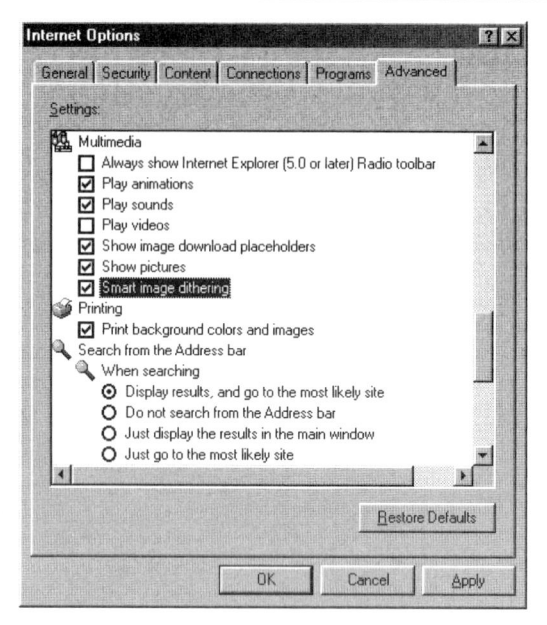

**Figure 10.8** Most **Advanced** options should be left at their defaults – click **Restore Defaults** if you think you may have messed them up!

## 10.5 Browsing the Web

Hypertext links provide an efficient means of following threads from page to page, but with so much information spread over so many pages on so many sites over the Web, the problem is where to start looking.

Your Internet Service Provider's home site will probably offer a directory with an organized set of links to selected sites, and Internet Explorer is initially set up to head to MSN (MicroSoft Network). This has a good directory, and a useful search facility. Leave it as your start point until you have found a better place, then change to that address in the **Internet Options** dialog box (page 137).

The directory approach is good for starting research on general topics, but if you are looking for specific material, you are probably better off running a search, and with Internet Explorer you can run a search at any time, no matter where you are on the Web.

## Running a search

❶ Click the 🔍 button to start the Search in the Explorer bar.
❷ Type a word or phrase to describe what you are looking for.
❸ Click the **Search** button.
❹ When you get the results, click on a link to view the page in the main window.

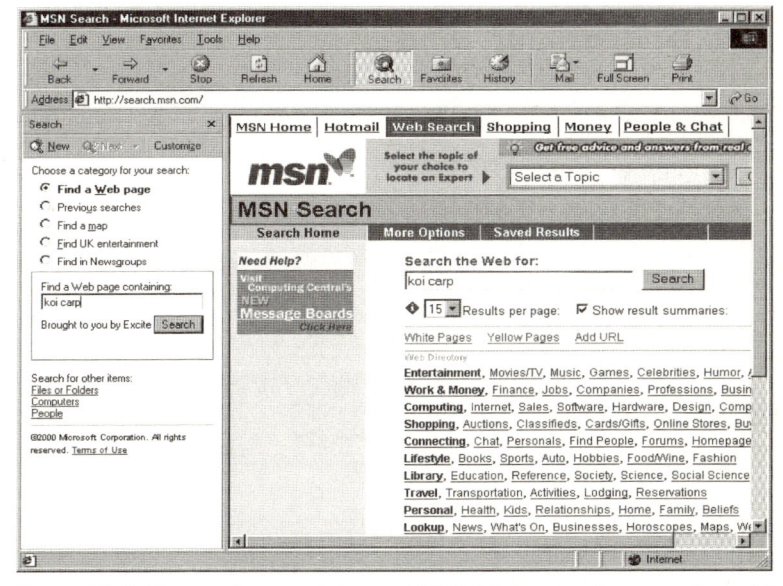

**Figure 10.9** The main panel shows MSN's **Web search** page. I could also run a search there. The two searches would produce different, but overlapping, sets of results. Every 'search engine' has its own way of finding and indexing sites, but some sites are very good at making sure that all the searches find them!

## Uniform Resource Locators (URL)

With all the millions of Web pages, files and other resources that can be reached over the Internet, a standardized way of identifying them is essential. URLs provide this. There are different styles of URL for each approach to the Internet, though they all follow much the same pattern:

　　type://hostcomputer/directory/filename

## Web pages

Many of these are instantly recognizable from their *html* or *htm* endings, which shows that they are hypertext pages.

http://sunsite.unc.edu/boutell/faq/www-faq.html

This one is a list of frequently asked questions (*faq*) and their answers, about the World Wide Web (*www*), stored in the Sun archives in the University of North Carolina (*unc*).

The URL of the top page of a site may just consist of the site address, with an (optional) slash at the end. This is the opening page at Microsoft's site:

http://www.microsoft.com/

If you know the URL of a page, you can jump directly to it.

Use **File → Open**, and type the URL into the panel, or type it into the **Address** toolbar.

The leading **http://** is not really necessary. The browser expects you to enter a World Wide Web URL. Thus:

http://uk.yahoo.com

can be entered as:

uk.yahoo.com

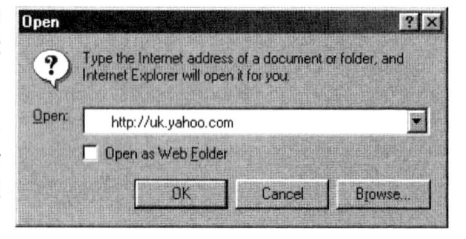

URLs must be typed exactly right for the routine to work. They are not case-sensitive – UK.YAHOO.COM works just as well as uk.yahoo.com – but watch out for symbols. Some URLs include a tilde (~). Where the URL is for the top page of a site, it will end with a slash (/). This can be omitted.

## Finding URLs

Before you can use a URL, you have to know it. There are several possible sources:

* As you browse the Web, you may find a hyperlink to a page that you do not want to visit at the time, but might like to drop in on later. Point to it, to display its URL in the Status bar, and make a note of it.

# INTERNET EXPLORER 147

- If you join any **newsgroups** (Chapter 11), you will often see postings about relevant pages on the newsgroup area of interest, particularly new ones.
- Internet magazines and newspaper columns often have 'What's new' features.

## Other start points

There are many places that you can use as start points for your surfing. Some that are well worth a visit include:

- Yahoo!'s main site – the original and probably still the best of the directories, at
  http://www.yahoo.com

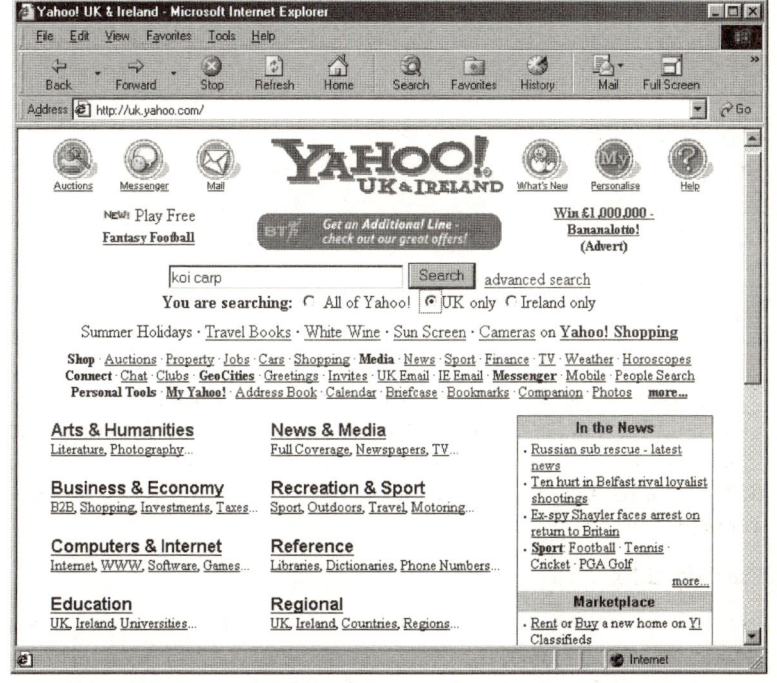

**Figure 10.10** There are Yahoo!s in the major countries, providing local links, but backed up by the central directory at www.yahoo.com. Yahoo! also offers Web e-mail, news, weather, shopping and auction services, games, and much more.

- Yahoo! UK & Ireland, at
  http://uk.yahoo.com or http://www.yahoo.co.uk
- The leading directory in the UK is UKDirectory, at
  http://www.ukdirectory.co.uk
- Excite offers an excellent directory, search and more, at
  http://www.excite.co.uk
- The most comprehensive search engine is AltaVista at
  http://altavista.digital.com
- The fastest – but very thorough – search engine is Google, at
  http://www.netscape.com

But before you can get to these, you need to know about URLs. Read on!

## History

When you want to return to a page, the simplest way is through the Back button and the list that drops down from it. This only works with those visited very recently – the Back list is wiped at the end of a session, and

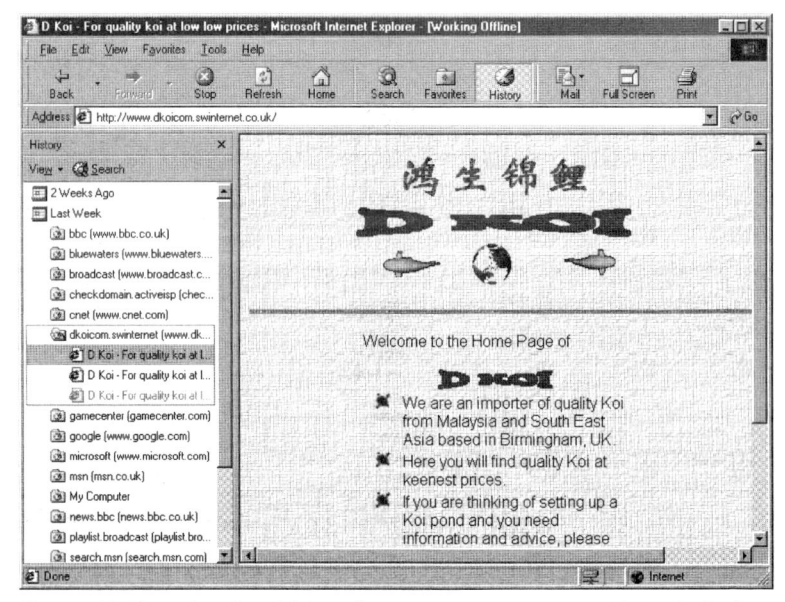

**Figure 10.11** Using the **History** list. Pages are grouped into their sites, making it much easier to find them.

INTERNET EXPLORER                                                                149

can be corrupted by movements within sites, especially those with complex, interactive page layouts. The most reliable way to revisit pages is by opening the History list in the Explorer Bar. The pages are grouped by day and then by site, making it easy to find the one you want.

## Favorites

The Explorer Bar can also be used to display the Favorites list. This has a few sets of ready-made links, but is really intended as a store of links to those places that you like to revisit regularly.

- When you find a page that you know you will want again in future, open the **Favorites** menu and select **Add to Favorites** or open **Favorites** in the Explorer Bar and click **Add…**
- Edit the name, if necessary – the page's title will be suggested.
- If you want to store the link in a folder, go to the **Create in:** list and choose it – a new folder can be created, if needed.
- Click **OK**.

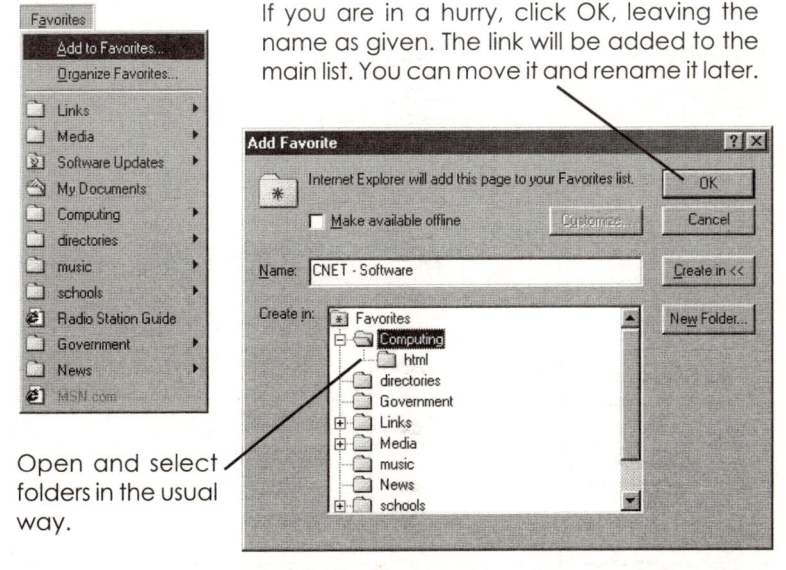

If you are in a hurry, click OK, leaving the name as given. The link will be added to the main list. You can move it and rename it later.

Open and select folders in the usual way.

**Figure 10.12** Adding a page to the **Favorites**. If – more likely when – your Favorites folders get crowded and messy, use **Organize Favorites** to open a display of the folders. You can then move, rename, delete and generally sort out your stored links.

## 10.6 Files from the Net

### Shareware sites

One of the great things about the Internet is that you can get from the Net virtually all the tools that you need to work on the Net. You already have a browser, of course, but there are more tools that you may like to acquire. The Internet is also a great source of games, audio and video clips, pictures, text files and more.

If you are looking for software, try these great shareware sites, both run by c|net – shareware.com (**http://www.shareware.com**) and download.com (**http://www.download.com**). Here you can search by keyword or program name, or browse by category. When you find something that you want, clicking on the program's name will start the download

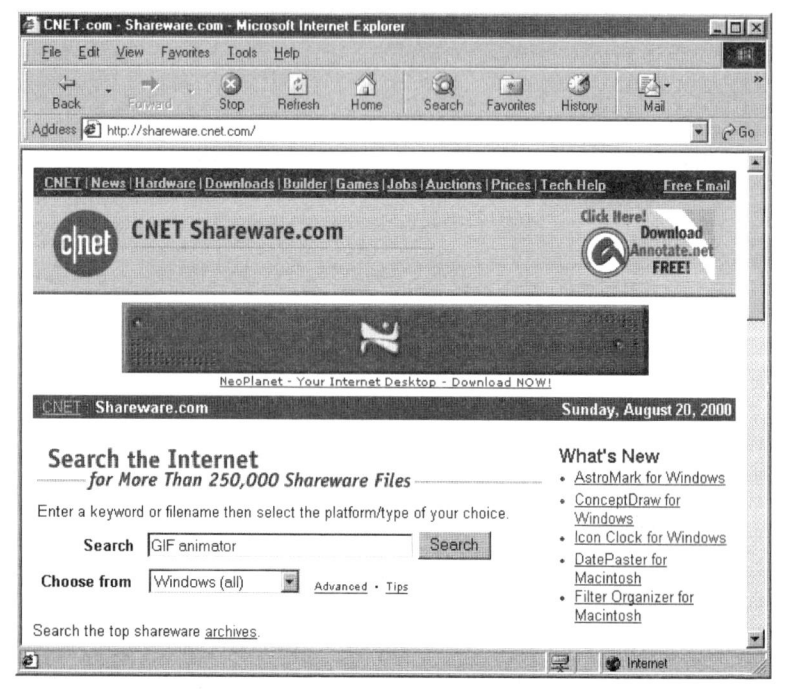

**Figure 10.13** shareware.com – a great source of software. Some of it is completely free, the rest is shareware – try it for free, but pay a (small) fee to continue using it.

**INTERNET EXPLORER** 151

– decide which folder to store it in, and sit back and wait. Downloading speeds vary, but average around 100Kb per minute.

---

**ZIPPED FILES**

Many of the files available over the Internet are ZIPped to save space. This can reduce file sizes, and therefore transfer times, by anything from 10% to 90%. You will need **WinZIP** to uncompress them. You can find a copy at shareware.com.

---

## Saving pages and images

You can revisit a page, offline, for as long as it is kept in the temporary files area, but if you want a permanent copy of a page you should save it.

- Wait until the page is fully loaded, then open the **File** menu and select **Save As** – you may need to change the filename to something more memorable. If you set the **Save as type** to *Web Page complete*, then any images and the component files of framed pages will be saved in a folder with the same name as the page.

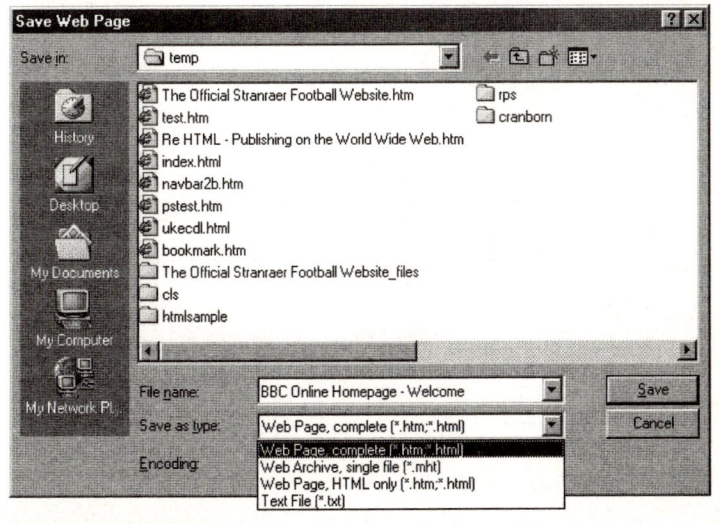

**Figure 10.14** Saving a Web page. If you just want the text of a simple page, set the **Save as type** to *Web Page, HTML only*. Use *Web Page complete* if you want to save all the associated files.

- When you want to view the page again, use **File → Open**, then browse through your folders to locate it.

If you don't want the whole page, but just an individual image from it, this can be saved separately.

- Right-click on the image and select **Save Picture As** from the short menu.

*or*

- If you really like the image and it is big enough to make a good background for your Desktop, select Set as Wallpaper.

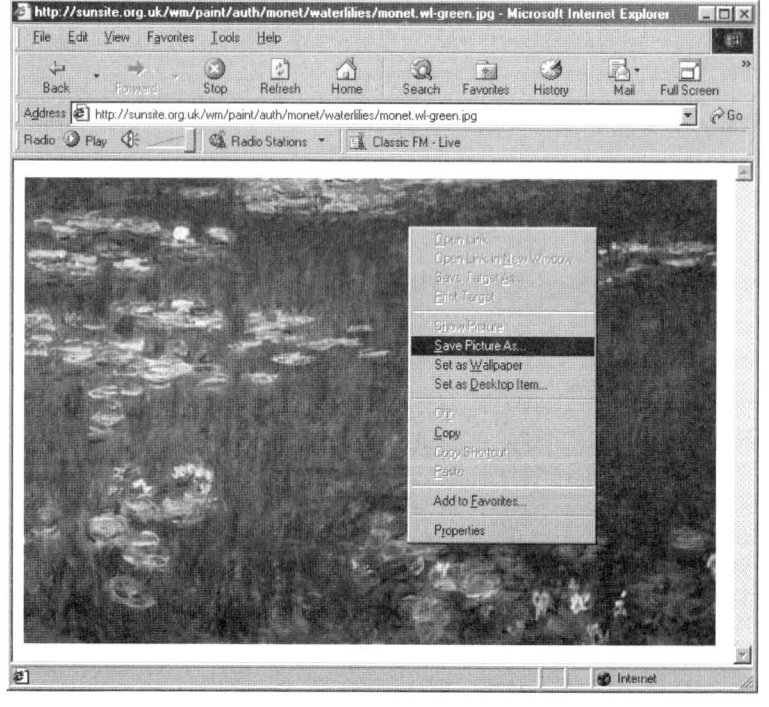

**Figure 10.15** Saving an image off a Web page. If you like art, try the Web Museum. There are 'mirrors' of this at many sites, including **http://sunsite.org.uk/wm** (Mirrors are identical copies of the files, held at different places so that more people can access them easily.)

## Windows Update

Windows Me comes with an automatic update system. This will check the Microsoft Web site regularly, when you are online, to see if there are updates available that you should have. If there are, the system will download and install them for you. You don't need to do anything about this – it just happens! If you prefer to control when and how your Windows Me software is updated, you can turn this facility off – open **Automatic Updates** in the Control Panel and switch to manual control.

If you choose to update manually, or want to see what optional updates are available, click on the **Windows Update** shortcut on the main **Start** menu. This is a highly automated page. It has routines that will check over your system to see if there are any files for which new replacements or 'patch' repairs are available. If there are any – or if you find any optional add-ons that you would like – they will be downloaded and installed for you.

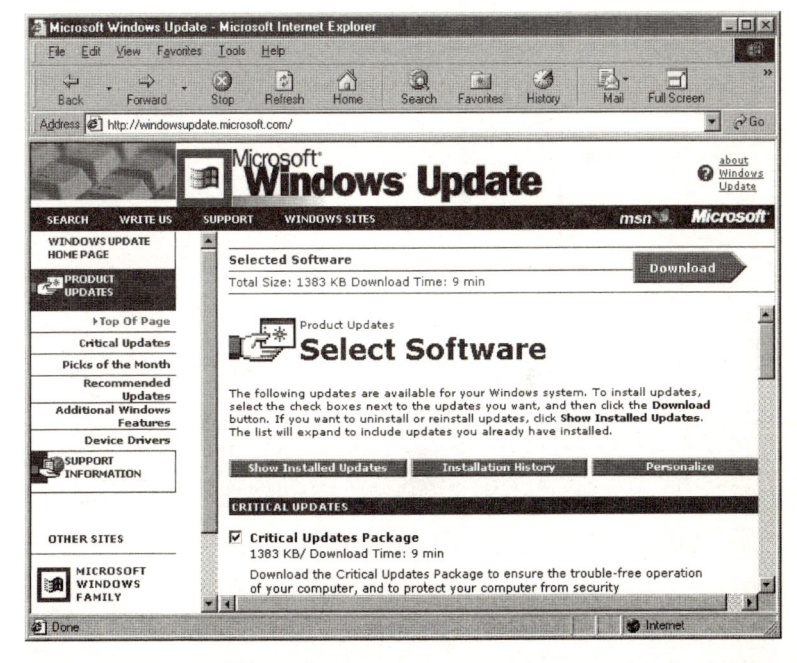

**Figure 10.16** The Windows Update page. My system has just been checked, and it seems that I need the **Critical Update Package**. Clicking Download will get that and install it for me.

## 10.7 Internet Radio

Want some music while you are surfing? Then turn the radio on! You can now listen to radio broadcasts from all over the world through your PC. Here's how:

❶ Turn on the Radio toolbar.

❷ Click on Radio Stations and select Radio Station Guide. This will take you to WindowsMedia, where they have links to radio stations all over the world.

❸ Pick a country from the list – and you are not restricted to your own, remember – then select a station.

❹ If you like the station and want to listen to it again, add it to your Favorites.

♦ You do not have to be at the station's site to listen to a broadcast. You can start it playing then surf on elsewhere.

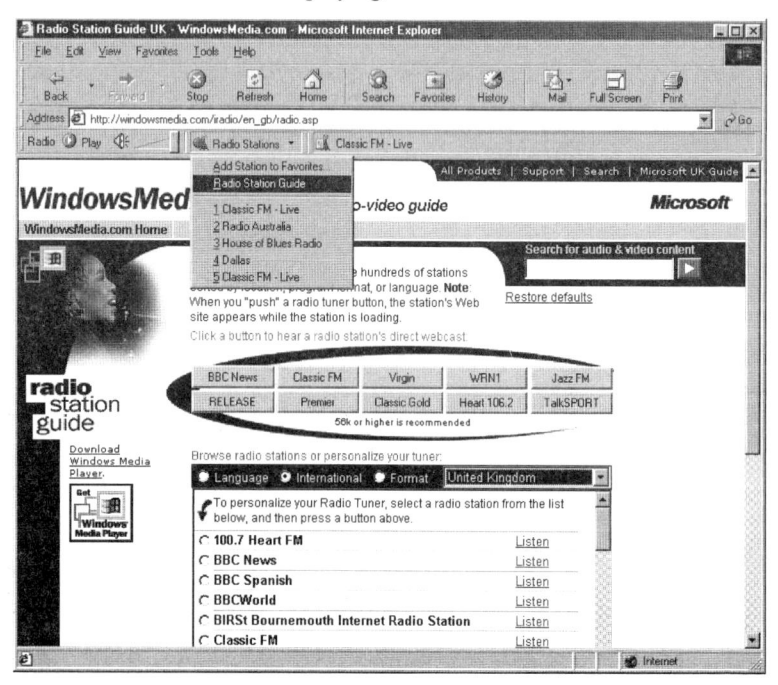

**Figure 10.17** Setting up a new radio station. Once the link is created, you can change stations by picking from the **Radio Stations** menu.

## EASY LISTENING?

The radio reception is not 100% brilliant, but it's not bad. The problem isn't in the quality of the sound – that is almost as good as a CD – but rather in its continuity. Modern compression techniques have greatly reduced the size of sound files, but they still take quite a bit of bandwidth, and there's not much to spare. If you get online through an ISDN line, you'll have no problem. If you link through a dial-up connection, data comes in from the Web at rarely more than 2Kb per second. That's about enough to cope with a broadcast, but if you are also surfing elsewhere, that will add to the overall quantity of data trying to come in. Expect occasional breaks in transmission of a second or so, and expect other sites to download slower.

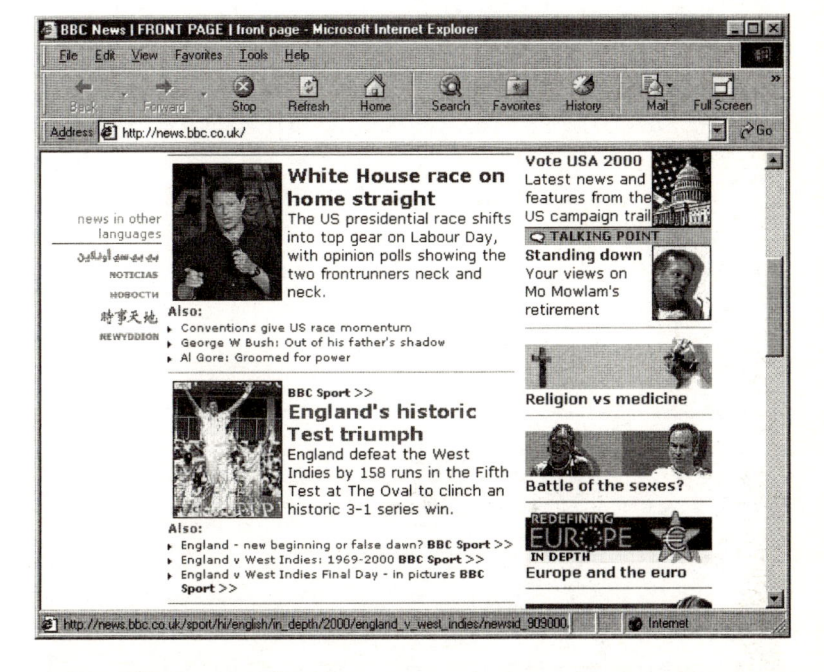

**Figure 10.18** And Internet TV! You can watch the latest BBC News (on a small, jerky screen) at any time via their online site. Head for **news.bbc.co.uk** and click on the Bulletin, News or Summary links.

## SUMMARY

- ✓ The Internet is the result of world-wide cooperation between computer networks in commercial, educational and other organizations.
- ✓ To get online, you need a modem, a convenient phone line and an account with a service provider.
- ✓ The Connection Wizard can be used to find a provider, or to set up a connection to an existing account.
- ✓ Internet Explorer is an integral part of Windows Me.
- ✓ Some of the Internet options should be set early on; others can be left until you have spent more time on the Internet.
- ✓ If children can get online from your PC, you should enable the Content Advisor.
- ✓ The Web consists of pages linked together by URLs given as hyperlinks in the pages.
- ✓ Every site on the Internet has its own unique address – its URL (Uniform Resource Locator). If you know the URL of a page, you can jump directly to it.
- ✓ Directories help you find your way around; Yahoo! is the most comprehensive of these. Search engines can be used to track down pages containing keywords.
- ✓ The Explorer Bar can be used to run an online search, or to open the History or Favorites folders.
- ✓ You can add pages to the Favorites folder, and organize them into your own set of folders.
- ✓ Files can be downloaded from many places on the Internet – shareware sites hold stores of free and cheap software.
- ✓ A Web page can be saved as a file. Pictures can also be saved separately.
- ✓ Use Windows Update to keep your system up to date.
- ✓ You can now listen to the radio through the Internet.

# 11 OUTLOOK EXPRESS

## AIMS OF THIS CHAPTER

Outlook Express can handle e-mail or access the newsgroups. In this chapter we will take a look at its main facilities, and cover some of the key points about e-mail and news.

## 11.1 Starting Outlook Express

Outlook Express can be started from the Desktop icon of the **Programs → Internet Explorer** menu. The initial screen should have the Folder List to the left of the main pane, with its icons for starting the various routines, and the usual toolbar and menu bar above. There are alternative displays – reach them through the **View → Layout** command.

- The **Outlook Bar** can be used as well as, or in place of, the Folder list for moving round the system.
- The **Folder Bar** can be turned on to provide a more substantial heading (it doesn't do anything else).

### The Folders

At first, there are only five folders – six if you have the news set up. More can be created to provide organized storage for any mail messages and news articles that you want to retain.

- The **Inbox** holds mail sent to you. The messages remain here, after reading, until you move or delete them.
- The **Outbox** provides temporary storage for messages, while they are waiting to be sent. If you compose your messages offline, you are only online to your service provider for as long

Outlook Bar    Folder Bar    Folder List

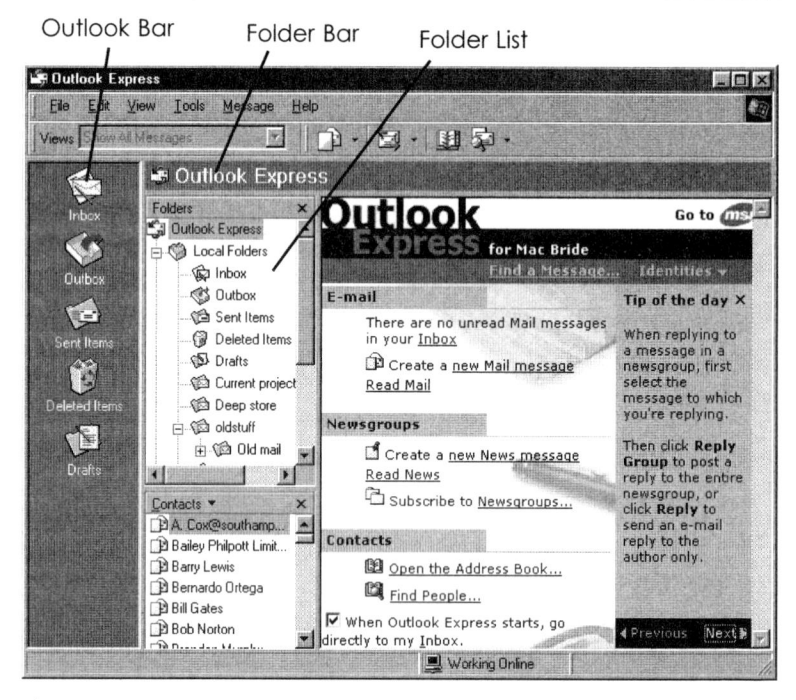

**Figure 11.1** The Outlook Express screen, with the optional elements displayed. Use either the **Outlook Bar** or **Folder List** to move around the system – you do not need both. The **Folder Bar** is just decorative. The **Contacts** display can be useful, but it is easy enough to get names from the Address Book (page 166) when you need them.

as it takes to send them and to collect incoming mail. It doesn't just reduce your costs, it also gives you time to check your text for typing and spelling errors first.

- The **Sent** folder keeps a copy of outgoing messages, if you choose to keep copies (see page 162).
- **Deleted Items** is where messages and articles are stored when they are first deleted. They are only removed completely when deleted from here.
- Use **Drafts** as a temporary store for messages that you want to work on some more before sending.
- If you have set up a news server, you will have a news folder.

## 11.2 Reading mail

All mail and news folders follow the same pattern. In the top pane are the message or article headers. These show the name of the sender, its subject and when it was received. They are normally in date order, but can be sorted by sender, subject or date, by clicking on the column name. If the message has not yet been read, its header will be in **bold**. When you select a header, the message is displayed in the preview pane (or in a separate window, if you have chosen this option).

When a message is displayed, these tools are available for dealing with it:

**Reply** – opens the New Message window, with the sender's name in the To: slot, ready to send back to them. This is neat as it means that you do not have to think about their e-mail address.

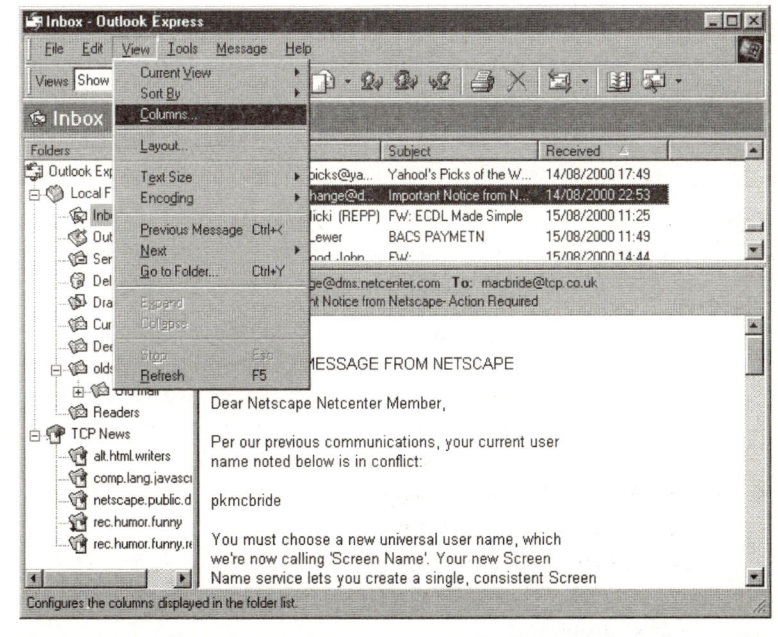

**Figure 11.2** The Inbox, with a message in the preview pane. The **View → Columns...** option lets you select which items to display in the headers lines, though *From*, *Subject* and *Received* are generally enough to be able to find and sort messages efficiently.

**Reply to all** – use this instead of Reply where a message has been mailed to a group of people, and you want your reply to reach the whole group! Your reply will then be mailed to all those who received a **To:** or **Cc:** copy (page 161) of the message.

**Forward** – copies the message into the New Message window, so that you can send it on to another person. This time you will have to supply the address, just as if you were sending a new message – see below.

**Delete** – moves the message to the Deleted folder. You can get Outlook Express to empty the Deleted folder for you on exit, or let them stay there, where they can be recovered if necessary – as with the Recycle Bin – until you delete them from there.

- You can also drag a message, at any time, from the header list to another folder for storage.

When people send you mail, it is stored in your mailbox at your Internet service provider.

If you work in an organization with a permanently open connection to the Internet, you can set up the options (page 161), so that Outlook Express checks the box and downloads new messages for you at set intervals.

If you get online through a dial-up connection, pick up your mail, and send any messages from your Outbox, whenever you are ready.

Click to send and receive all your mail, or drop down its list (or open the **Tools** menu) if you only want to **Send** or **Receive** at that time.

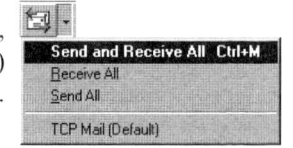

## 11.3 Sending mail

Outlook Express, like most modern mail software, can handle messages in HTML format (as used on Web pages), as well as plain text. This means that you can use different fonts, sizes and colours for your text, set bulleted or numbered lists and other layout options, and insert pictures. If you want colourful messages, without the bother of formatting them, there are a dozen Stationery styles. These give you decorative backgrounds and some also matching text formats already set.

# OUTLOOK EXPRESS

- Don't waste time formatting messages if the person to whom you are writing can only read plain text on their system.

To write and send a message:

❶ Click the **New Message** button, or use the menu command **Message ➔ New Message**.

*or*

❷ Open the New Message drop-down list, or select **Message ➔ New Message Using** and pick your Stationery from the list.

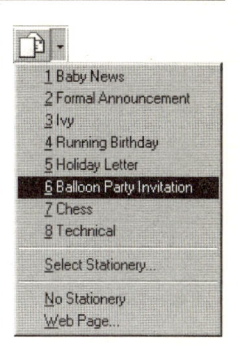

If you decide you don't like the Stationery, **Format ➔ Apply Stationery** will let you choose another style, or revert to a plain background.

**Figure 11.3** Composing a message using the Balloon Party Stationery – apply formats as in normal word-processing.

❸ When the Compose window opens, either type the recipient's e-mail address into the **To:** box, or click **To:** and select it from your Address Book (see page 166 for more on this).

❹ If more than one person is to get a copy, you can add addresses in the **To:** box (separated by semicolons or commas), or put them in the **Cc:** or **Bcc:** boxes.

**To:** the main recipients – you would normally expect to get replies from these people.

**Cc:** Carbon copies, sent mainly for information.

**Bcc:** Blind carbon copies – their names will not appear in the lists of recipients that normally accompany each message. Used for circulating mail to large groups.

5 Type a **Subject** for the message, so that your recipients know what it is about when they see the header in their mail window.

6 Type and format your message. If you don't have the spell checker set to run automatically, you should read the message through to check for errors.

7 Click the **Send** button. If the spell checker is turned on, it will run at this point. After you have worked through any errors it finds, the message will be sent immediately, or stored in the Outbox to be sent later – it depends on the settings (see below).

*or*

8 If you want to override your default send settings, open the **File** menu and select **Send Message** (i.e. now) or **Send Later**.

## 11.4 Outlook Express options

As with most software, the optional settings make more sense after you have been using it for a while, and the default settings are usually a safe bet to start with. However, there are a few that are worth checking and setting early on. Use **Tools → Options...** to open the **Options** panel.

The **General** tab deals with the interaction between Outlook Express and your system.

- Turn on '*Check for new messages every ?? minutes*', and set the interval, if you are permanently online or have long online sessions.
- Turn off '*Notify me if there are any new newsgroups*' if you don't bother much with the news.
- All the other options are probably best turned on at this stage.

The **Read** tab is mainly concerned with news articles.

- Some groups have hundreds of articles every day. You can set how many headers to download at a time.

- Where a set of articles has the same Subject (follow-ons start with 'Re:') they are grouped. If *Automatically expand grouped messages* is off, only the first is shown until you click ⊞.

The **Receipts** tab controls how you deal with receipts – you can request them when sending messages, and people may ask for them from you.

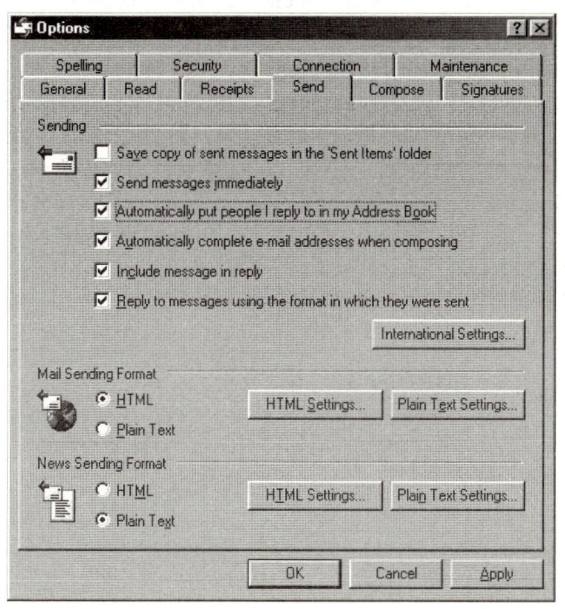

**Figure 11.4** The **Send** options.

The **Send** tab is mainly about message formats, see Figure 11.4.

- Turn on '*Save copies of sent messages*' only if you normally need to keep a copy for later reference.
- Turn on **Send immediately** if you normally deal with your mail online.
- Turning on '*Automatically put people I reply to in my Address Book*' is a good idea. It ensures that their address is correct – as it has been copied from their mail. If this includes some people you do not want, they can easily be removed.
- The '*Include message in reply*' option can be useful, especially if most of your e-mail is work-related. When replying, you can edit out any unwanted bits of the original message.

- Set your **Mail Sending Format** to *HTML* if most of your recipients are able to read HTML formatted messages, but select *Plain Text* for News.

The **Compose** tab lets you define your message format, setting the default fonts and stationery.

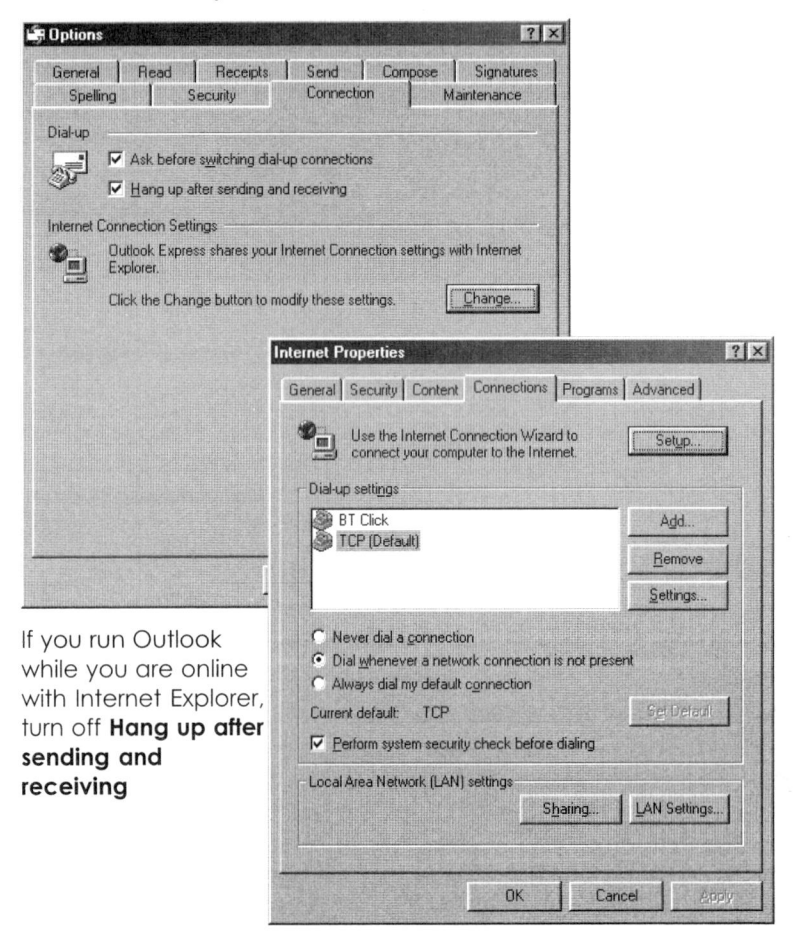

If you run Outlook while you are online with Internet Explorer, turn off **Hang up after sending and receiving**

**Figure 11.5** The **Connection** settings are shared with IE. Click **Change** to reach the **Internet Properties** dialog box. Selecting *Dial whenever a network connection is not present* will set it dialling (if necessary) when you try to access a Web site or send and receive mail.

The **Spelling** tab controls the way that the spell checker works. The main option is Always check spelling before sending – turn this on or off. Other options let you select the dictionary and define the kind of words that the spell checker should ignore.

The **Security** tab should be left alone for the time being – and can be ignored altogether if you are not bothered about the security of your mail.

The **Maintenance** tab is mainly about cleaning up messages.

- Turn on *Empty messages from the Deleted Items folder on exit* unless you tend to delete items in error regularly. If this is off, you will have to select and delete the messages in the folder yourself to remove them from your system.
- Compacting does not delete messages, but stores them more efficiently. Compacted messages take a fraction longer to open.
- The remaining message options all refer to newsgroup messages. How long – if at all – do you want to keep old newsgroup

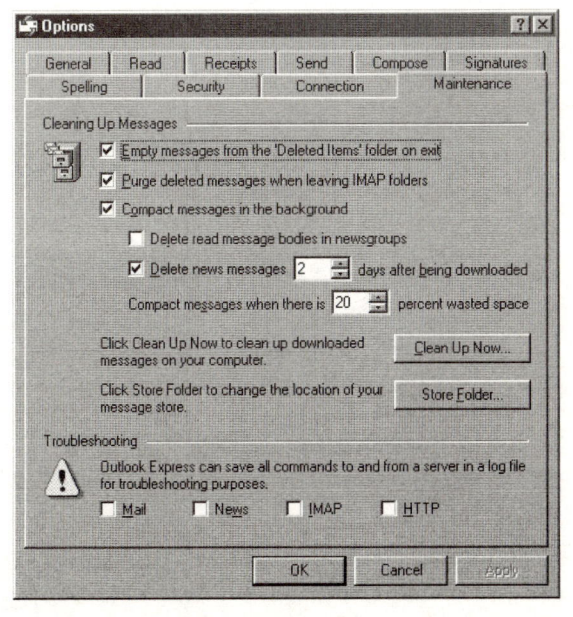

**Figure 11.6** Clearing out old messages doesn't just save space – rarely a problem with big modern hard disks – it also makes it far easier to see what's left and find the stuff you really want.

articles? Remember that selected messages can be copied to other folders for storage.

* The **Troubleshooting** options can be turned on if you have problems with your mail or news. The log files could provide useful information for whoever tries to solve the problems.

## 11.5 The Address Book

You must get e-mail addresses exactly right, or the post won't get through. Unfortunately, addresses are not always user-friendly and are rarely easy to remember.

The Address Book is a great idea. Once you have an e-mail address in here – correctly – you need never worry about it again. When you want to write to someone, you can select the name from the book and start to compose from there, or start the message and then select the names at the **To:** and **Cc:** boxes (see page 162).

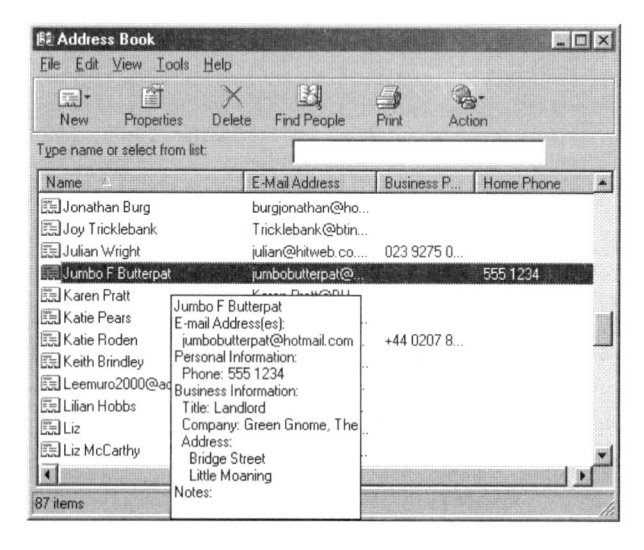

**Figure 11.7** My Address Book – you can store phone numbers and 'snail mail' address details here as well. If you do store phone numbers, you can get the Address Book to dial the number for you – the command is in the drop-down **Action** menu.

## Adding to the Address Book

❶ Open the **Address Book** from the **Tools** menu or click 📖.
❷ Click the **New** button and select **New Contact**. The **Properties** panel has tabs for lots of different contact information. Only the **Name** tab is essential.

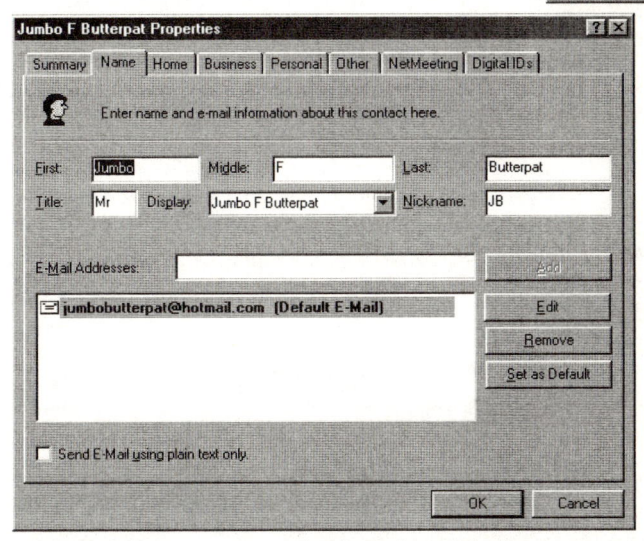

**Figure 11.8** Adding a new contact. First and last names and the address are the only essentials, and are quickly added.

❸ The First, Middle and Last names should be entered separately if you want to be able to sort the list by First and Last names. (**View → Sort By** has a number of alternative sort orders – very useful when you have lots of entries.)
❹ A **Nickname** can be entered, if wanted, and either this or the full name can be set as the **Display** value.
❺ Type the address *carefully* into the **Add new:** box, and click **Add**. If the person has more than one e-mail address, add the others then select one as the default.
❻ If you know that the person can only handle plain text on their system, turn on **Send E-mail using plain text only**.
❼ Switch to the other tabs to enter more details if required, then click **OK**.

> **COPYING E-MAIL ADDRESSES**
>
> If you have received an e-mail from someone that you want to add to the Address Book, the address can be copied in almost automatically. Start to reply to the person, then right-click on the name in the To: slot. Select **Add To Address Book** from the short menu. The name and e-mail address will be copied into place for you. If you don't actually want to reply to them at that time, just close down the window.

## Using the Address Book

If the Address Book is open already, you can start a new message to someone by selecting their name and picking **Send Mail** from the **Action** menu. The **New Message** window will open, with the name in the **To:** box.

If you start from the New Message button, click the icon to open the **Select Recipients** panel. This lists the names in your Address Book. Pick the recipients one at a time, clicking **To->**, **Cc->** or **Bcc->** to copy

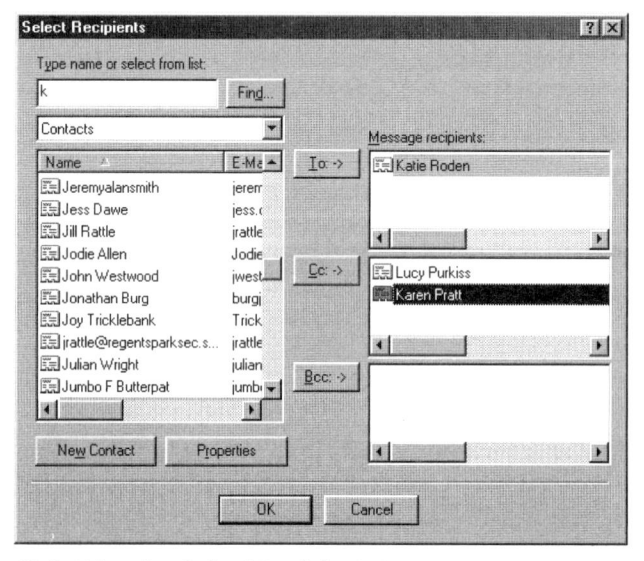

**Figure 11.9** Using the **Select Recipients** panel to get addresses from your Address Book. If you add a name by mistake, just select it and press the **Delete** key.

them to the appropriate categories. Click **OK** when you've done. The recipients will appear as names, rather than e-mail addresses – don't worry. They will be translated into addresses before sending.

## 11.6 Finding people

The simplest and safest way to get someone's e-mail address is to ring them up and ask them to send you an e-mail message. If this isn't possible, you may be able to find the address in one of the Internet's people-finding sites. These hold databases of names and addresses that they have compiled in various ways – none give complete coverage.

You are more likely to be able to find someone if they get online through an Internet Service Provider than if they connect through a business or other organization – these are often reluctant to release internal information to the people-finding databases. If you are looking for people in the USA, you can probably find their phone numbers easier than their e-mail addresses, as most of the sites have the US telephone databases. Having said all that, it's always worth a try. You may be able to find that long-lost schoolchum, or Uncle Arthur who emigrated in 1964.

You can run a search at half a dozen of the best sites through the **Find People** panel.

❶ Go online.
❷ Open the **Start** menu, point to **Search** and select **People...**
❸ Pick a site from the **Look in** list – it doesn't matter which.

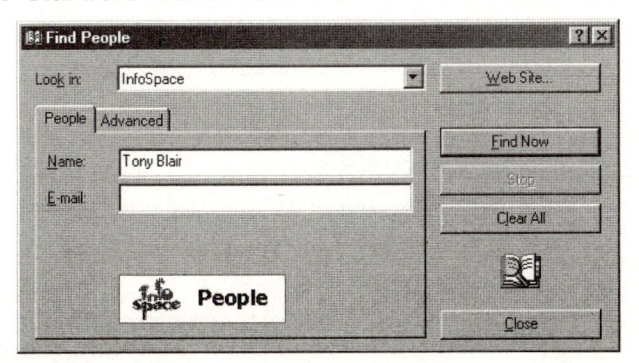

**Figure 11.10** Starting a search for an address. If InfoSpace has a 'Tony Blair' in its database, the panel will expand to show the results.

- ❹ Type in the first and last names.
- ❺ Click **Find Now**.
- ❻ If it doesn't work, try different sites. If you still have no joy, try with just the initial and the name – you cannot be sure how they gave their name when they signed up for e-mail. This will produce more unwanted hits for you to sort through.
- ❼ If your search produces too many results, you may be better going to the Web site – click the button to connect to the current **Look in** site. Most have advanced search facilities that will let you define your search more closely.

## 11.7 Newsgroups

Newsgroups are where people come together to share common interests and enthusiasms, to ask for and give help, to debate and to announce new discoveries and creations. There are over 20,000 of them, each devoted to a different topic, ranging from the seriously academic to the totally trivial. They are organized into about 20 major (and many more minor) divisions, subdivided by topic, and subdivided again where necessary.

Their names reflect this structure and describe their focus; for example, *rec.arts.animation* is found in the *arts* sub-division of the *rec* division and is devoted to *animation* as an art form. (There are other animation groups, with different focuses.)

Most newsgroups belong to one or other of these divisions.

**alt** – the alternative newsgroups, set up to cover topics that had not been included in the other main divisions. Hobbies, obsessions and fan clubs

---

**MODERATION**

Some newsgroups are *moderated* – someone checks articles and weeds out the irrelevant ones. Moderation is not really necessary for specialized academic or professional groups, as the quantity of articles tends to be low – and the quality high. With popular newsgroups – those on TV shows, pop stars, sports or anything to do with sex – moderation is more needed and frequently absent. These groups tend to generate huge numbers of articles – and the quality is highly variable.

form a substantial part of the *alt* groups, though there are also groups for professional interests and discussions. As a neat example of the diversity, here are three adjacent groups: *alt.architecture.int-design*, *alt.aromatherapy*, *alt.art.bodypainting*.

**biz** – business-oriented groups, carrying announcements of new products, job opportunities and discussions of market-related issues.

**comp** – a large set of newsgroups covering many aspects of computing, including languages, applications, hardware and standards.

**misc** – miscellaneous. Books, health, education, kids, for sale adverts and job opportunities make up the bulk of these.

**news** – amongst these newsgroups about newsgroups you will find several specially for new users. *news.newusers* is a good source of tips and advice, while *news.answers* may solve your problems.

**rec** – a very large set covering the whole range of recreational activities from arts through games to sports, with virtually everything in between. These three give an idea of the diversity: *rec.arts.sf.tv.quantum-leap*, *rec.games.xtank.programmer*, *rec.gardens.orchids*.

**sci** – academic and professional scientific discussion groups.

**soc** – most of the groups here are for discussions of different cultures, religions and social issues.

## 11.8 Reading the news

Outlook Express offers a simple but effective routine for finding and sampling or subscribing to newsgroups.

- ❶ Go to the news folder and click the **Newsgroups** button or use **Tools ➜ Newsgroups** to open the panel shown opposite.
- ❷ Type a word, or part of a word, into the **Display newsgroups which contain** box. The list is filtered to display only those groups whose names contain the given letters.
- ❸ When you see a group that looks interesting, select it and click **Go to**. (Or if you see a group that you know you want to read regularly, click **Subscribe**.) You will be returned to the main Outlook screen, with the selected group active.

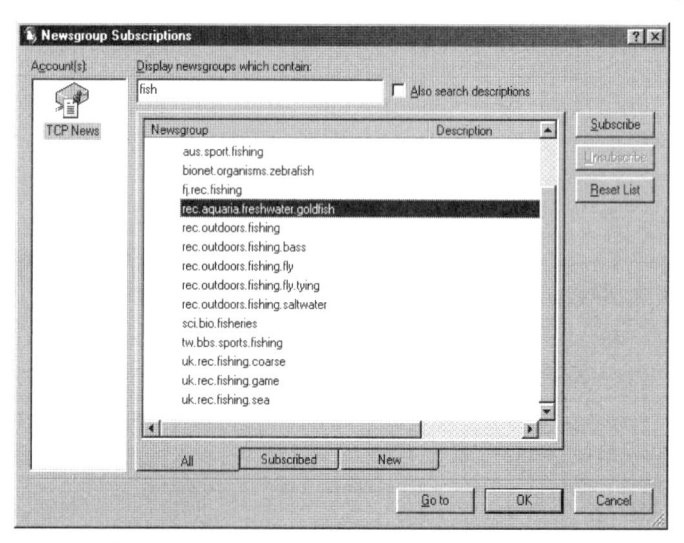

**Figure 11.11** Finding newsgroups. A simple keyword search will usually produce a good selection. Collect the list of new groups from your service provider, from time to time. Initially they will be listed on the **New** tab – use **Reset list** to move them to the **All** list after you've had a chance to look through to see if any interest you.

- If, after sampling its articles, you decide that you would like to add the group to your subscribed list, right-click on it and select **Subscribe** from the short menu. The group will be added to your news folder so you don't have to go and find it every time.

## Headers and articles

A newsgroup may generate hundreds of new articles every day. Even if you are fascinated by the topic of the newsgroup, you are unlikely to want to read every article. Read the Subjects in the headers in the top pane to find the nature of the articles, and whether or not you want to read them.

If you want to respond to an article, either send an e-mail to the author only, or post a follow-up article to the group. In general, if the original article was a request for information, reply to the author.

If you want to **follow up** on an article with your own contribution to the discussion, you would normally quote the relevant lines from the original article or give a brief summary of the key points that you want to pick up.

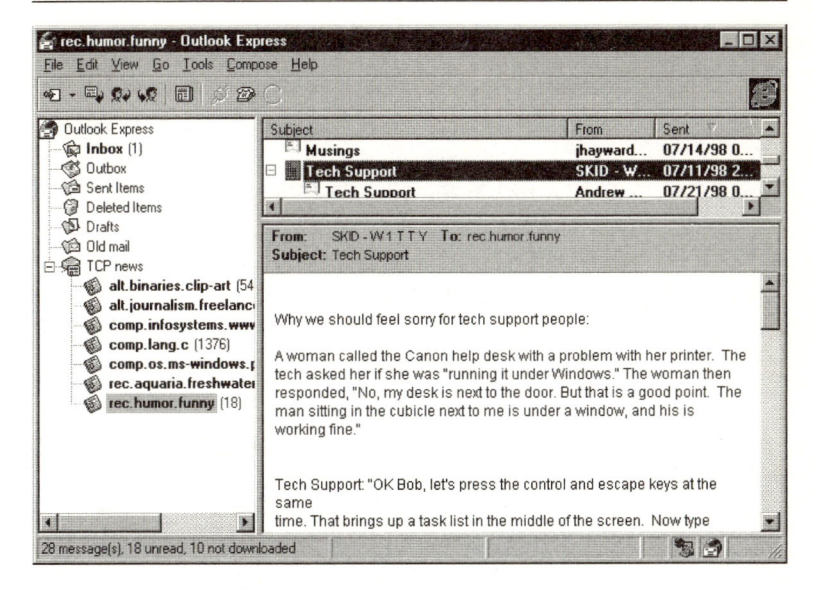

**Figure 11.12** Reading the news. Select a newsgroup and download the headers, and select from there to download and read articles.

If you want to put out your own request for information, or to start a new discussion, then you **post** your article to the group.

Don't rush into posting articles. There are few things existing members find more irritating than a 'newbie' asking obvious questions or rehearsing old arguments. Spend some time 'lurking' – reading without posting – to pick up the true flavour of the group and find out what topics have been discussed recently. You should also track down the group's Frequently Asked Questions list.

---

**WANT TO KNOW MORE?**

If you want to know more about using e-mail and the newsgroups, try *Teach Yourself the Internet*.

---

## SUMMARY

- ✓ Outlook Express handles mail and news through a set of folders. The key ones are the Inbox, where incoming mail is stored, the Outbox, where messages collect ready for sending, and the newsgroups folder.

- ✓ The subjects in the header lines should give you an idea of the nature of a message. You can easily reply to, or forward on, incoming mail.

- ✓ When composing a new message, you can use Stationery and apply formats to the text.

- ✓ Messages can be sent immediately, or stored for transmission later when you go online.

- ✓ The Options control your interaction with the system, and how and when messages are sent and read. Some options are more for newsgroups than e-mail.

- ✓ Use the Address Book to store the e-mail addresses of your contacts, and you will only have to type an address once!

- ✓ The Find People facility enables you to search some of the main people databases on the Internet.

- ✓ Newsgroups allow people from all over the world to share common interests and problems.

- ✓ There are over 20,000 newsgroups and mailing lists, covering almost every aspect of human (and alien!) life.

- ✓ Some groups generate huge numbers of articles – and of variable quality! You can go to a group to sample its contents, or subscribe if you intend reading regularly.

- ✓ Outlook Express has a good routine for finding groups, and lets you dip into them without subscribing.

- ✓ Don't post articles until you have got to know the nature and style of the newsgroup!

# 12 MAINTAINING YOUR DISKS

## AIMS OF THIS CHAPTER

Today's hard disks should give you years of trouble-free service. They will, however, give better service if they are maintained properly. Windows Me has tools that do all the donkey work, once you have started them off – you can even set them up so that they run automatically. Hard disks are now far more reliable than they were only a few years ago – it's unusual for them to become corrupted and lose data, even rarer to crash altogether. But these things do happen, and files can become corrupted through software errors or lost through human error. For all these reasons, it is important to protect your valuable data by backing it up regularly.

Floppy disks are more variable in quality, but reliable if treated properly. Initial formatting and checking, and careful storage is more important than regular maintenance for floppies.

## 12.1 The System Tools

These can all be reached from the **Start** button, through **Programs → Accessories → System Tools**. Open the System Tools menu and see what's there. You may well have a slightly different set from the one shown here.

Disk Cleanup, Disk Defragmenter and Scandisk – the main disk management tools – can also be run from the Properties panel of any disk, or be set to run automatically with the Maintenance Wizard. Get to know these, as well-maintained disks are essential for a reliable system.

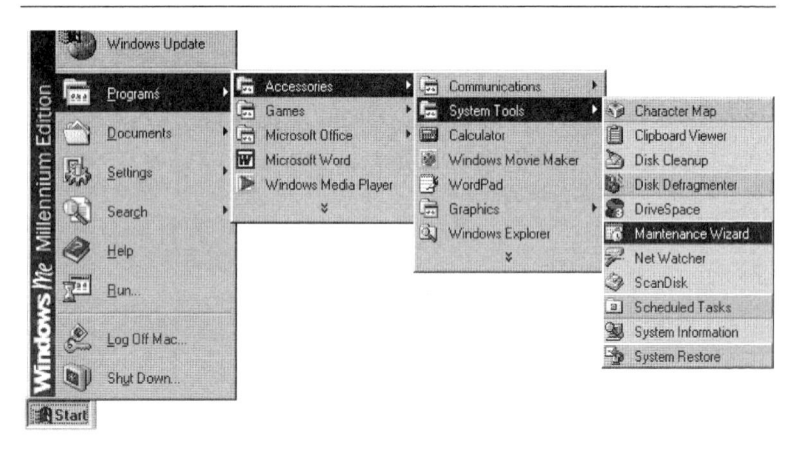

**Figure 12.1** The **System Tools** menu.

A disk – hard or floppy – is divided into *clusters*, each of which can contain all or part of one file. When a file is first written to a new disk, it will be stored in a continuous sequence of clusters, and the disk will gradually fill up from the start. If a file is edited and resaved – bigger than before – it will overwrite the original clusters then write the remainder in the next available clusters, which may well not be physically next to them on the disk. When a file is deleted, it will create a space in the middle of used area, and that later may be filled by a part of another file. Over time disks get messier, with files increasingly stored in scattered clusters. They are still safely stored, but a file that is held in one continuous chunk can be opened much more quickly, simply because the system does not have to chase around all over the disk to read it.

---

**DISKS AND DRIVES**

These words are often used interchangeably, but strictly speaking, a disk is that flat, round thing on which data is stored, while a drive is a logical area of storage identified by a letter (A:, C:, etc). The A: drive can have different disks put into it. A hard disk can be partitioned to create two or more drives.

---

MAINTAINING YOUR DISKS 177

## 12.2 Disk Properties

If you right-click on a drive in Explorer or My Computer, and select Properties from the menu, the Properties panel will open.

- The **General** tab shows how much used and free space you have on the drive.

Hard drives on new PCs are typically 10Gb or larger – you'll only start to run out of space if you store a lot of images, or audio or video clips.

Remove unwanted files

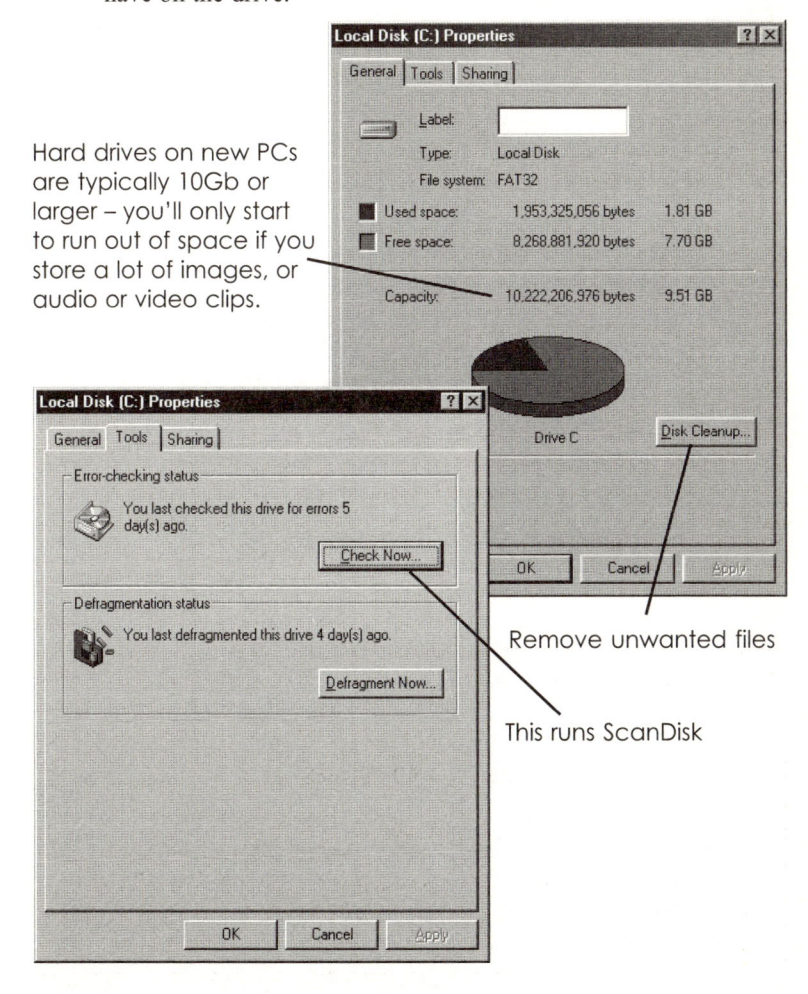

This runs ScanDisk

**Figure 12.2** The **General** and **Tools** tabs of the **Properties** panel for a C: drive.

- The **Tools** tab has buttons to start ScanDisk, Backup and Disk Defragmenter.
- The **Sharing** tab is only present if you are on a network.

## 12.3 Disk Cleanup

This is the simplest of the system tools, and one that should be run fairly regularly to free up space. It removes temporary and other unwanted files from the hard disk.

When you start Disk Cleanup, the first job is to select the drive – normally **C:**. You then select the sets of files to delete.

- **Temporary Internet Files** – don't remove these if you want to be able to revisit pages without having to go online again.
- **Downloaded Program Files** refer to Java or ActiveX applets (small programs) that you met on Web pages, and had to be stored on your disk so that they could be run.

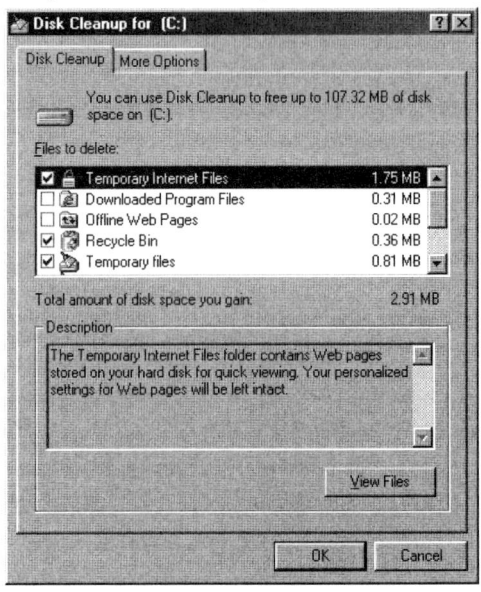

**Figure 12.3** Disk Cleanup. The **More Options** tab takes you to Add/Remove programs; on **Settings** you can opt to run Disk Cleanup automatically if you get short of space.

# MAINTAINING YOUR DISKS

- **Recycle Bin** – this just saves you having to empty the Bin as a separate operation.
- **Temporary files** refers to those created by applications – typically automatic backups and print files. They are normally cleaned up when the application is closed, but may be left behind especially if it ends with a crash. Disk Cleanup will not touch new files, which the application may still be using.

After you have made your selection and clicked **OK**, you will be prompted to confirm the deletions – they are irreversible – before the cleanup starts.

## 12.4 ScanDisk

ScanDisk will find and fix errors on a disk. It can be run at two levels.

- A **Standard** scan checks that all files and folders are where they are supposed to be on the disk. This is the one that you would normally use, and takes only a few minutes.
- A **Thorough** scan also checks that the disk surface is sound, and that data can be written to and read from it correctly. Use this when first checking a disk, after significant errors have been shown by a Standard check, and as part of an occasional overhaul of your system. It takes up to an hour to run on a hard disk – start it, then go and do something useful.

If the **fix errors** option is turned on, ScanDisk will move data from dodgy areas of the disk – if it finds any – and store it more safely elsewhere.

The **Advanced Options** apply to all scans. The key options here are:

- **Lost file fragments** – data-filled clusters that are no longer linked to their files. They can be converted to files (named FILE001.CHK, FILE002.CHK, etc., and stored in C:\). If the data is text it may be possible to recover it from here by opening the files in a word-processor. Other forms of data are generally not recoverable.
- **Cross-linked files** – where the same data is linked to two files. The data can only belong to one of the two – and may, in fact, belong to neither. Making a copy may leave one of the files intact.

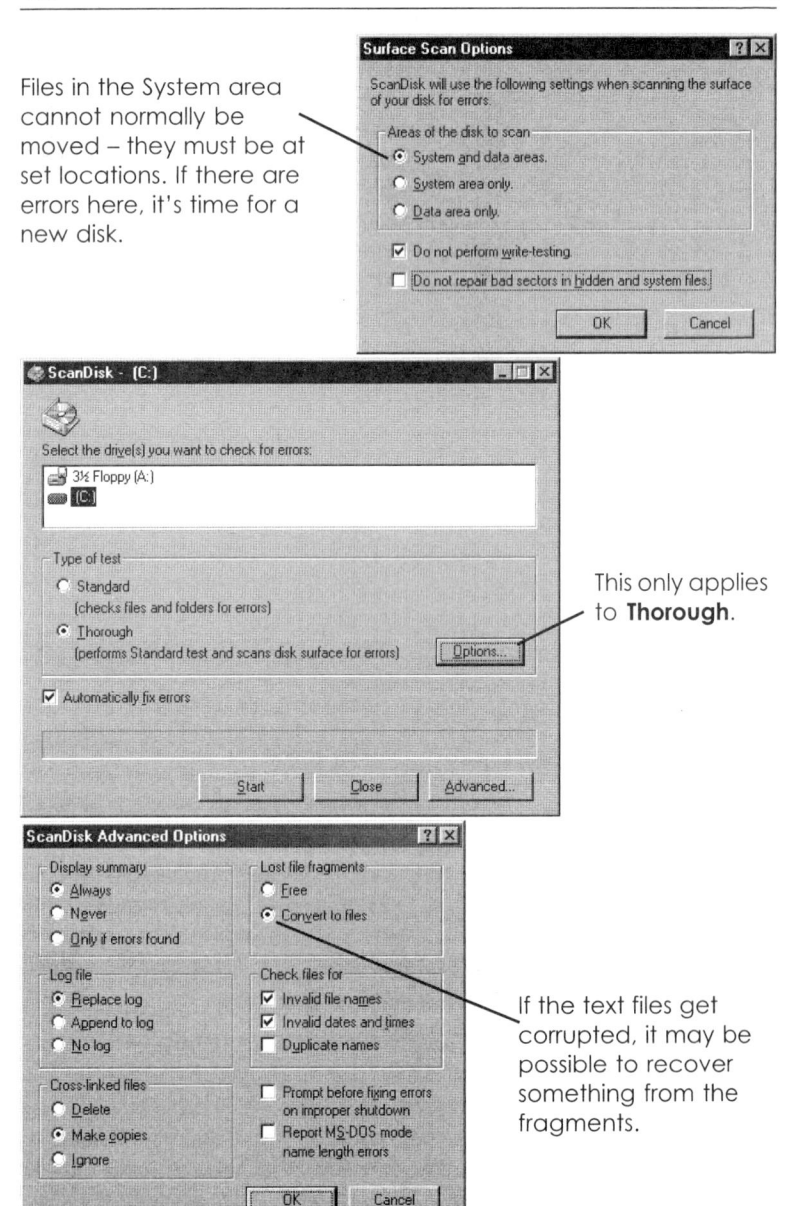

Files in the System area cannot normally be moved – they must be at set locations. If there are errors here, it's time for a new disk.

This only applies to **Thorough**.

If the text files get corrupted, it may be possible to recover something from the fragments.

**Figure 12.4** Setting the **ScanDisk** options.

MAINTAINING YOUR DISKS 181

**Figure 12.5** ScanDisk has given this drive a clean bill of health. To a certain extent, 'bad sectors' do not matter – ScanDisk will mark them off so that Windows does not try to store data there. If you have a high proportion of bad sectors – over 5% or so – throw a floppy disk away and think about replacing a hard drive.

## 12.5 Disk Defragmenter

We noted earlier that the storage space on a disk is divided into clusters, and that a file may occupy any number of clusters, each linked to the next. On a new, clean disk, each file will normally be written in a set of clusters that are physically continuous on the disk. Over time, as the disk fills up, and as files are written, rewritten (larger or smaller) and deleted, it gradually becomes more difficult to store files in adjacent clusters – the disk is becoming *fragmented*. The files are still safe, but they cannot be read as quickly if the reading heads have to hop all over the disk.

Disk Defragmenter reorganizes the physical storage of files on the disk, pulling together the data from scattered clusters. Though it improves performance, the gains are in the order of a few seconds for starting a program or loading a data file, and it is a very slow job – allow an hour on a 2Mb disk. It is only worth doing regularly if your disk is almost full – so that new files are being stored in a limited area – or if you have a high turnover of files from working on large databases or reports, or from installing and removing demos, shareware and other programs.

❶ If any other program writes to the disk while Disk Defragmenter is running, it will restart from scratch. Shut down any applications that may write temporary files to the disk. You should also open the Desktop's **Properties** panel and turn off the screensaver. This may also write to the disk.

❷ Start Disk Defragmenter from the **System Tools** menu.

Select the drive, then check the **Settings** before starting

The job will take ages anyway, so you may as well do it properly!

It's worth watching Defragmenter at work – for a little while – just to see what it does.

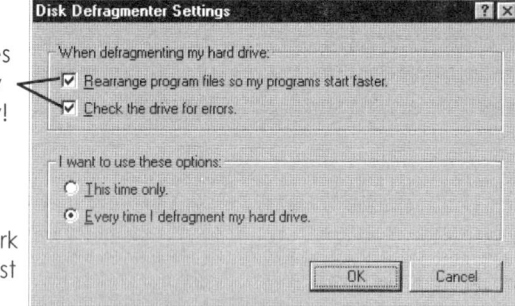

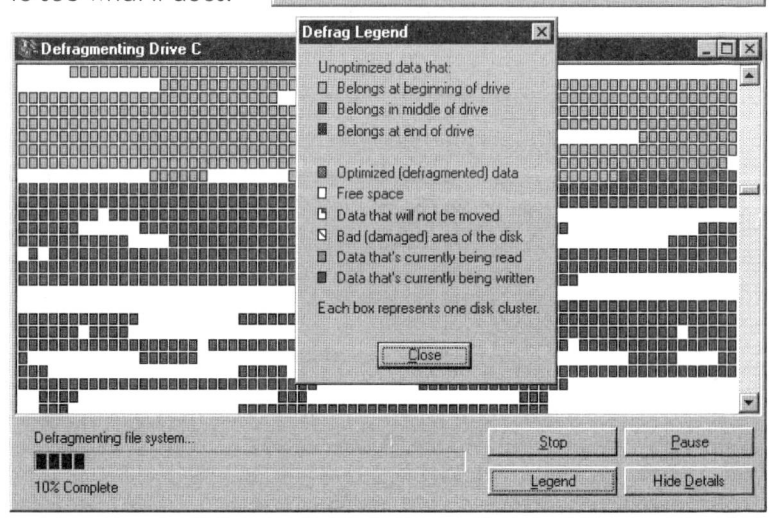

**Figure 12.6** Defragmenting the drive – a slow job, but worth doing when the drive starts to fill.

❸ Select the drive and click the **Settings** button. If you have scanned the disk recently, you can clear the **check for errors** option to save a little time.

❹ Click the **Show Details** button if you want to see what's going on, then turn on the **Legend** so that you can understand it!

❺ When you get bored, go and do something else for an hour.

---

**RESTORING CORRUPTED FLOPPIES**

If a floppy disk becomes corrupted so that you cannot read its files, try running it through ScanDisk then Disk Defragmenter, It doesn't take long to process a floppy and it will sometimes recover the lost files.

---

## 12.6 Maintenance Wizard

You can set up Disk Cleanup, ScanDisk and Disk Defragmenter to run automatically at set times – in fact, they may already have been set up when Windows Me was installed. Whether you are doing it for the first time, or checking and adjusting the settings, use Maintenance Wizard.

❶ At the first panel, select **Express** if you are happy to let Windows Me make your decisions, or **Custom** if you would like to see – and control – what's going on.

❷ Pick a convenient time for maintenance – it must be when you will not be using the machine. If you have chosen the Express route, click **Finish**, otherwise click **Next**.

❸ If there are any programs in your Startup folder – i.e. ones that run automatically when Windows starts – you will be asked if you want to run them.

❹ You will see a panel for each of Disk Defragmenter, ScanDisk and DiskCleanup. All follow the same format. If you choose to run the utility, you can change when and how often it runs by clicking **Reschedule**, and set its options by clicking **Settings** – this leads to the utility's normal options panel.

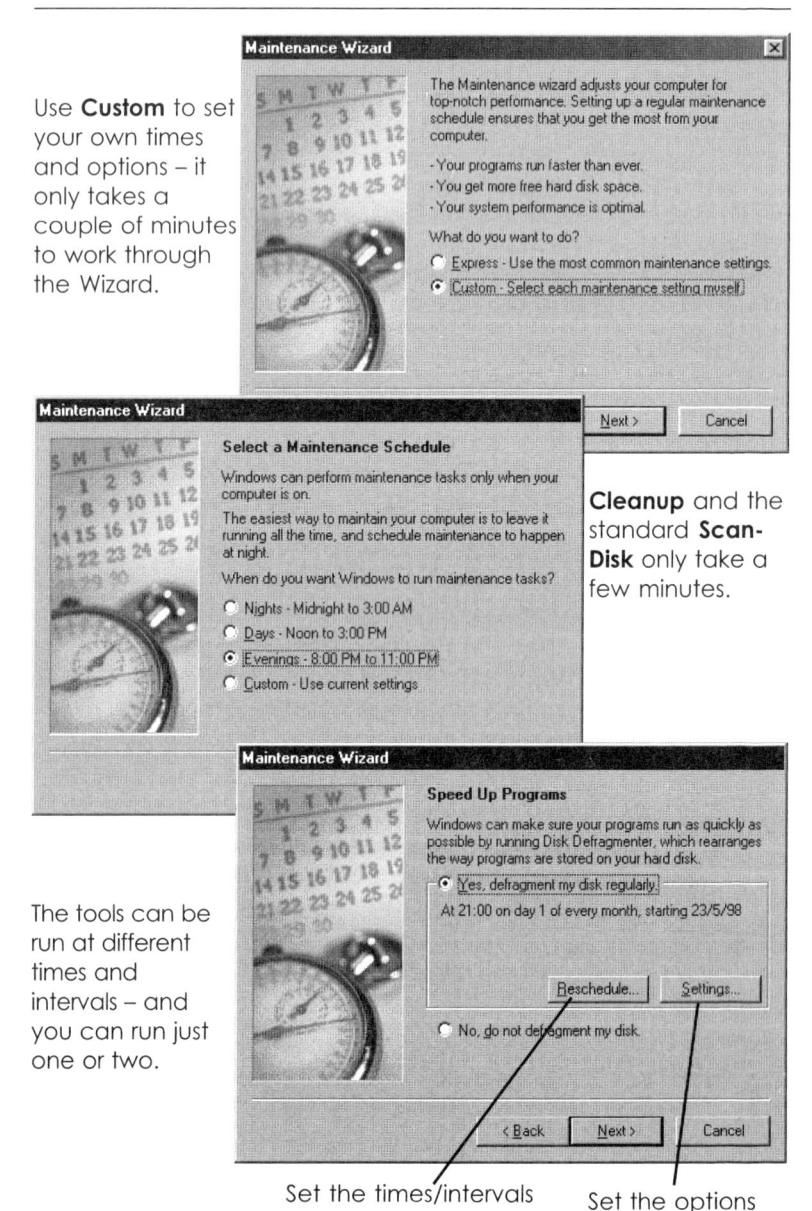

Use **Custom** to set your own times and options – it only takes a couple of minutes to work through the Wizard.

**Cleanup** and the standard **ScanDisk** only take a few minutes.

The tools can be run at different times and intervals – and you can run just one or two.

Set the times/intervals    Set the options

**Figure 12.7** Running the **Maintenance Wizard**.

# MAINTAINING YOUR DISKS

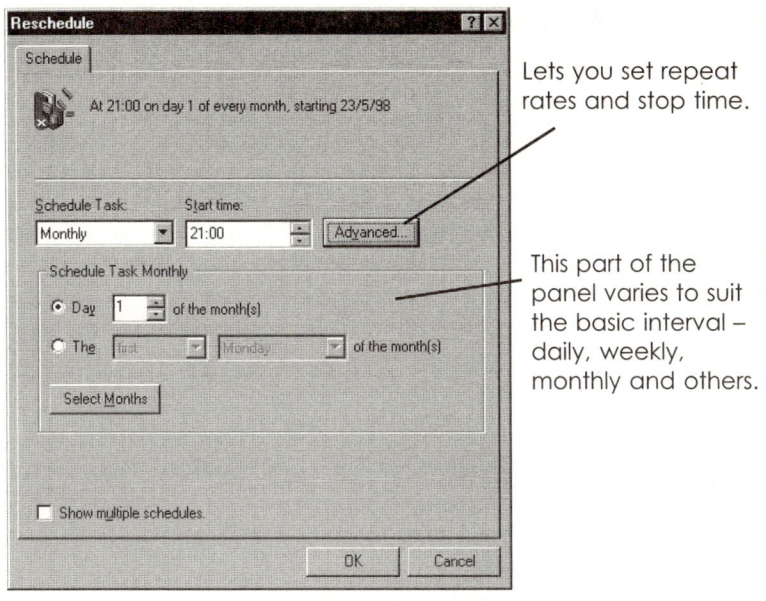

**Figure 12.8** Adjusting the schedule for a task.

Lets you set repeat rates and stop time.

This part of the panel varies to suit the basic interval – daily, weekly, monthly and others.

## Scheduled Tasks

After the Maintenance Wizard has been run, the settings are stored in the **Scheduled Tasks** folder. This can be opened from the **System Tools** menu. Click on an icon here to enable or disable a task, or to change its schedule or settings.

If you have another program that you want to run regularly, at set times, click here to set it up as a scheduled task.

**Figure 12.9** The **Scheduled Tasks** folder. Clicking an icon simply opens its configuration panel – it does not start the tasked program.

## 12.7 System Restore

With any luck you'll never need this, but it's good to know that it is there. Windows Me automatically stores a backup copy of your important system files, known as system restore points, at regular intervals. If these files become corrupted for any reason – e.g. 'user error', new software installation problems or hardware failure – System Restore will get your system running again.

To restore your system:

- ❶ Go to the **System Tools** menu and select **System Restore**.
- ❷ At the first stage, select **Restore my computer ...**
- ❸ At the next panel, pick the most recent checkpoint when you know that the system was running properly.

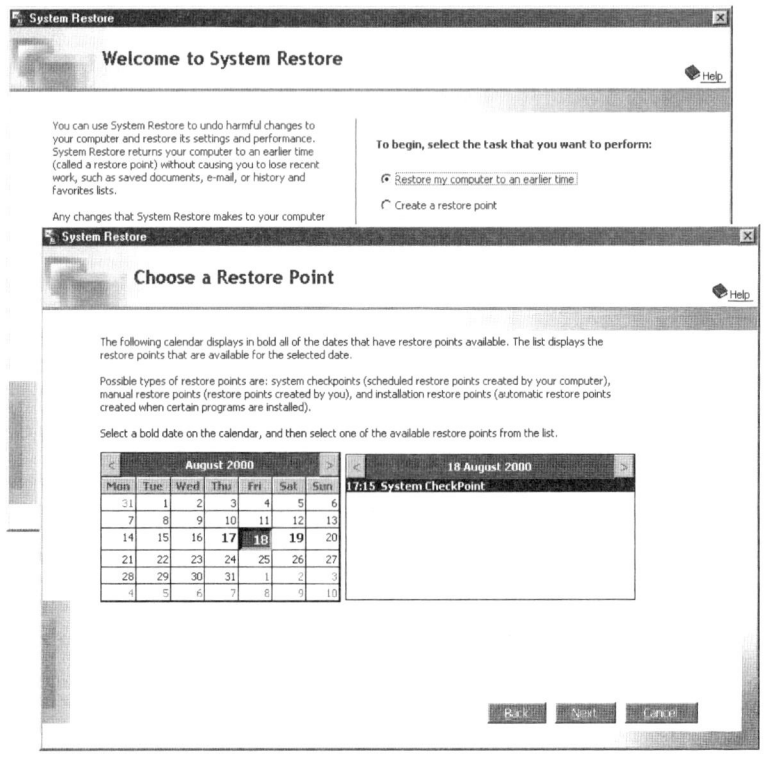

**Figure 12.10** Using **System Restore**.

### Creating a restore point

A Windows Me computer is robust; modern software and hardware is normally reliable and thoroughly tested, but things do go wrong. Before you do anything which might upset the system, such as installing new kit or making any other major changes, create a restore point. It takes only a few minutes and could save you endless hours of pain!

- ❶ Start **System Restore** and select **Create a restore point**.
- ❷ Type in a description to help you identify it – the point will have the date and time added, so this is not too crucial.
- ❸ Click **Next** to start the process.

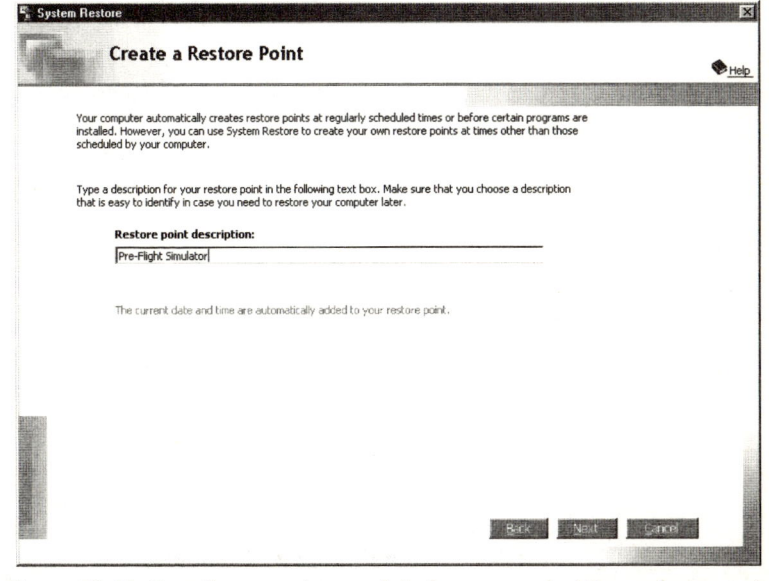

**Figure 12.11** Creating a restore point – insure against the unforeseen!

## 12.8 Backups

System Restore is purely there to ensure the safety of your system files and settings. It does not backup your application files or documents. These also need to be looked after.

Application files – the ones that make up the programs – should be less of a problem. Just keep their original CDs safe so that, if necessary, you could reinstall them. Reinstallation will not affect any documents that you may have created with the software – unless by pure fluke you have given them the same names as the software's sample files!

To ensure that your documents are safe, you must take backup copies of them on another PC or on some form of removable media. The important thing is that the backup should not be on the same machine. If it gets stolen, destroyed or becomes corrupted, your data is lost.

- If you don't have much essential data, it can be backed up onto floppy disks – if you compress it first with WinZip, you can typically fit 3 to 6 Mb of data on a floppy.
- If you have a lot of data – and photos and videos tend to be large files – then you should be using an IOmega Zip or a tape backup system or a CD writer.
- If the PC is on a network, you can backup data in a folder on the other machine.

## 12.9 Floppy disks

These are mainly used for backups and for copying files from one PC to another. Before use they will need formatting – unless you have bought them ready-formatted.

- ❶ Place an unformatted disk in the floppy drive.
- ❷ Right-click on the **A:** icon in My Computer or Explorer and select **Format...** from the menu.
- ❸ At the Format dialog box, in **Format Type**, select *Full*. A *Quick* format will erase files from a formatted disk; *Copy system files* is used to create a startup disk.
- ❹ Type a **Label** if wanted – the paper label is more use for identifying floppies.
- ❺ Click **Start**.

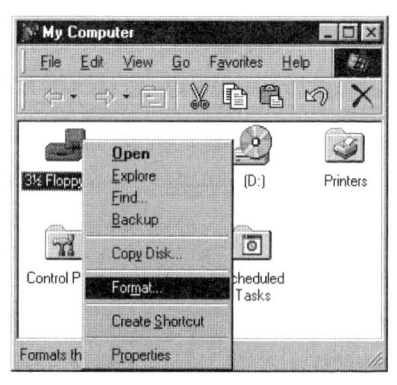

# MAINTAINING YOUR DISKS

**Figure 12.12** The Format dialog box, ready to start a full format on a 3½" floppy.

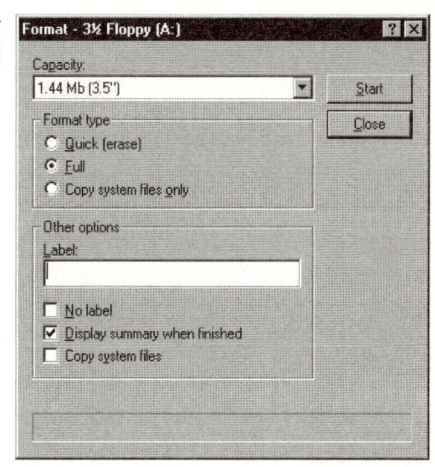

Formatting destroys all the data on a disk. **Do not format the C: drive!** The option is there, but it should only be used as a last-ditch attempt to recover something from the ruins of a major virus attack or other total failure – and only ever with professional advice.

---

**FLOPPY CARE**

Floppies are quite robust, but their files can be corrupted if exposed to heat or magnetism. Keep them away from radiators, magnets, heavy machinery and electricity cables.

## SUMMARY

- ✓ Hard disks need regular maintenance to keep them in good condition. Windows Me provides tools for this.
- ✓ The maintenance utilities can be started from the System Tools menu, or from the Tools tab of the Disk Properties panel.
- ✓ Disk Cleanup will remove temporary and unwanted files.
- ✓ Use ScanDisk regularly to check that your files and folders are intact and correctly stored. Run it in Thorough mode occasionally to check the condition of the disk surface.
- ✓ Disk Defragmenter will reorganize the disk so that files are stored in continuous sequences for faster reading.
- ✓ You can use the Maintenance Wizard to arrange for the disk tools to be run at set times as scheduled tasks.
- ✓ System Restore can help to recover the system from calamity.
- ✓ Document files should be backed up on floppy or other removable disk, or on another PC.
- ✓ Floppies must be formatted before use.

# 13 | PRINTERS

## AIMS OF THIS CHAPTER

With Windows Me, much hardware is simply plug and play – just connect it up, and Windows will configure the system so that the new kit is ready to run. Printers are a bit different. If you want to get the best out of one, you must use the right driver – the program that converts the PC's formatting codes into ones that the printer understands. In this chapter we look at how to install a new printer, and how to control it in use.

## 13.1 Adding a new printer

If your printer dates from before Spring 2000, the drivers on the Windows Me CD are probably newer than those supplied with the printer. If it is more recent, dig out its installation disk.

The **Add Printer Wizard** makes installation simple.

❶ Open the **Printers** folder, from the **Start → Settings** menu.

❷ Click (or double-click) **Add Printer** to run the wizard.

This system has several printers already – the Xerox is the default (shown by ●); the Brother is on the network.

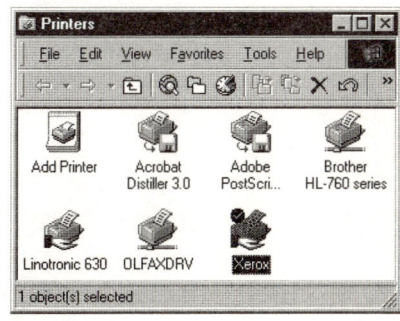

❸ At the first screen, select *Local printer*, if it is attached to your PC, or *Network printer* if you access it through your office Local Area Network.

❹ If you are using one of the Windows Me drivers, select the **Manufacturer** from the list, then the **Printer** model. If you are using the drivers supplied with the printer, click **Have Disk**, then select the model from the list that is drawn from the disk.

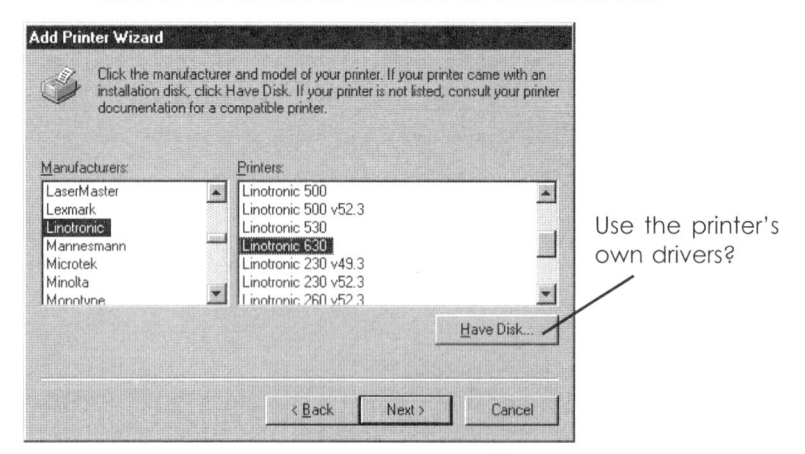

Use the printer's own drivers?

❺ For a local printer, you need to choose the port – normally LPT1. If you have a (rare) serial printer, use a COM port – COM4 may be free.

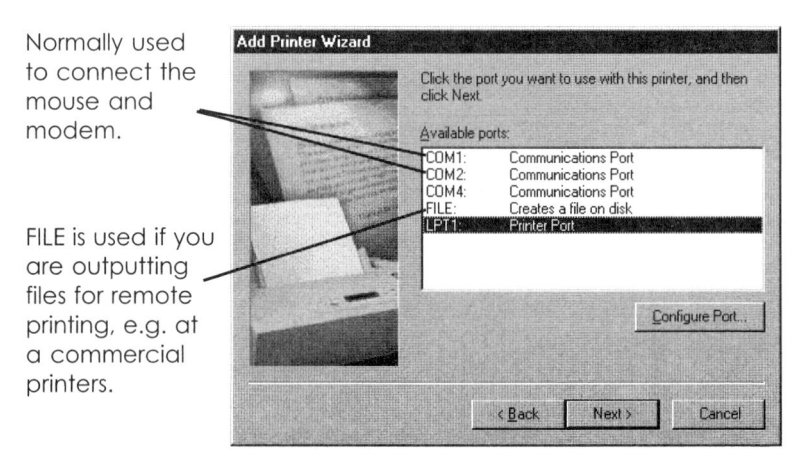

Normally used to connect the mouse and modem.

FILE is used if you are outputting files for remote printing, e.g. at a commercial printers.

- ❻ For a network printer, browse the network to find the printer you want to use.
- ❼ You may want to edit the full manufacturer/model name into something shorter to label the icon in the Printers folder.
- ❽ If you have more than one printer, one is set as the default – the one that applications will use unless you specify otherwise when you start a print job.
- ❾ At the final stage, accept the offer of a test print – it's as well to check! Once you click **Finish**, the Wizard will load the driver from the disk and install it in your system.

## 13.2 Printer Properties

Before you use the printer, check its properties. If nothing else, you may well need to change the paper size, as it is often set to the US 'Letter'. The standard UK paper size is A4 (210 × 297mm).

Right-click on the new icon in the Printers folder and select **Properties**. Different printers have different Properties panels, but you should find:

- A **General** tab, where you can type a comment. This is only useful on a network, to inform others of any special requirements that you or the printer have.
- A **Details** tab, where you can select a new port or driver if needed. The **Timeout** settings define how long Windows should wait before reporting an error; the **Spool** settings determine whether the file is sent directly from the application to the printer, or through a temporary memory buffer. Spooling frees up applications, as they can generally send data out faster than the printer can handle it.
- A **Paper** tab, where you can set the default paper size. The other options here are best left at their defaults, though you may well want to change them just before printing specific documents – the printer properties can be accessed from the Print routines of applications.
- A **Device Options** panel. Check the **Memory** value (normally only with laser printers). If you have added extra memory to the printer – a good idea if you print pages with lots of graphics – tell Windows about it.

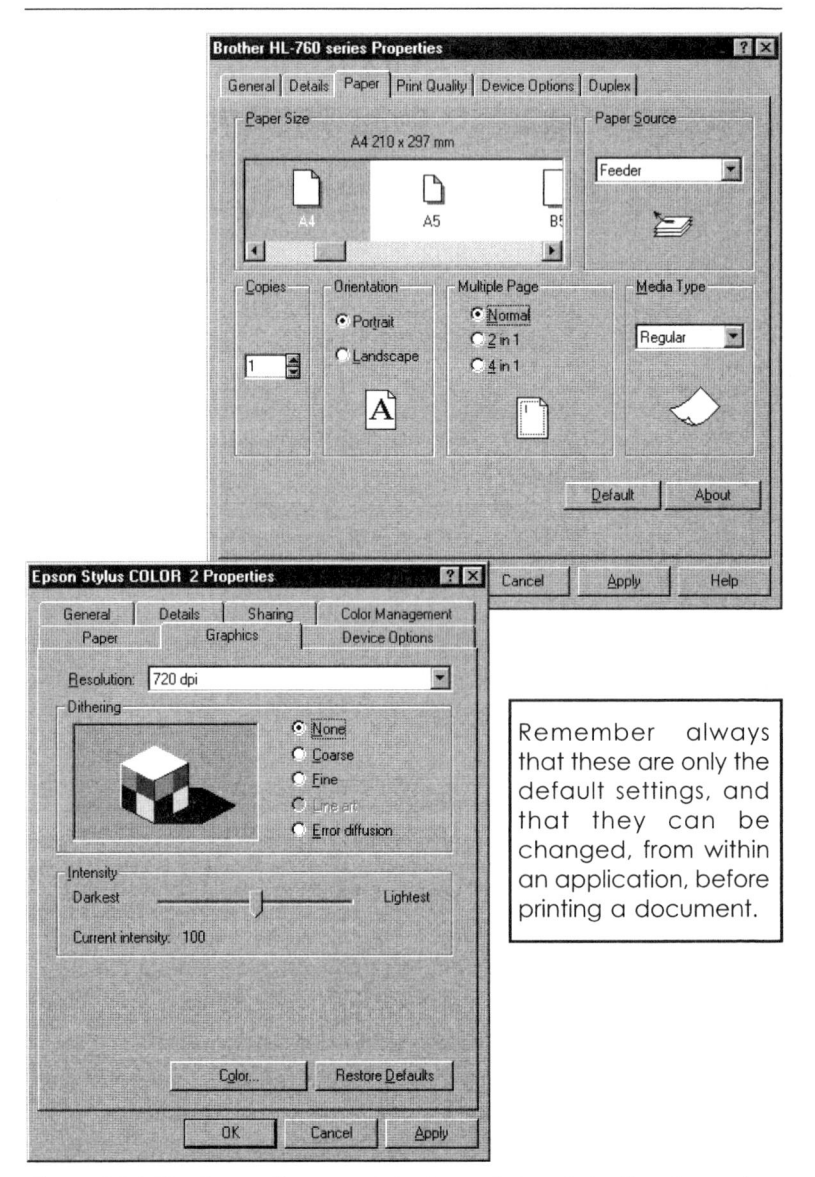

Remember always that these are only the default settings, and that they can be changed, from within an application, before printing a document.

**Figure 13.1** The **Properties** panels for two printers. Take time to explore yours to see what options are available, and what defaults have been set – not all may make sense at first!

## 13.3 Printing from applications

The Print routines in applications are all much the same. There will usually be a 🖨 toolbar button, and clicking on this will send the document to the printer using its current settings – whatever they are. The first time that you print something, it is best to start by selecting **Print** from the **File** menu. This will open a dialog box where you can define the settings – the key ones are which pages to print and how many copies.

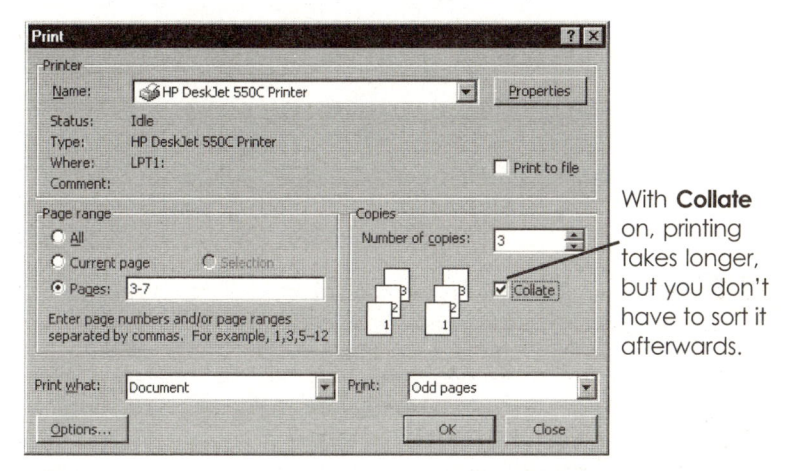

With **Collate** on, printing takes longer, but you don't have to sort it afterwards.

**Figure 13.2** The Print dialog box from Word. Other applications have different options, but **Page range** and **Copies** are common to all.

If you need to change the layout, print quality or other printer settings, clicking the Properties button will open the printer Properties panel – this may look slightly different from the panel opened from the Printers folder, but gives you access to the same settings.

## 13.4 Controlling the print queue

Unless you are exceptionally disorganized or have very unreliable hardware, most of your printing will run smoothly. But things go wrong even at the most organized desk...

When a document is sent for printing, it goes first to the print queue. If it is the only print job, it is then processed directly. If not, it will sit in the queue and wait its turn. As long as a document is still in the queue, you can do something about it – but if it is just one short, simple document, it will almost certainly be through the queue before you can get to it.

- If you discover a late error, so that printing is just a waste of paper, a job can be cancelled.
- If you have sent a series of documents in succession, you can change the order in which they are printed.

When the printer is active, you will see [icon] on the right of the Taskbar, next to the clock. Click on it to open the printer's folder, where the queue is stored.

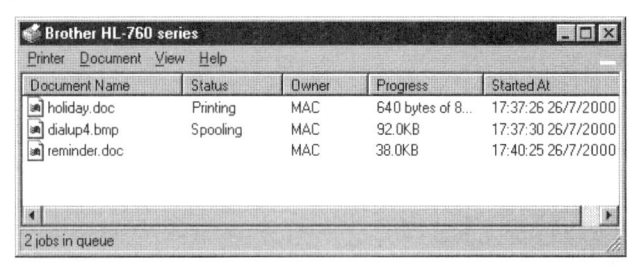

| Document Name | Status | Owner | Progress | Started At |
|---|---|---|---|---|
| holiday.doc | Printing | MAC | 640 bytes of 8... | 17:37:26 26/7/2000 |
| dialup4.bmp | Spooling | MAC | 92.0KB | 17:37:30 26/7/2000 |
| reminder.doc | | MAC | 38.0KB | 17:40:25 26/7/2000 |

2 jobs in queue

- *To cancel a print job*, select the document, then use **Cancel Printing** from the **Document** menu.
- *To cancel all the queued jobs*, use **Purge Printing** from the **Printer** menu.
- *To change the order of printing*, select a document and drag it up or down the queue as required – this only works with those documents that are not already being spooled or printed.

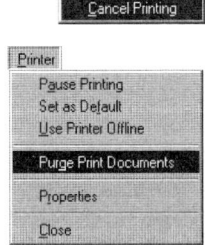

### DON'T JUST TURN OFF!

Turning off the printer is not a good way to stop a print job. If the document is partially printed or still waiting in the queue it will simply start to print again as soon as the printer is turned back on – and if partially printed, will be probably be garbled. You must clear the queue to get rid of a print job.

## 13.5 Printing from file

If you have Windows Explorer or My Computer open, you can print a document directly from there, as long as you have an associated application which can handle it. Windows Me will open the application, print the document, then close the application for you.

To send the document to the default printer:
* Right-click on the file and select **Print** from the short menu.

To send to any other printer:
1. Open the printers folder and arrange the screen so that you can see the document file and the printer icon.
2. Drag the document across the screen and drop it onto the printer icon.

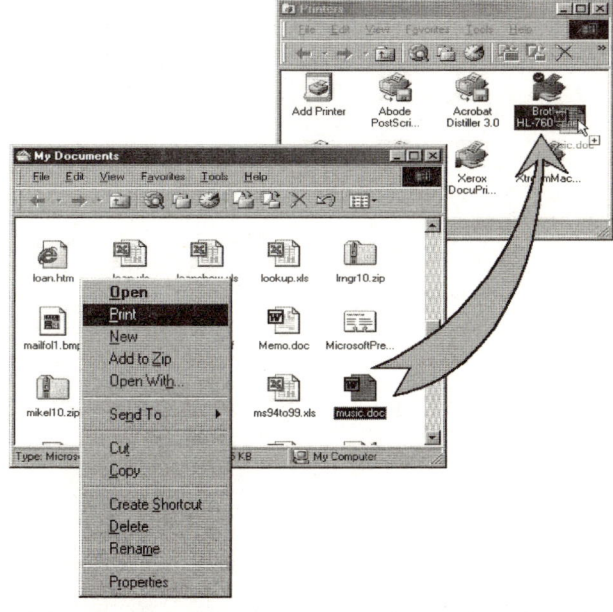

**Figure 13.3** You can print a document directly from file, either from the short menu or by dropping it onto a printer icon.

## SUMMARY

- ✓ To install a new printer, use the Add Printer Wizard in the Printers folder. Windows Me has drivers for almost every known printer model.

- ✓ Check the printer's Properties panel before use, to make sure that the default settings – especially the paper size – are suitable.

- ✓ When printing from an application, you can usually set the page range and number of copies. If required, the printer Properties can be adjusted before printing.

- ✓ Documents are taken to the print queue before output. By opening the queue you can cancel a print job or change the order in which they are printed.

- ✓ A document can be printed from Explorer or My Computer.

# 14 THE ACCESSORIES

## AIMS OF THIS CHAPTER

The Windows Me package includes a host of accessories – some very useful, others just for fun. In this chapter we will be looking at a selection of these. Even if you never use any of these accessories in earnest, it is worth experimenting with them, as the skills and knowledge that you learn here can be applied to other Windows applications.

## 14.1 WordPad

Don't underrate WordPad just because it's free. It has all the facilities that you would have found in the top-flight software of just a few years ago, and compares well with today's commercial packages. It's fine for writing letters, essays, reports, source code for computer programs and anything else where you want to be able to edit text efficiently, formatting it with fonts, styles and colours, and perhaps incorporating graphics or other files.

- When entering text, just keep typing when you reach the edge of the page – the text will be wrapped round to the next line. Only press the **Enter** key at the end of a paragraph.
- Existing text can be selected, with the normal techniques, then moved, deleted or formatted.
- Most formatting can be done through the toolbar. Select the text, then pick a font or size from the drop-down lists, or click the **B** bold, *I* italic, U underline, colour or other buttons.
- The left, centre and right alignment buttons determine how the text lines up with the edges of the paper.

Standard toolbar – with the main filing and editing tools

Formatting toolbar    Ruler

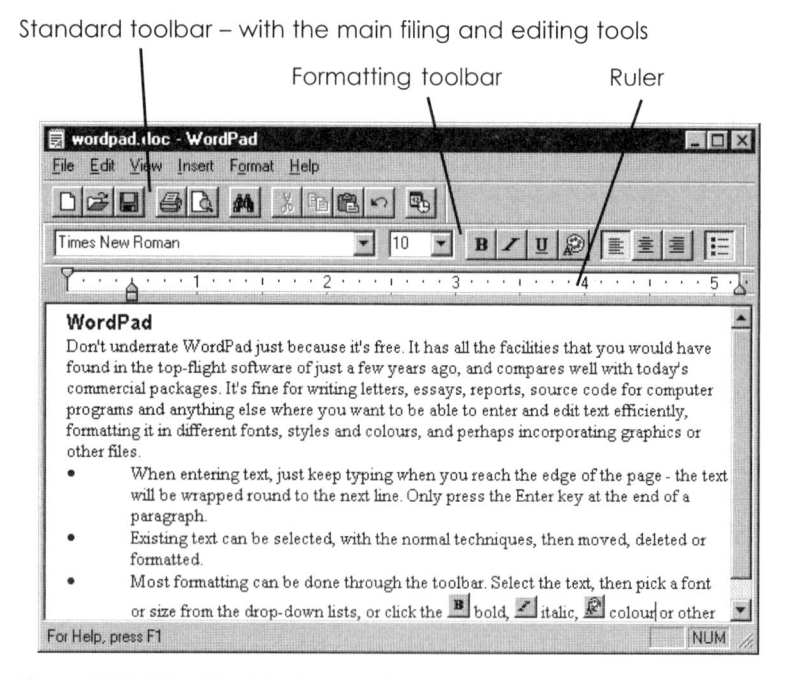

**Figure 14.1** WordPad, being used to create the text for these pages!

- The bullets button indents text from the left, with a blob at the start of each paragraph.
- Alignment and bullet formats apply to whole paragraphs. You do not need to select the whole paragraph – if the cursor is within it, or part of its text is selected, the paragraph will be formatted.

### Indents and tabs

These are best set from the ruler. Select the text where new indents or tabs are required then drag the icons to set the indent; click to set a tab point.

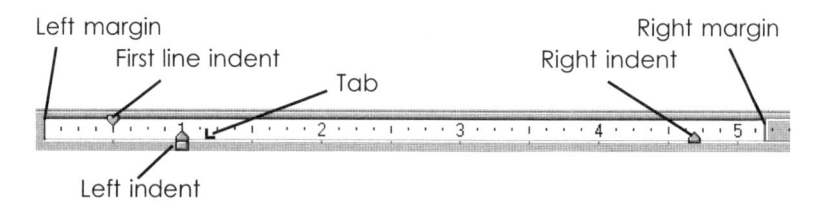

Left margin                                                    Right margin
    First line indent                        Right indent
                          Tab

Left indent

## Full font formatting

Though you can set almost all font options from the toolbar buttons, you get better control through the **Font** panel – open it with **Format → Font**. Here you can set all aspects of the selected text, and preview the effects of your choices. Watch the **Sample** text as you change the settings.

**Figure 14.2** The **Font** panel.

You will find similar panels in all applications that use fonts.

Click **OK** when you like the look of the **Sample**.

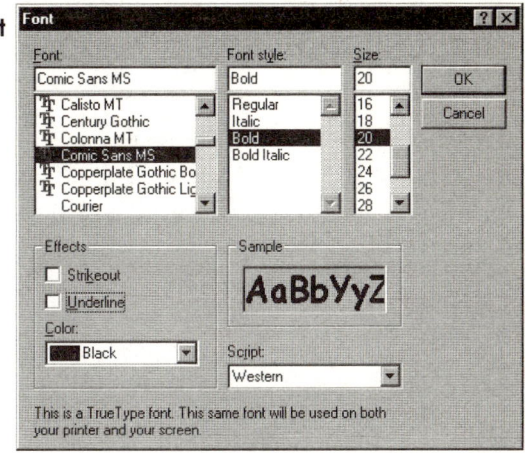

## Page Setup

The **Page Setup** panel, opened from the **File** menu option, controls the basic size and layout of the page – for all pages in the document.

- The **Paper Size** and **Source** settings rarely need changing – if you've set your printer properties correctly. If you are printing on card or special paper, change the **Source** to *Manual*, if the option is available.
- In the **Orientation** area, *Portrait* is the normal way up; use *Landscape* if you want to print with the paper sideways.
- The **Margins** set the overall limits to the printable area. You can use the indents to reduce the width of text within the margins, but you cannot extend out beyond them.
- Click the **Printer** button to reach its **Properties** panel to change any settings at that level – you might, for example, want to switch to a lower resolution for printing a draft copy, or a higher resolution for the final output. (At low resolution, the printer will work faster and use less ink or toner.)

**Figure 14.3** The **Page Setup** panel in WordPad.

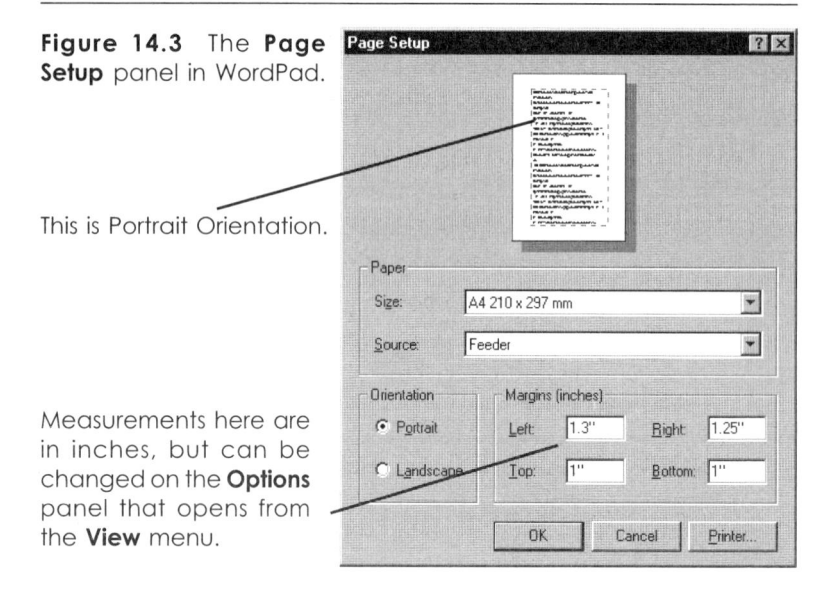

This is Portrait Orientation.

Measurements here are in inches, but can be changed on the **Options** panel that opens from the **View** menu.

## Graphics and other objects

WordPad is not limited to text only. Pictures, graphs, spreadsheets, audio and video clips – in fact just about any object that can be produced by any Windows application – can be incorporated into a WordPad document. The technique is much the same for any object.

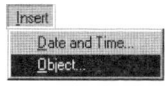

① Open the **Insert** menu and select **Object...**
② If the object does not yet exist, select the **Object Type** and click **OK**.

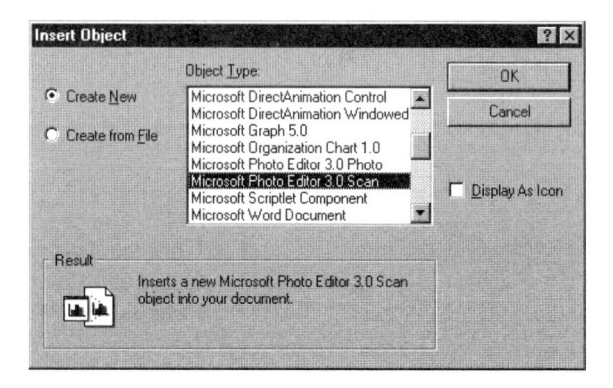

The appropriate application will open. When you have created the object, save it if you want to keep a separate copy for future use, then select the new **Exit & Return to Document** option from the **File** menu.

❸ If you want to use an existing object, select **Create from File**, and browse through your folders to locate it.

❹ Back in your WordPad document, you can resize the object if necessary.

Select the object – it will be outlined with handles at the corners and mid-edges.

Point to a handle to get the double-headed arrow then drag in or out as required. The position of the object across the page can be set by using the alignment buttons.

---

You can't do fancy layouts with WordPad. An image can sit by itself, separate from the text above and below, or can be embedded in a single line. That's it.

---

**Figure 14.4** Adjusting the size of an image in WordPad. An inserted object can be edited by double-clicking on it – this opens the source application. Use **Exit & Return** when you have finished editing.

## Print Preview

Like almost all applications, WordPad has a Print Preview facility. Working on screen, it is often difficult to tell how a document will look on paper – you may not be able to see the full width of the page and you certainly won't be able to see the full height. Use the Preview to get a better idea of the printed output, before you commit it to paper. Are your images or headings large enough to make the impact that you want? Do you get awkward breaks in the text at the ends of pages? If you are happy with the look of your document, you can print from here by clicking the **Print** button, otherwise, click **Close** to return to WordPad for that final tweaking.

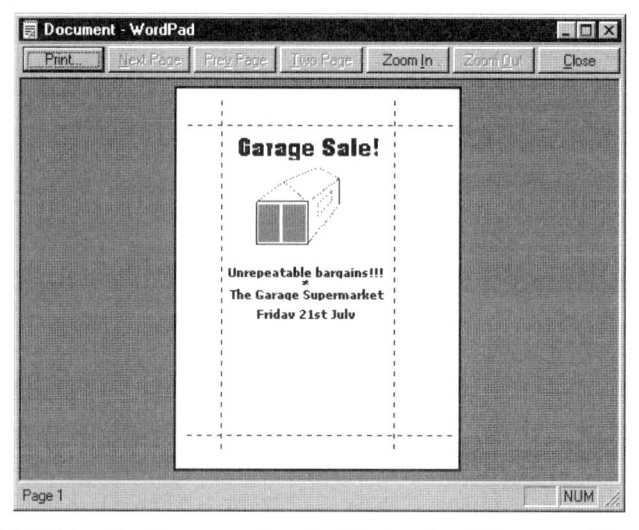

**Figure 14.5** Using the Page preview facility to check the overall layout of a page. You can print from here, or close to return to editing.

## Saving and opening files

In WordPad as in all applications you should save early and save often! Don't wait until you have finished writing that eight-page report before you save it. Applications can crash, hardware can fail, plugs get knocked out and we all make mistakes! The first save may take a few moments, but later saves are done at the click of a button.

## THE ACCESSORIES

To save a file for the first time:

- ❶ Open the **File** menu and select **Save As...**
- ❷ At the dialog box, select the folder.
- ❸ Change the default 'Document' in the filename to something that will remind you what it is about.
- ❹ If you want to save in a different format, pick one from the **Save as type** drop-down list.
- ❺ Click **Save**.

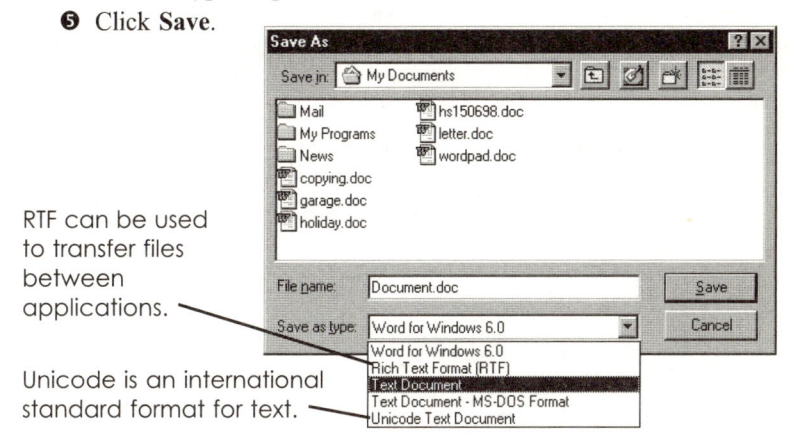

RTF can be used to transfer files between applications.

Unicode is an international standard format for text.

To resave the current document:

- Click 🖫 – that's it!

When you close the document, or exit from WordPad, if you have not saved the document in its final state, you will be prompted to do so.

Next time that you want to work on the document, open it from the **File** menu. Either:

- Select **Open** and then browse for the file – the dialog box is used in almost exactly the same way as the Save dialog box.

*or*

- If it is one of the files that you have used most recently, it will be listed at the bottom of the File menu. Just select it from here.

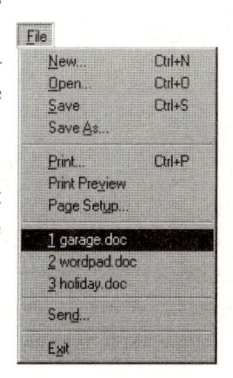

## 14.2 Notepad

This is a text editor, not a word-processor. Text can be typed and edited here just as it can in WordPad, but it cannot be formatted. Because it is such a simple program, it starts up faster and uses less memory than any word-processor. It is the one to use if you want to produce plain text files – such as memos, program code and text which is to be handed on to someone else for formatting.

```java
import java.awt.*;
import java.applet.*;

public class MoveText extends Applet
{
        Font header = new Font("SanSerif",Font.BOLD,24);
        String text;
        String temp;
        int delayLimit;

        public void init()
        {
        text = getParameter("message");
        if (text == null)
                text = "nothing to say";
        temp = getParameter("limit");
        if (temp == null)
                delayLimit = 10000;
```

**Figure 14.6** Editing a program in Notepad. You can set the font, but only for the screen display of all the text.

Apart from the normal File and Edit commands, the only significant facility offered by Notepad is a search routine – useful in programming for tracking down variables.

**Search → Find...** opens the **Find** panel, where you can specify what to look for.

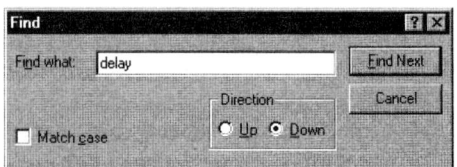

**Search → Find Next** simply repeats the last search.

THE ACCESSORIES 207

## 14.3 Character Map

You will find **Character Map** on the **System Tools** menu – don't ask me why! It's a useful tool and one that I like to have close to hand. It allows you to see the characters available in any font, and to copy individual characters from there into a document.

❶ Pick a font from the drop-down list – Symbol, Webdings and Wingdings are the main fonts for decorative characters, and you will find foreign letters and mathematical symbols in most other fonts.

❷ Hold down the left button and move across the display – the character under the cursor will be enlarged.

❸ To copy characters into a document, click **Select** – the current one will be added to the **Characters to copy** display – then click **Copy** when you have all you want. Return to your document and use **Edit ➙ Paste** – the character(s) will be copied in, formatted to the chosen font.

*or*

❹ Make a note of the **Keystroke** in the bottom right corner. If it says '**Alt+...**', you can get that character by holding down **Alt** and typing the numbers (with the leading 0) into the *Number keypad*. Remember that the appearance of the character depends upon the font.

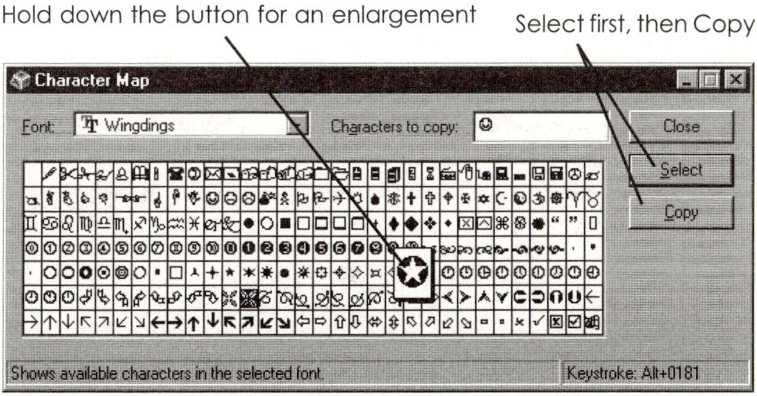

Hold down the button for an enlargement    Select first, then Copy

**Figure 14.7** Character Map. If you are likely to want to use a character regularly, make a note of its **Keystroke**.

## 14.4 Paint

Graphics software falls into two broad groups. With some, including Paint, the image is produced by applying colour to a background – with each new line overwriting anything that may be beneath. Using these is very like real painting. You may be able to wipe out a mistake while the paint is still wet, but as soon as it has dried it is fixed on the canvas. (Paint allows you to undo the last move; some will let you backtrack further.)

The second type works with objects – lines, circles, text notes, etc. – that remain separate, and can be moved, deleted, recoloured and otherwise changed at any point. **Imaging** works this way (see page 212).

I use Paint regularly – it's ideal for trimming and tidying screenshots for books, though I don't expect many of you will want it for this purpose. Though it can be used to produce intricate images, these require a great deal of time and skill – and can be created more successfully on a computer art package, with a full set of shading, shaping and manipulating tools. Paint is probably best used to draw simple diagrams, or as a children's toy, or to get an idea of how this type of graphics software works.

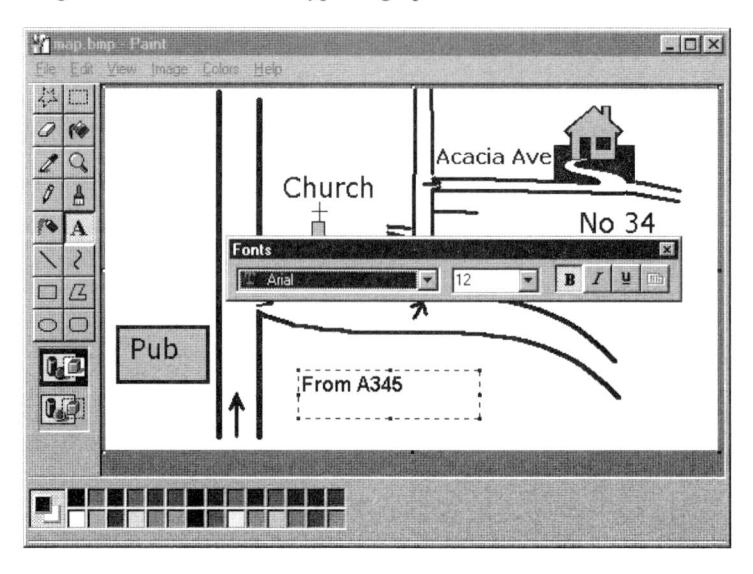

**Figure 14.8** Using Paint to create a diagram. The **Text toolbar** gives you the full range of fonts and the main style effects.

## The Toolbox

There is a simple but adequate set of tools. A little experimentation will show how they all work.

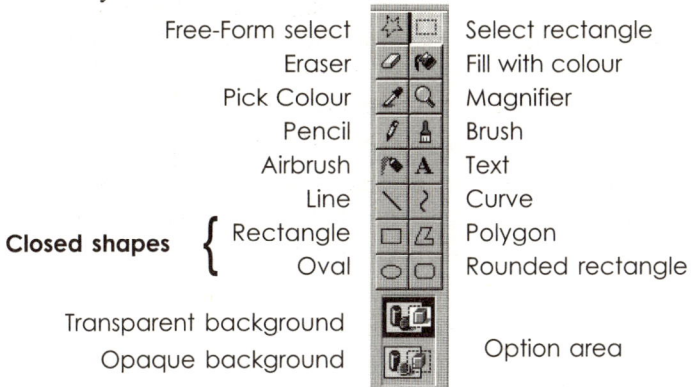

| | |
|---:|:---|
| Free-Form select | Select rectangle |
| Eraser | Fill with colour |
| Pick Colour | Magnifier |
| Pencil | Brush |
| Airbrush | Text |
| Line | Curve |
| **Closed shapes** { Rectangle | Polygon |
| Oval | Rounded rectangle |
| Transparent background | |
| Opaque background | Option area |

Most of them have options that can be set in the area below the toolbar.

- When you select an area (or paste an image from file or from the Clipboard) the background can be transparent or opaque.
- You can set the size of the Eraser, Brush, Airbrush, Line and Curve. N.B. the Line thickness applies to the closed shapes.
- The Magnifier is 4× by default, but can be 2×, 6× or 8×.
- The Pencil is only ever 1 pixel wide.
- Closed shapes can be outline or fill only, or both.

The Curve is probably the trickiest of the tools to use. The line can have one or two curves to it.

❶ Draw a line between the points where the curve will start and end.

❷ Drag to create the first curve – exaggerate the curve as it will normally be reduced at the next stage.

❸ If the line is to have a second curve, drag it out now – as long as the mouse button is down, the line will flex to follow the cursor.

❹ For a simple curve, just click at the end of the line.

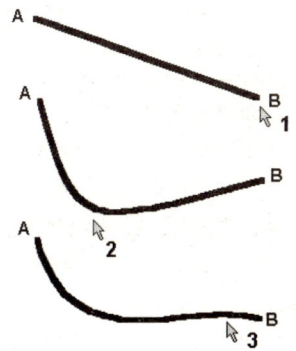

> **UNDO IT!**
> If you go wrong any time – and you will with the Curve – use **Edit → Undo**. This removes the effect of the last action.

## Working with selected areas

The rectangular and free-form selectors can be used to select an area of the screen. Once selected, an area can be:

- Deleted – use this for removing mistakes and excess bits.
- Copied – handy for creating repeating patterns.
- Saved as a file – use **Edit → Copy To...** and give a filename.
- Dragged elsewhere on screen.
- Flipped (mirrored) horizontally or vertically, or rotated in 90° increments – use **Image → Flip/Rotate** for these effects.
- Stretched – to enlarge, shrink or distort, or skewed, either horizontally or vertically – use **Image → Stretch/Skew**.

## Colours

The colour palette is used in almost the same way in all Windows programs. You can select a colour from the basic set – use the left button for the foreground colour and the right button for the background – or you can mix your own colours.

Double-click on a colour in the **Color Box** or use **Colors → Edit Colors** to open the **Edit Colors** panel. Initially only the **Basic colors** will be visible. Click **Define Custom Colors** to open the full panel.

To define a new colour, drag the cross-hair cursor in the main square to set the Red/Green/Blue balance, and move the arrow up or down the left scale to set the light/dark level. Colours can also be set by typing in values, but note that you are mixing light, not paint. Red and green make yellow; red, green and blue make grey/white; the more you use, the lighter the colour.

When you have the colour you want, click **Add to Custom Colors**. The new colour will replace the one currently selected in the Color Box on the main screen.

THE ACCESSORIES 211

Set the Red/Green/Blue balance.

Light/dark

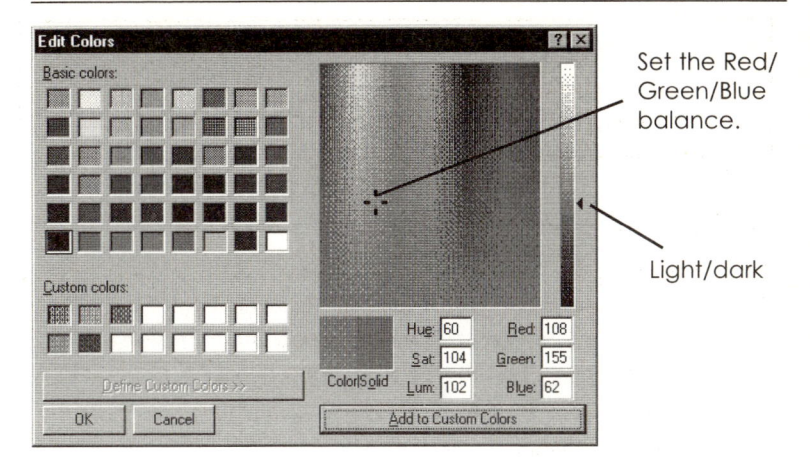

**Figure 14.9** Editing colours in Paint.

## Filing

Saving and opening files is the same here as in WordPad. You can also use **Edit → Copy To...** to save part of an image (see page 199) and **Edit → Paste From...** to open a file so that you can combine its image with the existing picture. The image will come in as a selected area, which can be positioned wherever required. Set the background to transparent to merge the two images, or to opaque for the new file to overlay the old image.

---

**SCREENSHOTS**

If you press the **Prt Sc** (Print Screen) key, the whole screen display will be copied into the Clipboard. If you press **Alt** + **Prt Sc** then only the active window will be copied into the Clipboard. The image can then be pasted into Paint, or any other graphics program, and saved from there. That's how the screenshots were produced for this book.

## 14.5 Imaging

You can use this to take images in from a scanner or from file and add simple annotations to them. And the annotations are simple. Text can be added on a transparent background, or on a yellow 'Post-It®' note. There are drawing tools only for freehand or straight lines, and filled or open rectangles – so you are not going to be doing much more than simple diagrams with these!

When you use a tool, the object appears in the default colour, thickness and font. These can be changed by right-clicking on the object and selecting **Properties** from the shortcut menu. The defaults for a tool can be changed by right-clicking on its button and opening its **Properties** panel – well worth doing if you want to use the same tool several times with the same effects.

One of the interesting aspects of this program is the way that the image is formed. Each note, line or rectangle is a separate object. You can click on it at any point and move, resize or delete it, or change its colour, font or thickness. This is true even after the image has been saved and reopened.

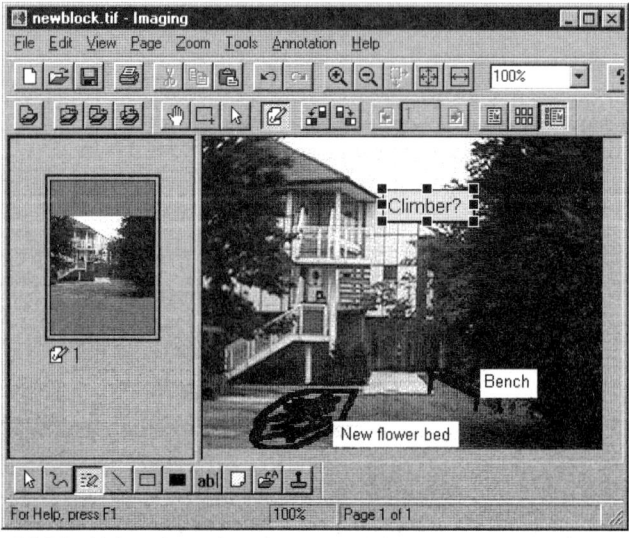

**Figure 14.10** Using Imaging to annotate a scanned picture. The screen is seen here in **Page and Thumbnail View**. Switch to **Page View** and increase the **Zoom** level for close-up work.

Imaging has a few, limited editing facilities: you can cut, copy and paste rectangular areas, and the whole image can be rotated.

On the positive side, Imaging can read images in most major formats and can save as TIFF files (a high quality and very portable format, handled by many applications), as BMPs (like Paint) and AWD (fax format). You can use it to create multi-page documents, and these can be printed, faxed or e-mailed.

**Figure 14.11** A typical **Properties** panel in Imaging. The **Palette** button opens the same **Edit Colors** panel that you met in Paint.

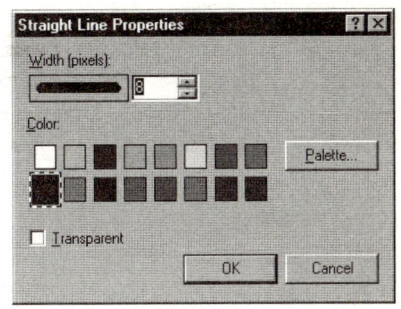

## 14.6 Calculator

Pack away that pocket calculator. You don't need it on your desk now that you have one on your Desktop!

The Calculator can work in two modes – Standard or Scientific. In either case, you use them the same way that you would a hand-held one. Enter the numbers, arithmetic operators and functions either by clicking on the screen keys, or by using your keyboard. (If you want to use the keyboard in the Scientific mode, look in the Help file for the keyboard equivalents.)

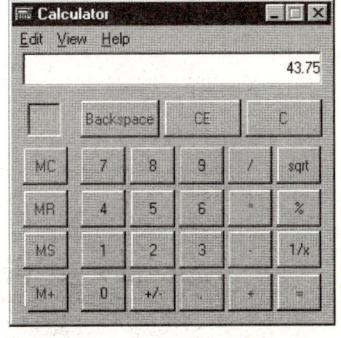

It has the same limitations as a pocket calculator – you can only store one value in memory at a time (**MS** to store it, **M+** to add to the value in memory, **MR** to recall it and **MC** to clear it); and you cannot print your results. If you want more than this, use a spreadsheet!

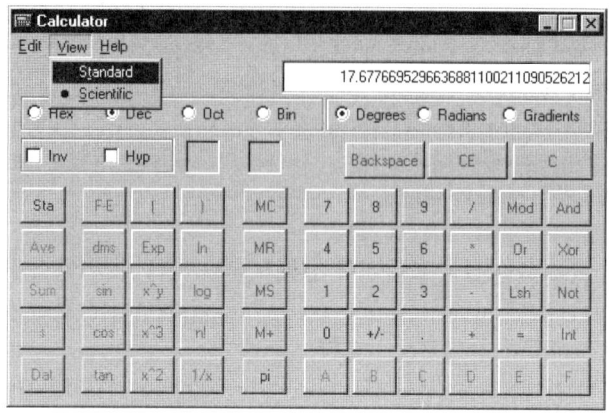

**Figure 14.12** The Calculator in Scientific mode. In either mode, it works to 32 digit accuracy – is that close enough for you?

## 14.7 Phone Dialer

Phone Dialer is on the **Programs → Accessories → Communications** menu. To use it, you must have your modem plugged into the phone line. To use it conveniently, you should have a phone on your desk.

You can dial a number here, rather than on the phone, but that's scarcely worth doing unless the phone keypad is difficult to reach for some reason.

The real benefit of Phone Dialer is in the **Speed dial** facility, which can act as an extension to, or in place of, any memory buttons on the phone. (Setting up and changing Speed dial numbers here is far simpler than on my phone!) Up to 8 numbers can be stored.

**To set up a Speed dial number:**

❶ Click on an unused Speed dial button.

❷ Enter the **Name** and **Number**.

❸ Click **Save**, or **Save and Dial** if you want to call immediately.

**To edit a number:**
  ❶ Open the **Edit** menu and select **Speed Dial...**
  ❷ Click on the button.
  ❸ Edit and click **Save**.
  ✦ New numbers can be set up here – click a blank button to start.

**To make a Speed Dial call:**
  ❶ Click on the button.
  ❷ When you get through, click **Talk** at the prompt.
  ❸ When you have done, click **Hang up**.

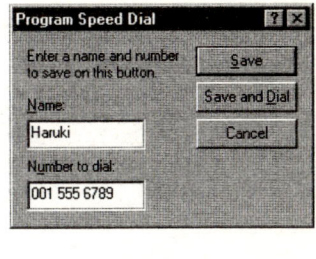

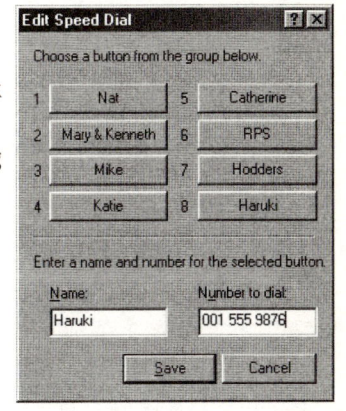

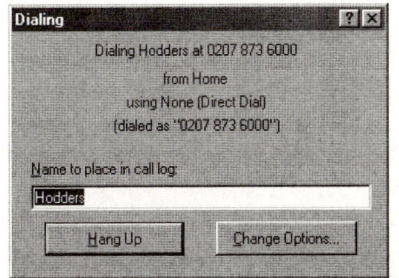

The **Dialing** prompt appears as soon as the modem starts work. You can click **Hang Up** any time after you have connected – as long as you have the phone off the hook you will stay online.

On the **Call Status** prompt, click **Talk** when you get through, or **Hang up** if there's no reply.

## 14.8 Media Player

Media Player is a multi-purpose audio/video player. It can handle sound files in MIDI and in the native Windows format, WAVE – as well as audio CDs – or video in the standard Video for Windows (AVI), Media Audio/Video (WMA and ASF) or the many ActiveMovie formats.

### CD Audio

Want some music while you work? Let Media Player play a CD for you.

❶ Start Media Player.
❷ Click the **CD Audio** button.
❸ Load in the CD and wait for a moment for Media Player to read the track information.
♦ The CD will play in the tracks in their playlist sequence – initially this will be the standard order.

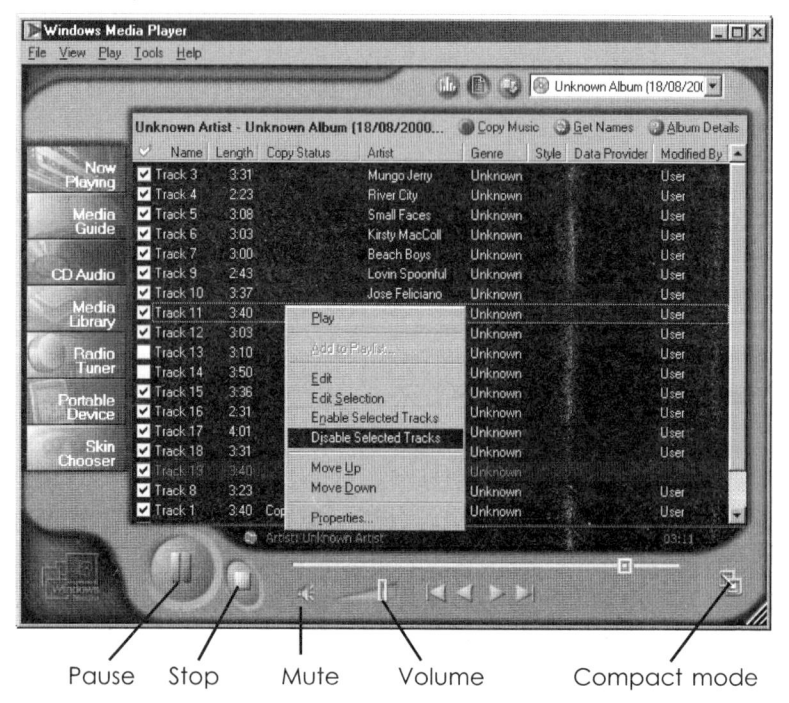

**Figure 14.13** Media Player, showing the playlist for an audio CD.

# THE ACCESSORIES

❹ To change the order of tracks, click on one to select it, then drag up or down.

❺ To skip over tracks, select them, then right-click and choose **Disable** from the shortcut menu.

*It's worth taking time over this, as any choices or other information that you enter here are recorded by Windows in a file (on the hard disk – it can't write to the CD) and will be reused next time the same CD is loaded.*

Once the playlist is set up and the CD is playing, you can switch into compact mode. This doesn't just occupy less screen space, it also has some great 'skins'. This is my favourite – it's sooo tacky.

This has the default 'visualization' running in it. If you don't like it – and I do – there are plenty of alternatives. Open the **View** menu, point to **Visualization**, select a set then pick from there. The names are not terribly helpful – you'll have to watch them to make a proper choice.

## Radio

This offers another way to get radio over the Internet (see page 154). There are a dozen pre-set stations, catering to a range of tastes, or you can use the Station Finder facility to pick from the hundreds of stations that are now broadcasting. You will find, when choosing a station, that Internet Explorer will normally open to show you the station's Web site. This can be closed down, if not wanted, to save screen space and speed up download of the broadcast.

Obviously, if you are paying for your phone time when you are online, this is not an efficient way to listen to the radio!

---

**PORTABLE DEVICE**

CD audio tracks and files, from the Internet or elsewhere, in MP3, WAV, WMA or ASF formats can be copied through Media Player onto your MP3 player or other portable device.

---

**Figure 14.14** Listening to Jazz FM, while looking to see what stations offer classical music – there are dozens, how do I choose one?!

## Video

Newer, faster hardware and more efficient software has significantly improved the quality of videos on PC, but they are still small and jerky – or run them in full-screen mode and they are large and blocky and jerky!

The main sources of videos are multimedia packages, where Media Player can be called up automatically to play the clips, demos and samples on CDs, and – most of all – the Internet.

There are three main ways in which you will get video from the Internet:

- Clips for downloading – the new high-compression formats have brought a better balance between download time and playing time. 1Mb of video gives you around 90 seconds of playing time, and will take up to 10 minutes to download – and you must have the whole file on your disk before you can start to play it.

**THE ACCESSORIES** 219

- Streaming video in TV and webcam broadcasts and, increasingly, in movie and pop video clips. Here the videos are played as they download. The images are jerkier, but at least you don't have to wait to see whether they are worth watching at all.
- Home movies e-mailed to you by relatives, who also have Windows Me and have been playing with its Movie Maker.

So let's have a quick look at Movie Maker.

## 14.9 Movie Maker

You can use this to edit digital video, taking images in directly from your camera. The video is automatically split into clips, which can then be split further or trimmed and set into a new sequence. You can merge in other video clips, or add still pictures, for titles and credits, or a voice-over or background music. Altogether, this is quite a competent editing suite. If you have the time and the skill, you can produce some good movies.

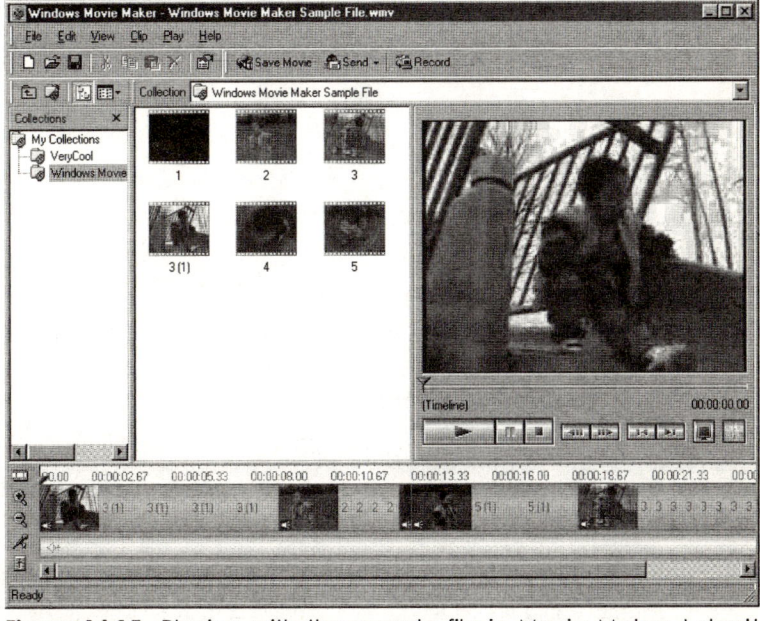

**Figure 14.15** Playing with the sample file in Movie Maker. I don't think I've got a future in the movies, but you may have!

The Movie Maker format takes around 10Kb for each second of playing time. This means that video files are not small, though they are very much more compact than the ones produced by older formats, and sharing them with distant friends and relatives via the Internet is now quite feasible.

There are two ways to do it:
- Send the movie by e-mail. Files are increased in size by 50% when attached to a message (it's to do with the way that data is transferred through the mail system), but you can normally download e-mail at 3Kb or more per second.
- Upload the file to your home page, and just send the URL to people. There are two catches to this: you have to have at least a basic grasp of putting home pages together, and download times from the Web are typically less than 2Kb per second.

What it boils down to is that it is going to take your distant friends and relatives around one minute to download 100Kb of video, which will play for 10 seconds. That 10 minute video of the little one's birthday party will take over an hour to get, and as for the school's Christmas panto…

## 14.10 Home networking

Setting up even a small network used to be a real chore. Windows 95 introduced some tools which simplified it, but it was still not a job for the faint-hearted or the non-technical. But the Home Networking Wizard transforms the business. It is so easy to use – with two provisos.
- Networking is quite straightforward as long as you are just connecting Windows Me PCs together. You can also connect to older Windows 95 or 98 PCs, but you won't get quite the full range of facilities through the link. If you want to share an Internet connection, the PC with the modem must be an Me PC.
- You still have to open the PCs' boxes and install the network cards, and their software, then cable them together.

The Home Networking Wizard takes care of setting up the Windows' networking software. All you need to do is tell the Wizard a few things about your system, and decide what to call your machines and which folders and printers to share – and that is it!

# THE ACCESSORIES

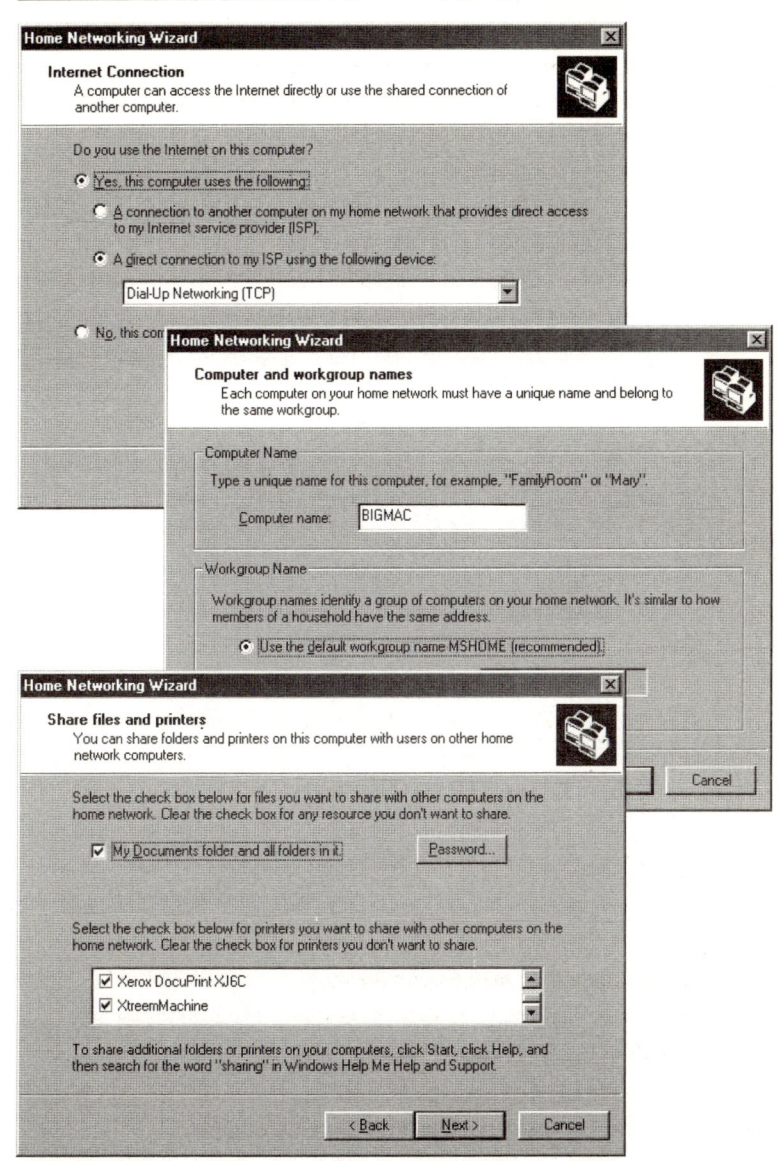

**Figure 14.16** Working through the Home Networking Wizard. If the PC has an Internet connection, the Wizard will ask for details. You can adjust how you share folders and printers at any time.

Once the network is in place, you can then run the Internet Connection Wizard on the PC that does *not* have the modem. Tell it you want to set up the connection manually and through a LAN (Local Area Network).

The crucial stage is this one. The PC with the modem is acting as a *proxy server* – one making the connection for another. Don't try to configure it yourself – that option is there for special situations and keen techies – select Automatic discovery of proxy server and let the Wizard sort it out for you. It may take a minute or so. The rest of the Wizard collects details of your e-mail account.

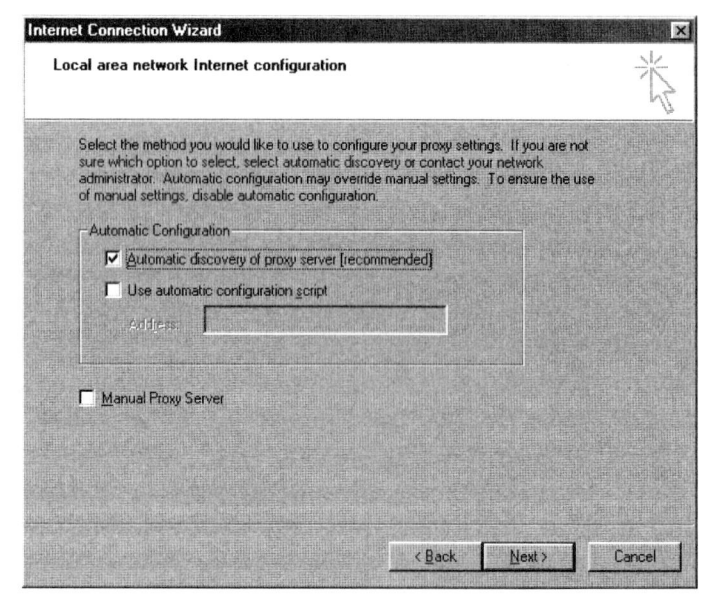

**Figure 14.17** The most technical bit of setting up a shared Internet Connection – tick the Automatic option!

The connection is fully shared. Not only can all the networked machines use the connection, they can use it at the same time.

---

**ISPs AND CONNECTION SHARING**

Internet connection sharing may not work with some ISPs. If you have problems, check that they can handle it.

## SUMMARY

- ✓ The techniques and skills that you learn using the accessories can be applied to many other Windows applications.
- ✓ WordPad has enough formatting and layout facilities to cope with many word-processing jobs.
- ✓ If you want only plain text output, Notepad will handle this very efficiently.
- ✓ Character Map will let you examine the characters in any font. Characters can be copied from here and pasted into documents.
- ✓ Paint is a simple graphics program that can be used for creating diagrams, fun pictures and for editing and saving screenshots.
- ✓ With Imaging you can add annotations to scanned or imported images.
- ✓ Calculator will do the job of a simple or a scientific pocket calculator.
- ✓ Use Phone Dialer to extend or replace the memory functions of your telephone.
- ✓ Media Player can play audio CDs, and audio and video files in most formats.
- ✓ You can produce your own movies with Movie Maker.
- ✓ The Home Networking Wizard makes it very simple to network your PCs together, and with Internet Connection sharing, they can all get online through the same modem.

# INDEX

Accessibility 104
Active content 140
Active Desktop components 15
Add Printer Wizard 191
Add/Remove Programs 106
Address Bar 79
Address Book 166
alt. newsgroups 170
Appearance, of screen 21
Application 1
   buttons 6
   defined 56
   Help 46
   windows 5
Assisted support 44

Background to screen 20
Backups 187
Bcc: (Blind carbon copies) 162

Calculator 213
Cc: (Carbon copies) 162
CD Audio 216
Change View, Help 43
Character Map 207
Check boxes 13
Clipboard 69, 71
Clipboard Viewer 70

Clock 5
Closing programs 61
Colours, editing 210
comp. newsgroups 171
Content Advisor 142, 143
Context menu 11
Control menu 28
Control Panel 103
Cookies 140, 143
Crashes 61
Cut, Copy and Paste 69

Date/Time options 109
Desktop 2, 3, 15
   customizing 18
   shortcuts 59
   themes 110
Dialog boxes 11
Directories, Web 130
Disk Cleanup 178
Disk Defragmenter 181
Disks
   and drives 176
   and folders 75
   properties 177
Document 6, 56
Drag and drop 71
Drop-down lists 13

E-mail 132
  forwarding 160
  reading 159
  replying 159
Explorer Bar 78
Extensions 63

Favorites, Internet Explorer 149
File Types 87
Filenames 63
Files 93
  deleting 97
  displaying and sorting 82
  moving and copying 95
  renaming 96
  restoring after deletion 98
  saving and opening 204
  selecting 93
  sending 97
FilterKeys 106
Find, people on the Internet 169
Finding stuff 130
Floppy disks
  formatting 188
  restoring 183
Folder Options 17, 84
Folder views 85
Folders 75
  creating 90
  organizing 89
Follow up, newsgroups 172
Font formatting 201
Fonts 111
Formatting disks 188
Forward, e-mail 160
Frequently Asked Questions 173

Graphics, selecting 67
Greyed out 8

Headers 172
Help
  and Support 39
  Contents 46
  dialog box 51
  Index 48
  Search 49
  Starting 39
Hibernate 37
High Contrast schemes 23
History, Internet Explorer 148
Home networking 220
Home Page 131
HTML (HyperText Markup
  Language) 21, 132
Hyperlink 130

Icons 2
Imaging 212
Inbox 159
Inserting objects 202
Install/Uninstall 107
Internet
  defined 129
  integration with Windows 3
Internet connection sharing 222
Internet Connection Wizard
  133, 222
Internet Explorer 135
Internet Service Provider 133
Internet Society 129
Intranet 140

Java 144

Keyboard
  accessibility options 106
  important keys 7

responses 113
shortcuts 9
Keystroke, special characters 207
Keywords 42
   in newsgroups 172
   in searches 49

Links 79
Lists 13

Maintenance Wizard 183
Maximize 28
Media Player 216
Menu bar 28
Menus 8
Minimize 28
Modem 133
Moderation, newsgroups 170
Mouse
   configuring 114
   moves 6
Movie Maker 219
My Computer 58, 76
My Documents 89

news. newsgroups 171
Newsgroups 132
   main categories 170
Notepad 206

Objects, deleting 69
On-line sales 130
Operating system 1
Options, setting 13
Outlook Express 157
   newsgroups 171

Page Setup, WordPad 201

Paint 208
Paper size 193
Paste 69
Phone Dialer 214
Pictures, and Web pages 143
Plug and Play 2
Posting articles 173
Print from file 197
Print in applications 195
Print Preview, in WordPad 204
Print queue 195
Printer Properties 193
Printers, adding 191
Privacy 140
Programs 55
   starting 58

Quick Launch toolbar 5

Radio
   and Internet 154
   and Media Player 217
Radio buttons 14
RASCi 143
Reading mail 159
rec. newsgroups 171
Recreational Software Advisory
   Council 143
Recycle Bin 98
Reply, e-mail 159
Restore 28
Restore points 187
Restricted sites zones 140
Root 75

Safe surfing 142
Scheduled Tasks 185
Scraps 72

Screen layouts 30
Screen Saver 21
Screenshots, capturing 211
Scroll bars 30
Search 99
Search engines 130
Security, and the Internet 140
Shareware sites 150
Shortcuts 4, 92
Shut Down 36
Sliders and number values 14
Sounds, and events 117
Speed dial 214
Start menu 56
Stationery, e-mail 160
Status bar 28
StickyKeys 106
Suspend 37
System Restore 186
System Tools 175

Tabs, in dialog boxes 11
Taskbar 4
   buttons 31
   options 119
   toolbars 59, 120
Text
   boxes 13
   selecting 66
Thumbnails 83
Tip of the Day 82
ToggleKeys 106
Toolbar
   Internet Explorer 137
   Windows Explorer 80

Toolbars 28
   Taskbar 120
Tooltips 51
Tours and tutorials 45
True Type fonts 112
Trusted sites zone 140

Uniform Resource Locators
   (URL) 145
Utilities 2, 56

Video 218
Viruses 140

Web Page mode 15
Web page URLs 146
Web page view, Explorer 85
Window size 33
Windows
   basic concepts 26
   keyboard control 34
   moving 36
   tabbing between 33
Windows Explorer 58, 77
   Toolbar 80
   Views 81
Windows Setup 107
Windows Update 153
WinZIP 151
WordPad 199
World Wide Web 130
   Browsing 144

ZIPped files 151